MOTHERING
THE MOVEMENT

MOTHERING
THE MOVEMENT

he Story of the San Francisco Women's Building

SUSHAWN ROBB

Outskirts Press, Inc.
Denver, Colorado

Outskirts Press, Inc.
http://www.outskirtspress.com

ISBN: 978-1-4327-8105-7

Outskirts Press and the "OP" logo are trademarks belonging to Outskirts Press, Inc.

PRINTED IN THE UNITED STATES OF AMERICA

CONTENTS

INTRODUCTION

I first visited The Women's Building in 1981 while attending the national conference of the Reproductive Rights National Network. At the time, I lived in Seattle and was just beginning to work with the Alliance Against Women's Oppression. When I moved to the Bay Area in 1982, The Women's Building was one of the things that attracted me to the region. Throughout the 1980s, I worked closely with women who were very involved at The Women's Building. Though I was never a member of the collective, I thought of the Building as my second home in the city. In 1994, I was invited to join the Board of Directors, where I served until 2000. At that year's annual board/staff retreat, I looked around the room and realized that though many of the women in the room had been involved with the Building for much of the previous decade, I was the only one present who had been around during the 1980s. As my final contribution, I agreed to write a short, basic chronicle of the San Francisco Women's Centers. As I researched the early, pre-building years, it became clear that this history should be more than an internal document used only for orientation purposes.

Too often, individual women and their contributions are lost to history. Thankfully, that is changing, and this book both represents and is indebted to that change. It could never have been written without the Gay, Lesbian, Bisexual, Transgender Historical Society. This institution, based in San Francisco, houses the archival files from The Women's Building and dozens of audio tapes containing interviews of women involved with The Women's Building and the Women's Centers. The tapes were the product of the Women's Building History Project, which was formed in the 1990s to gather and organize the vast collection of written materials and begin the process of interviewing individuals. The goal of this committee and of the historical society is to preserve original material for use by historians. I joined this committee in 2003 and have been involved in integrating recent files into the archives and conducting some of the oral history interviews.

There are hundreds of files and many hours of oral history in the GLTB Historical Society archives, and it would be easy to get overwhelmed by the vast accumulation of paperwork and the rich, detailed stories recounted in the interviews. Every single woman involved has her own story, many of which can be heard in the tapes. It was my task to tell the story of the institution while honoring the stories of the individuals.

First, the individuals. In the Prologue, this book is dedicated to the long list of women who played a role in making The Women's Building the success that it has become. I want to honor these women, and I do so by naming them. You will find many lists of women who were involved in various meetings and projects. I include quotes from some of the dozens of hours of tapes, with only the lightest of editing in order to preserve the sound of the women's voices. Any errors in spelling, omission of names or giving inaccurate or incomplete credits are mine alone, for which I apologize. Whenever possible, I have used both first and last names, but record keeping, especially in the early days wasn't always complete, so in some cases I couldn't locate last names.

But this is the memoir of an institution, not of any of the individuals involved. (If you know any of them, ask them for their part of the story.) Thus I have tried to respect privacy by telling very few details about their personal lives and relationships. I have told specific personal stories only where those are important to understanding the history of the institution. I only rarely attribute specific actions or positions to specific individuals, as most decisions were based on a consensus process that brought most to the same general position. Any opinions are mine alone.

Some of the personal stories from 1979 to 1981, when the Building was purchased and first occupied, are dramatized in *She Rises Like a Building to the Sky*, a play based on oral histories that is reprinted here. The playwright, Mercilee Jenkins, was also a member of the Women's Building History Committee (where I met her and we fell in love in 2004, yet another relationship given birth to by The Women's Building). Though people who know the real cast of characters will see similarities with the play's characters, there is no direct correlation, and the dialogue is imagined.

The Women's Building has helped birth new organizations, promote movement building, and support the individuals who make up our communities. It is a product of a unique time, place, and individuals. The Building can't be directly replicated, but that doesn't mean we can't learn from her experiences and be inspired by her success.

PROLOGUE

This book is the story of an institution. But behind all good institution are a few good women. Or, in the case of the Women's Building,
scores of women. Too often, the names behind our history are forgotten. One of the purposes of writing this book was to make sure that
our history is not forgotten and there is a record of who made that
history. Especially in the early years, it is very hard to say who did
what when. It was truly a collective effort, where everyone did a little
bit of everything. You'll see some of these names as you read through
the rest of the book. Many of the names won't appear again, but all
of them have their own stories about the Women's Building or of the
years prior to the building being purchased. To the best of my ability,
I've listed the names in chronological order of their first contact with
the organization. I'm sure I'm wrong about some of the years and
unfortunately have probably left names off the list. For these errors, I
apologize. I dedicate this book to all here, and any missed. Without
you, there would be no Women's Building.

Jean Crosby, 1969

Karen Folger Jacobs, 1969

Dorothy Martin, 1969

Jennifer Gardner, 1969

Brenda Brush, 1969

Pat Condry, 1969

Barbara Harwood, 1973

Jodi Safier, 1973

Corky Sullivan, 1973

Jan Zobel, 1973

Del Martin, 1973

Phyllis Lyon, 1973

Karen Jacobs, 1973

Anna Maria Bartlett, 1973

Linda Rothacker, 1973
Jodi Bienstock, 1973
Edie Asrow, 1974
Fran Ziegler. 1974
Jane Kenner, 1974
Holly Reed, 1974
Linda Breckinridge, 1974
Linda Jupiter, 1974
Elaine McKinley, 1974
Billie Rose, 1974
Roma Guy, 1974
Edith Davidson, 1974
Marylou Donnelly, 1974
Nancy Henderson, 1974
Pan Haskins, 1974
Adrienne Bergh, 1974
Judy Coulter, 1974
Karin Krut, 1974
Karen Greenhill, 1974
Christine Kowalsky, 1974
Beverly Beinstock, 1974
Ana Mahoney, 1975
Marcia Settel, 1975
Anne Warren, 1975
Pam Brennan, 1975
Sylvia Bursztyn, 1975
Sharon Hurley, 1975
Liz French, 1975
Jesse Miller, 1975
Janis Greenberg, 1975
Cheryl Thurman, 1975
Jo Kuney, 1975
Jean Livingston, 1975
Chris Cecchettini, 1975

Eddie Schein, 1975
Sue Goedtel, 1975
Peggy Cleveland, 1975
Pam Waldo, 1975
Katie Knudson, 1975
Dana Smith, 1975,
Lynn Lonidier, 1975
Gail Friedlander, 1976
Lore Politzer, 1976
Susie London, 1976
Barbara Boraff, 1976
Linda Leavitt, 1976
Sally Goldin, 1976
Mary Beavins, 1976
Becky Schnelker, 1976
Sharon Hallas, 1976
Elisa Baker, 1976
Laurie Field, 1976
Sandy Swanson, 1976
Kate Werhane, 1976
Pat Friday, 1976
Barbara Starkey, 1976
Diane Jones, 1976
Cherie Pies, 1976
Nan Schlosberg, 1976
Elizabeth Ross, 1976
Marya Grambs, 1977
Tiana Arruda, 1977
Carmen Vasquez 1980
Cathy Merschcel, 1977
Margaret Puffer, 1977
Jeanette Lazam, 1977
Rebecca Sandridge, 1977
Sara Leong, 1977

Melissa Williams, 1977

Snake, 1977

Tanya Brennan, 1977

Louise Guy, 1977

Toby Salk, 1977

Sheila Kirschbaum, 1977

Shay Huston, 1977

Cheri Collins, 1977

Dvora Hongstein, 1977

Jill Sager, 1977

Tina Logan, 1977

Alana Schindler, 1977

Bonnie Bartlett, 1977

Gretchen Walsh, 1978

Tracy Gary, 1978

Jeanne Adelman-Mahoney, 1978

Jeanette Lazam, 1978,

Marge Nelson, 1978

Mimi Young, 1978

Anne Pollack, 1978

Margo Adair, 1978

Rapunzel Olsen, 1978

Anne Worthington, 1978

Grace Dumman, 1978

Joyce Lucarotti, 1978

Joyce Garay, 1978

Willow Allen, 1978

Pat Durham, 1978

Nita Winters 1978

Dorinda Moreno 1979

Kim, 1979

Carmen Vazquez, 1980

Suzanne De Groot, 1980

Jan Adams, 1981

Graciela Perez Trevisan, 1981

Leslie Kirk Campbell, 1981

Celeste Smeland, 1982

Janice Toohey, 1982

Meryl Sunshine, 1982

Deena Cleavenson, 1982

Barbara Kotacka, 1982

Ali Marrero, 1982

Alicia Maddox, 1982

Flavia Maucci, 1982

Isabel Irigoyan, 1982

Happy Hyder, 1982

J. Castleberry, 1983

Jacque DuPree, 1983

Arlene Eisen, 1983

Monifa Anjanaku, 1983

Adrianne Lauby, 1983

Anne Vanderslice, 1983

Lucreta Bermudez, 1983

Summer Tips, 1983

Ambar Canales, 1984

Jaime Baldino, 1984

Mirta Beal, 1984

Lisa-Lyn Sharpe, 1984

Rawna Romero, 1984

Flo Tumolo, 1984

Nelly Reyes, 1984

Holly Fincke, 1985

Denise Curtis, 1985

Lisa Milos, 1986

Regina Gabriel, 1986

Rose Arrieta, 1987

Deb Riley, 1987

Rita Cummings, 1987

Cecilia Rodriquez, 1987
Janice Falco, 1989
Marta Ames, 1990
Pam Weatherford, 1990
Laurencia Strauss 1990
Debra Castro, 1990
Cherise Gould, 1990
Lilia Sarria
Shellie Stortz, 1990
Kris Balloun, 1990
Joy Scheffer, 1990
Shoshana Rosenberg, 1990
Kim Lau, 1991
Teresa Mejia, 1993
Deborah Miller, 1991
Shirley Kennedy, 1991
Suzanne Peck, 1991
Donna C, 1992
Silja Talvi, 1993
Josefina Velazquez, 1993
Elisa Odabasian, 1993
Molly Brennan, 1993
Sonia Wong-Johnson, 1993
Anita Countee, 1993
Susan Pedrick, 1994
Mary Schmidt, 1994
Marsha Carter, 1994
Mary Schmidt 1994
Consuelo Rojas, 1994
Cyndi Cain, 1994
Noemi Zulberti, 1994
Anna Marie Torres, 1994
Jane Donaldson, 1994
Patricia Tamayo, 1994

Lisa deHaas, 1994
Wendi Raw, 1994
Carla Sarvis 1995
Gemma del Barrio Cubero, 1996
Esperanza Macias, 1996 Raquel
Jimenez, 1996
Cyndi Cain, 1996
Rachel Timoner, 1996
Page McGraw, 1995
Maria Pilar Gonzalez 1998
Joanna Carichner, 1998
Charlotte Burchard, 1998
Denhi Donis, 1998
Michon Blount, 1998
Denhi Donis 1998
Marya Sealover, 1998,
Liza Ziebel, 1998
Kelly Lockwood, 2000
Liz Longfellow, 2000
Amity Mead, 2000
Zulma Oliveras, 2000
Chrisina Trujillo, 2000
Katy Young, 2000

Muralists

Yvonne Littleton
Susan Kelk Cervantes
Miranda Bergman
Juana Alicia
Meera Desai
Irene Perez
Edyth Boone

Reinforce the Dream Leadeship Committee

Marta Drury
Ayse Kenmore
Libby Denebeim
Sofiah Dickerson
Susan Hisrsh Simmons Alina Laguna
Jeanette Lazam
Meghan McVety
Beth Rosales
Mary Schmidt
Lois Shapiro
Vikki Barron
Myra Diaz
Claire Lachance
Christine Olague
Lele Santilli
Deb Montesinos
Andrea Shorter
Tricia Stapleton

Board Members (1989 – 2000)

Norma Del Rio
Leticia Pena
Leni Marin
Hilary Crosby
Moli Steinert
Lily Wu
Judith Klain
Diane Jones
Jeanette Lazam

Deborah Whitman
Carmela Rombawa-Bey
Linda Feliz
Sally Hershey
Rowena Pineda
Cynthia Gissler
Meridith Wilson
Sushawn Robb
Yolanda Marrow
Rosa Bernard
Barbara Richard
Ces Rosales
Theresa Ramirez
Robin Gilbrecht
Claire LaChance
Katey Mulligan
Donna Wan
Brewster Wyckoff
Nancy Corrigan
Vikki Barron
Lisa Kramer
Marta Drury
Julie French
Elizebeth Gettelman
Mangui Irizarry
Anne Marie Siu Yuan
Kim Walton

Women Building History Committee

Roma Guy
Marge Nelson
Laura Bock

Anna Dunham
Kaye Hoxter
Mercilee Jenkins
Frances Doughty
Carla Sarvis
Jill D. Giovanni
Chris Fitzpatrick
Tyler Lee
Patricia Kess
Susan Pedrick
Susan Ford
Suzanne Pullen
Elizabeth Clark
Sushawn Robb

CHAPTER 1

BEGINNINGS

IF YOU LOOKED at the San Francisco Women's Building today, you would see a traditional nonprofit organization with a small staff, a volunteer board, and an annual budget of about one million dollars. The only thing that sets it apart from most nonprofits is that the organization owns its own building, valued at $7-8 million. The programs of the Women's Building are relatively modest: information and referral, educational services relating to jobs, taxes, and legal rights, and low-rent office space for emerging organizations.

But there is nothing modest about the contributions of the scores of organizations that have been housed at the Building and incubated over the years through the sponsored project program. A list of these groups, probably incomplete, can be found in appendix 1. It reads like a virtual Who's Who of organizations that make up the San Francisco Bay Area women's movement. In terms of size, public visibility, and impact on public policy, many of these groups far surpass The Women's Building. And as a good mother, The Women's Building is content with her contribution. Participants may at times chafe over the lack of recognition the Building receives, but there has been no serious impulse to mortgage the Building in order to launch a big, glamorous, and expensive program that would grow the organization.

This modest stance is no accident. It started at the beginning, with the very purposeful formation in 1970 of the San Francisco Women's

Centers. The milieu was a spirit of egalitarianism, borne of the 1960s. Among the radical feminists who formed the group, competition was out. Cooperation despite differences was the goal. This spirit stood in stark contrast to the sectarianism and dogmatism that was so prevalent in the broader socialist/left movement of the time. It probably also reflected the internalized sexism of women who habitually undervalued their own work. In any case, the idea was to exist in the plural, providing a pool that would support a multitude of efforts, each with its own center to direct its own work.

Getting Started

The San Francisco Women's Centers was formed during a time of societal upheaval. Across the country, the 1960s were going out with a bang. People were regularly out on the streets, expressing their differences with all forms of the status quo and challenging the current dominant institutions. The San Francisco Bay Area was one of the nation's centers of activity. Blockades at the Oakland army base by antiwar protesters, the student strikes in San Francisco and Berkeley, demanding ethnic studies programs, and activities of the Black Panther Party were among the nationally publicized struggles, and many more were taking place under the radar of the national mainstream media.

By the early 1970s an energetic and chaotic "anti-establishment" attitude was making its mark on U.S. society as a whole. The civil rights movement had laid the foundation for other social movements, arising from many sectors of the population and addressing a variety of societal inequalities. On a national scale, the dominant voices challenging the status quo, whether on behalf of race, gender, or working conditions, were asking for a fairer share of the current system.

At the local level, much of the organizing was carried out by collectives and organizations that offered a more radical critique of the establishment and its underlying economic system. The student and antiwar movements of the sixties were evolving into a myriad of revolutionary organizations.[1] Other revolutionary organizations were formed within many communities of color, drawing inspiration from the role the Black Panther Party had played before it was decimated by agents of the U.S. government.[2] The Stonewall Rebellion in 1969 brought the homosexual rights movement into the public eye and gave birth to the radical gay liberation movement, adding yet another dimension to the left-wing politics of the day.

Up until 1973 and the formal "end" of U.S. involvement in Vietnam, opposition to the war had been the one common point of agreement among all these diverse groups. As this reference point became obscured, organizers became more ensconced in specific communities or in work around single issues, and the "movement" became as segregated as the broader U.S. society. And within each of these segregated movements, there were often dozens of different organizations, focused on different issues and/or bringing different ideological perspectives to the work.

The Women's Movement

Thus the women's movement was also comprised of many organizations, addressing many different issues and operating from varied analyses of the root source of sexism. Hundreds of organizations and collectives took on the wide range of "women's" issues—domestic violence, rape, and other misogynist violence; the range of reproductive health concerns; media and cultural representations of women and girls; employment issues; education access—the list goes on at length. Lesbians were active in every social movement of the time, but were particularly active around women's issues.

Indeed, almost everything was still very male focused. Forty years later, it's hard to believe how institutionalized the inferior position of women was. The legal system provided fewer rights to women,

---

1   Examples include the October League, the Weathermen, and Democratic Socialists of America.
2   Examples include the Young Lords Party, the Puerto Rican Socialist Party, the La Raza Unida Party, and the American Indian Movement.

who were denied the right to enter into contracts, to pursue certain careers, to access full health care, or even to wear what they wanted to wear. By its silence, the judicial system effectively condoned abusive treatment of women by men. Cultural images in entertainment and advertising further underscored the subservient and inferior position of women. Across the country, and across the globe, women were standing up to challenge these assumptions, and by the seventies some aspects of institutionalized sexism were beginning to be dismantled.

But there were also sexist barriers to institution-building. Some community organizations were able to access the institutional resources of churches and unions to get started. In many cases, however, these institutions were unavailable to advocates of women's liberation. So short-term campaigns and local community-based organizations often began as informal collectives, with varying degrees of internal structure and regulation. For a group funded largely by its own membership or small donations from its base, internal systems of accountability sufficed, with no need to establish a formal relationship to the state. However, once substantial amounts of money became involved, greater accountability was also called for. For any effort hoping to obtain grants from private foundations or public funds or offering tax deductions to large donors, formal corporate status was a necessity. Some groups went through the hoops to obtain, and then maintain, their own nonprofit corporate status with the government; others looked for an existing nonprofit organization with a similar mission to sponsor their efforts. For organizing around women's issues, this latter was often not an option.

It was to begin to fill this need that a number of Bay Area women's organizations met, including the National Organization for Women (NOW), Daughters of Bilitis, and San Francisco Women's Liberation. In 1969, they applied for and were granted nonprofit status for a new organization, San Francisco Women's Centers (SFWC). The founders didn't want yet another organization that would exist for itself. Rather, they wanted an organizational structure, with a governmental recognition as a nonprofit, with the goal of supporting existing organizations and helping to nurture new organizing efforts on behalf of women. The 1969 incorporation papers were signed by Jean Crosby, Karen Folger Jacobs, Dorothy Martin, Jennifer Gardner, Brenda Brush, and Pat Condry. With incorporation in place, they wrote a grant proposal and went in search of money.

As a group of feminists, many with radical critiques of mainstream society, the SFWC founders found the usual corporate structure of offices and officers to be "male" and anathema. In fact, traditional corporate structure represented the very thing they hoped to change about society. So in order to fill in the required blanks for "president," "secretary," and "treasurer" of the new corporation, the group drew straws, a symbol of the randomness that those terms would involve for the group. From its inception, the SFWC was to be a collective endeavor, drawing energy and contributions from members of the organizations that were promoting the new group. But it was a lucky stroke of fate that Jean drew the "secretary" straw and held on to the paperwork.

At the time, Crosby was on staff for one of the projects of Glide Memorial Church. Under the leadership of the Rev. Cecil Williams, Glide played a leading role in the civil rights movement in the Bay Area, as well as supporting other progressive efforts of the time. (This is a role it continues to play to this day, with a special focus on meeting the needs of poor and homeless people who have been cast off by recurring economic downturns.) In her work at Glide, Jean saw that an established institution could be instrumental in working for radical social change.

One model that inspired the SFWC founders was that of the Urban Young Adult Action Center, which operated under the auspices of Glide Church. Rather than taking on direct organizing efforts itself, the center worked to offer technical support and funds to grassroots organizing efforts. Of course, the center enjoyed some resources that the SFWC lacked, like the resources to hire a staff to work with organizing efforts and a building for meetings and programs. To start, all it had was a bold concept, a few individuals willing to offer considerable time and expertise in pursuit of the dream, and a vibrant community that would rise to the call time and time again in the years to come.

A Long Gestation

The euphoria of starting a new organizing effort soon gave way to a holding pattern. After two years of trying to raise money, the original collective had exhausted its energy. The effort to secure foundation funding hit a wall, for several reasons. For one thing, the money just wasn't there. A study done in the mid-70s by the Funding Feminist Coalition (a project operating under the auspices of the SFWC) found that in 1972-74, only one-fifth of 1 percent (that is, two cents out of every one thousand dollars) of foundation grant making went to programs to improve women's status. It's not surprising that without a track record, the SFWC didn't get any of these pennies. Another reason was that a few of the women in the group moved away, and others were busy with existing organizations and campaigns.

However, rather than drop the whole thing, Crosby made a commitment to maintain the SFWC by keeping up with the annual paperwork the State of California required of nonprofit corporations. None of the women involved wanted their initial work of acquiring nonprofit status to go to waste, even though the original idea of a coalition effort among existing organizations seemed unlikely to happen. So they started looking for a current organizing effort that could adopt the SFWC articles of incorporation and state nonprofit status to its own project.

By now it was 1972, and the women's liberation movement was beginning to have an impact on broader U.S. society. The historic *Roe v. Wade* decision would be issued in January 1973, representing a major political advance for women. At the time, the idea of women controlling their own bodies was still new and liberating. Feminist clinics were springing up in many cities, and *Our Bodies, Our Selves* went quickly into multiple printings (and remains a bestseller to this day). Women's presses and bookstores, usually operated by a collective, were coming to life across the country. Defense committees on behalf of battered women who fought back were bringing the issue of domestic violence to the fore, right next to the battle against rape. The organizations that had initially come together to form the SFWC were deeply immersed in their own projects, with no time or money to put into a coalition effort that didn't directly address their issues.

In San Francisco, two women with extensive ties to the world of feminist publishing agreed to join in an effort to get the SFWC project off the ground as a collective of individuals. Barbara Harwood and Jody Safier started by moving the SFWC from Crosby's closet to their apartment. A simple structure for the organization was drawn up to enable various levels of involvement. The highest decision-making body was to be a General Assembly, which would meet monthly and operate with consensus to reach decisions. A Coordinating Council, representing groups and projects working under the SFWC umbrella, would meet more frequently.

The list of issues that made up the initial vision of this Coordinating Council is a good reflection of the base and issues of the center: "feminist counseling, legal counseling, rape counseling, health group, phone hotline, library, liberation school, lesbian office, funding committee, NOW and *Off Our Backs* [a national radical feminist weekly newspaper]."[3] The final organizational level was an office collective, which would handle administrative demands.

A lawyer was hired to complete the process of obtaining tax-deductible status from the IRS. In the meantime, the three women, Jean, Barbara, and Jody approached Glide Memorial Church to request fiscal sponsorship by the Urban Young Adult Action Center. This enabled the SFWC to apply for an employee allowance to VISTA, Volunteers in Service to America. A federal program, VISTA was a remnant of the

---

3   Coordinating Committee notes, July 1972. Gay, Lesbian, Bisexual, and Transgender Historical Society (hereafter GLBTHS), Women's Building Archives (hereafter WBA), main collection, series 1, subseries A, box 1, file 8.

"Great Society," launched in 1965 as part of President Johnson's War on Poverty. Akin to the Peace Corps, its purpose was to provide small subsidies to volunteers who took on specific tasks for underfunded nonprofit organizations.

Once this funding came through, the group's first project was to organize a woman's music festival, one of the first of its kind in the country. The day-long event featured twenty-two performers and was well attended. The event was also successful in raising about $1,100 to get the organization off the ground.[4] Over the years, numerous other musical fundraising events would be held, featuring well-known performers like Sweet Honey in the Rock and Alix Dobkin, as well as local groups like Berkeley Women's Music Collective and Sweet Chariot.

After three years, the vision of forming a group whose purpose was to help develop the organizations that would define the women's movement was now reality. Though it no longer functioned as a coalition of groups, the women kept the name "San Francisco Women's Centers." In naming the organization, the use of the plural word "centers" was very deliberate. Roma Guy, who would play a key leadership role in developing The Women's Building, described this vision of plurality:

> I was very motivated by the vision and inspiration that "s" in the phrase "San Francisco Women's Centers" meant. It wasn't San Francisco Women's Center. It was San Francisco Women's Centers. [This meant] that it was activist oriented, and it [expressed] the idea that it could be a women's center, where women and others who wanted to support women's rights could drop in and get information and referral, and events could be organized there, however small it was. . . . So the approach was to organize and then to let go of those organizations, then they would either become their own 501c3 or join other efforts and broaden

---

4   The details of this event have been lost—one of the consequences of having no office space to call their own.

out. But we would be the incubator for those ideas. And if we had anything to do with it, we would try to implement it around progressive politics and be broad-based and not just focused on women's rights per se. The idea was that women's rights cannot be gained or achieved without broadening out and including other people's rights, that women's rights were part of everyone's rights and part of the general oppression in our society. Without taking that into view and using that to organize ourselves, then as a movement we would be severely limited.

At the same time, there are issues that women mobilize around [that] addressed women clearly as women. So for example, reproduction and how women were oppressed as it relates to our reproductive rights tends to attract women first, and the same thing around battered women—[these issues] had to be focused on very specifically. Not because violence against men doesn't occur, but we had to bring women's perspective into the issue of violence. That was what we could do for the larger community — bring our issues in. For example, how does violence affect women and what are the causes? And then also to join other coalitions, like police violence against certain communities of color or around sexuality and the lesbian and gay community, for example. Obviously, women are found in every one of those communities, so clearly that was the vehicle we could use because women are everywhere, in every class, every race, every disability or ability.

So that was the vision and that was the strategy of the "s" in Women's Centers. In our community today, the Women's Building is the most cohered and the most visible of that politic and that strategy. In essence, that's what it represents. So a range of organizations live at The Women's Building.

In practice, the General Assembly soon evolved into a board, with monthly meetings open to any woman involved with the SFWC in any way. In keeping with legal requirements, notes were taken to reflect the nomination of new members, the resignation of others, and the annual "election" of officers, but the group functioned as a collective process and decisions were made by consensus. When the SFWC began to pay staff directly, those paid rotated off the board to avoid any perception of conflict of interest. Legal requirements prohibit board members from receiving significant funds from the organization, and though the pay levels never reached this threshold, the organization took the safe road. Committees were formed as needed and desired by the participants, and the concept of a Coordinating Council was abandoned.

The first board meeting was convened in June 1973. Two of the founders, Jean Crosby and Brenda Brush, joined Barbara and Jody on the board, and others were invited as well. Corky Sullivan and Jan Zobel joined the board, and by year's end, Del Martin and Phyllis Lyon (founders of Daughters of Bilitis), Karen Jacobs (another original signer of the incorporation papers), Anna Maria Barton, and Linda Rothacker had joined the board.

Thanks to the VISTA allowance of $286 a month, at least one volunteer was able to devote a significant amount of time to the organization. Even in 1973 terms, $286 wasn't a lot of money, but with food stamps to stretch the budget and sharing rent on still affordable apartments, a frugal single woman could get by. Many volunteers held other part-time jobs as well. Over the first few years, various women were paid, sometimes more than one at a time. In the first five years, dozens of women were involved in many aspects of the centers' work, with regular rotation of who, if any, was paid for their efforts.

Most of the women involved in these first few years were white and lesbian. Though they came from a variety of class backgrounds, most were also in their twenties and thirties, making for a fairly homogenous group. However, older women were also drawn to the SFWC, forming Options for Women Over 40, one of the most successful groups to have its beginning as a SFWC-sponsored project. Influenced by the civil rights movement and opposition to the Vietnam

War, the SFWC brought a commitment to antiracist politics and an internationalist perspective, but it would be some years before the composition of the group reflected this commitment.

Moving to a Bigger Home

It wasn't long before the SFWC reached the limits of its office in Barbara and Jody's living room, and plans were made to locate an office that could be rented fairly cheaply. In 1973 the SFWC approached the San Francisco Women's Switchboard (the Switchboard) about the possibility of joining forces to open a new office. This was a natural choice, as there was significant overlap in volunteers, a common feminist philosophy, and complementary purposes.

The Switchboard had been formed in October 1972 to provide a centralized location for access to information about services for women. It provided information about women's centers throughout the United States and Europe, as well as local listings for jobs, rides, housing, crisis counseling services, legal and health services, and other miscellaneous information. The intent of the Switchboard was to provide women with direction for getting assistance, but many callers were desperate for immediate help or at least a sympathetic ear. So volunteers were often providing direct counseling services over the phone. Dozens of women volunteered for weekly two-hour shifts to staff their two phone lines every day, and a VISTA volunteer coordinated the effort. Free office space was provided by the San Francisco YWCA.

When presented with the idea of sharing a rented space with the SFWC, the Switchboard took some convincing, since currently their only significant expense was the cost of the phone lines and a minimal stipend for the coordinator, paid by VISTA money. Now they were being asked to share rent as well. Ultimately, however, the idea of sharing offices with more like-minded women won them over. It didn't hurt that the SFWC agreed to provide free rent for one year in their joint space (once it was located), and to pay for the phone and two staff women for several months, to offset the cost to the Switchboard of moving from the YWCA.

Jointly, SFWC and the Switchboard applied for and received a grant from Cerredwyn, one of the first foundations dedicated to women's issues. This gave them enough money to start looking for an office and pay the first and last month's rent and security deposit. After several months of searching, an office was located at 63 Brady Street, on the edge of the Mission District.

It was soon clear that running an office without regular office hours was a losing proposition. Three members of the core collective, Jean Crosby, Holly Reed, and Linda Breckinridge all held part-time jobs at the time. Each made a commitment to be at the new SFWC office during work hours when they were not at their paid jobs. As a result, the new office was able to maintain daily hours.

In their first year one and a half in the Brady Street office, the SFWC organized a series of five fundraising workshops for over sixty women's social change groups. They also held community forums on the following topics: Sexism and Racism in Employment, Lesbianism/Coming Out, the IUD Scare, Women and Electroshock, Abortion, Rape, and Women in Vietnam. They helped convene a funding coalition of ten to fifteen groups to explore ways to develop resources for the women's movement, and they coordinated and led numerous consciousness-raising groups. The SFWC began publishing a monthly newsletter, with a mailing list of two thousand, mostly women, by October 1974.

Once the new office was up and running a resource library was established. A meeting room was made available to other organizations, and groups like Non-Traditional Employment for Women, Golden Gate Methodist Women's Caucus, the Peace and Freedom Party, and San Francisco Women Against Rape all used the space. The number of groups that the SFWC sponsored grew apace, including Daughters of Bilitis, Women's Art Center, Allyssum, Press Collective, the Switchboard, San Francisco Women's Newsletter, 5 Trees Press, Amazon Quarterly, Women's Skills Center, Counterpoint Films,

Essential Films, San Francisco Women Against Rape, Union Wage, and Options for Women Over 40.

Tiana Arruda, a member of the collective from 1976 remembers those early years:

> There were four people there, and we did everything. We staffed the phones. We answered calls. . . . It was different than the Switchboard—the Switchboard was just more giving out information—but at the Women's Centers since we did have an office all day, people also called there. Sometimes you would refer to the Switchboard later in the day or you'd answer the phones related to the projects that were going on. And the Women's Centers was like a community organizing . . . place, so there were lots of activities, a lot of support groups and new projects going on, like Options for Women Over 40 was starting; the women's building project. We had a newsletter that was monthly, and we had to type, gather material, and then do the layout. In those days we did everything on the typewriter. No computers yet, not even typesetting. And then we had a membership that renewed their subscriptions every month. So there was a mixture of work. Some paperwork, office work, organizing internally, and other things. A little bit of everything.

Money was always short. Grant proposals, even those to progressive foundations, were regularly turned down, so money for salaries was sporadic and the paid staff had to find other part-time employment. Fortunately, events like the Woman's Music Festival, a program featuring lesbian writer Rita Mae Brown, and an office-warming party brought in funds, as did newsletter subscriptions. In addition, the group established a membership fee of five dollars a year, two dollars for the unemployed. While the SFWC itself had minimal success with grants, some of its sponsored projects did secure grants that passed through the organization, and a 5 percent administrative fee bolstered the center's income.

This was the early seventies, and personal computers, fax machines, cell phones, and photo copiers were not readily available. As an underfunded, volunteer group of women, the SFWC had limited access to even current top-of-the-line technology, even something as basic as a self-correcting IBM typewriter. Tiana remembers the space:

> The Women's Centers had one little room, the Switchboard had another one. Then there was another room, called a drop-in room, where all the flyers and housing postings and all kinds of different information was posted, and also that was the meeting room for groups like support groups. And then there was another little room in the back, narrow and long, that was also used for meetings. There were all these pieces of old furniture and broken couches. But the only . . . desks were one desk in the Switchboard room and three desks in the Women's Centers room that we shared, because there was more staff than there were desks.

One early donation to the SFWC was a printing press. Barbara was a printer by trade, and teaching women to use a press was seen as a critical means of giving women their own voice. The list of sponsored projects at the time reflects the overlap of the SFWC's base with the world of feminist publications. Unfortunately, the press was old and soon broke down. What they had hoped would be a source of revenue threatened to become a drain on resources, and the press project was abandoned.

Common Values

At any point during the SFWC's first few years, one to two dozen women were active in the core collective. Among them there was a broadly shared assumption of feminist values, and many held a radical critique of U.S. capitalist society, But there was no attempt to drawn up firm political points of unity. In terms of issues and specific demands, the politics of the SFWC were principally defined by the projects for which the SFWC provided fiscal sponsorship. In terms of how the group functioned, however, the politics were classic radical feminism. Capitalism was a problem, but the patriarchy definitely was the enemy.

Opposing patriarchy meant finding feminist ways of doing things. This was particularly true for a group whose purpose wasn't directly taking on the patriarchy but supporting the efforts of others to do so. Hierarchy and formal leadership structures were to be replaced by a collective and the rotation of responsibilities. Process and feelings were as important as getting the work done, and in some ways, this value was probably essential to the group's survival. The task the group had set for itself was enormous, and the woman power of the collective was under constant strain. A nurturing environment and the opportunity to vent helped avoid, or at least assuage, the inevitable burnout. One drawback of this focus was an increased homogeneity within the collective, even as its membership turned over.

Begun by white women—some of working class backgrounds, others middle class—the group remained predominately white. The original core members were also mostly lesbian. Straight women and women of color, especially lesbians of color searching for a political home, were involved in the collective throughout the seventies, but at first glance the SFWC could easily be described as a white lesbian group. New collective members were most often friends of current members, which in our segregated society was (and is) usually someone of the same racial background. Women of color were more likely to come in contact with the group through its programs or events, but it's a big step from there to attending regular meetings.

After two years of functioning, the collective held a discussion to re-evaluate just exactly what they were about. This list is taken from the notes of a May 1975 meeting:

- A core staff which coordinates a newsletter, initiates women's consciousness raising groups, sponsors other women's groups, and staffs a women's resource development group

- Provides services, particularly facilitates activities and communications among women's groups
- Communicator on issues with other women's groups
- Works collectively, learning new ways to work together
- Emphasizes process in activities and objectives
- Works on a consensus basis
- Acts as a communications nerve center
- Offers physical space for groups to meet[5]

Although the collective recognized the need to involve more women of color, this list shows that this goal was yet to be integrated into its program.

One of the agenda items for the May 1975 meeting was a discussion of how the group made decisions. Technically, decisions were made by consensus, but in fact decisions were made daily and weekly by the individuals or subcommittees about the work they were doing at the time. These ad hoc decisions were not yet seen as a significant problem. A growing number of collective members were paid at least part time to work for the SFWC, but there was still far too much to do for a handful of part-time staff to take on alone. Nor was the salary for the paid collective members very high; they were often forced to find other part-time work in order to survive. With the establishment of formal memberships, there was also the issue of how to include this base of women in making decisions.

By March 1976, the SFWC adopted a new operational structure. The board would now be composed of the core staff/volunteers, representatives from internal projects, and a liaison for the Switchboard. Meetings were open to anyone interested, and scores of women took part on all levels of the organization's work.

One of the most important efforts undertaken at the time was the Staff Support Program. Basically, the core collective, along with their friends, agreed to make regular monthly donations to the SFWC in

---

5 May 1975 meeting notes. GLBTHS, WBA, main collection, series 1, subseries A, box 2, file 1.

order to provide secure funds for paying staff. Unlike grants and special events, these were funds that could be counted on from month to month. Even though it was never a large amount of money, this allowed the SFWC to make plans with the knowledge that at least some paid staff would be available to coordinate the work.

The Bay Area Feminist Federal Credit Union

There were several projects that the women from the SFWC put a tremendous amount of energy into during those first formative years. One of these was the Bay Area Feminist Federal Credit Union. This organization would have a fairly short life, founded in 1975 and disbanded in 1979. It was a collective effort that ultimately failed to adapt the collective approach to the demands of its business. Yet it was an important contribution to the lives of individual women, and it represented part of the growing demand that society give women equal economic access. It all began in 1974, when the SFWC ran into problems in finding a landlord who was willing to rent to a bunch of women. From this immediate grievance, they began exploring the idea of a credit union.

In the early 1970s, women were definitely second-class citizens when it came to financial affairs. The ability to get a credit card, even to buy gasoline, was not a given for women. Any contract for a major purchase, from appliances to vehicles to houses, had to be cosigned by some male, either a father or a husband. Women were routinely turned down for personal and business loans that would have been routinely granted had the gender on the application been marked "male."

Feminist credit unions had already been set up in other cities—the Detroit Feminist Federal Credit Union was an initial model and inspiration for women in the Bay Area. One of its members attended early planning meetings and offered technical assistance. This was long before the banking "reforms" that led to the demise of many credit unions. Credit unions were a still a respected means for a community to pool its resources for investments and then loan money back to community members. The National Credit Union Administration (NCUA) chartered credit unions and insured their deposits. In return, it set strict restrictions on how the funds could be invested and defined the boundaries of healthy balance sheets.

The SFWC put out a call to local women's movement organizations to join in an effort to form a credit union for women as a means to increase their economic clout. Many groups attended the initial meetings in 1974, and eventually four organizations signed on as sponsoring organizations in applying for a charter: the SFWC, Black Women Organized for Action, Daughters of Bilitis, and the Golden Gate chapter of NOW. The defined common bond, required by the NCUA charter process, was feminism. The goal was to provide a financial alternative that would promote economic self-sufficiency for women through a process of saving, borrowing, and counseling. The charter was granted in June 1975, and the Bay Area Feminist Federal Credit Union was born.

There was overlap in personnel between the SFWC and the credit union, but with the NCUA charter, the credit union became its own corporate entity, with a distinct Board of Directors. Nearly the entire core of the SFWC collective was in some way involved in the discussions leading up to the charter, and some members were very involved with the credit union for the next few years, including Linda Jupiter, Ana Mahoney, Pan Haskins, Linda Breckenridge, Barbara Rellick, Elaine McKinley, and Billie Rose.

The credit union opened its own office and hired a small staff, complemented with a lot of volunteer time. The first year was exhilarating, with growth far beyond expectations. The funds grew 720 percent in the first year, and members were paid 5 percent dividends the first three quarters of 1976. But the down side of operating a business with minimal staff, especially one that involved the distasteful task of dunning women to repay loans, led to burnout by the end of the 1976.

To overcome the burnout, the number of staff was expanded to seven half-time people and one full-time position. Each position had well-defined responsibilities, with the full-time position as the overall coordinator. In keeping with the credit union's feminist principles, responsibilities were rotated monthly. Daily decisions were made collectively by the staff, with broader policy issues left to an open board meeting, to which all members were invited. In addition to the coordinator position, staff jobs were screening loan applications and interviews, monitoring cash flow, basic bookkeeping and office operations, pass-book processing, and compiling the treasurer's report. The most distasteful task, collecting outstanding loans, was left to the board's Executive Committee.

One year later, the reorganization clearly hadn't worked. Collections continued to be delayed while the who and how of the "dirty work" was worked out, the rotation of staff tasks meant that all the staff members were constantly learning new jobs, and because outside sources of funds for the increased salary expense weren't found, the credit union was soon operating in the red.

After a round of recriminations over what went wrong, the group came back together with renewed efforts to find a way to save the operation. The staff was cut to three positions at thirty hours a week (at a pay of three dollars an hour; the minimum hourly wage in 1976 was $1.65). A treasurer from outside the organization was found to ensure timely and accurate reports, and staff energy was devoted to collections and delinquent accounts. In October 1977, the auditor from the NCUA declared the credit union financially insolvent because of the large number of delinquent and unsecured loans compared to the amount of savings deposits. It was given until 1978 to either reduce the delinquency rate by 10 percent or close its doors.

An appeal was made to members to make new savings deposits, take out secured loans, and pay back delinquent loans. 1978 began on a hopeful note: delinquency rates were slowly dropping, deposits were up, and most active volunteers and board members made the commitment to stay for the next year. Two additional staff positions were added.

The year of stability came to an abrupt end in 1979. The outside treasurer resigned for personal reasons, and the funding for three of the five paid positions came to a sudden end with the end of the government-funded Comprehensive Employment and Training Act program. An attempt to computerize the system in order to ease the workload had so many bugs that more work was created. The resulting errors in statements also damaged relations with the members of the credit union, undermining efforts to increase deposits. The ongoing discussion of the past two years about whether to keep the doors open intensified, and in July 1979, most of the Executive Committee members met to discuss their future.

A final appeal was made to the two remaining sponsoring organizations, the SFWC and Black Women Organized for Action (Daughters of Bilitis and Golden Gate NOW had disbanded since the credit union had first formed.) Both groups had separate meetings to discuss the issue, and it became clear that neither was in a position to assume leadership of the credit union. Black Women Organized for Action worked out a liquidation plan, and all business except loan collection ceased on August 23, 1979.

Though its doors were closed after five years, for a time the credit union did what it set out to do. It loaned out over 1 million dollars to women (of which $60,000 was delinquent at the time the doors were closed). Of these loans, many were amounts too small to be considered profitable by most banks. Others were to women who wouldn't have qualified anywhere else. For investors, it was a place to keep money that they knew would be used by women. The credit union's financing helped scores of women-owned businesses and organizations, as well as individuals—contributing to the strength of the women's movement.

By the time the credit union disbanded, the Equal Credit Opportunity Act was in place. Its provisions included one that prohibited creditors from discriminating against any applicant on the basis of sex, marital status, race, color, religion, national origin, age, receipt of income from public assistance programs, or good faith exercise of rights under the consumer credit protection act. Nor could creditors demand information about an applicant's childbearing intentions, capabilities, or birth control practices. Women still faced barriers, but things were beginning to change.

The organizers of both the SFWC and the Bay Area Feminist Federal Credit Union came to the work as feminists, and most as radical feminists who explicitly rejected the capitalist system. The strategic goal was the liberation of women in a world free of oppression. For many feminists, opposing oppression meant challenging power relations. As often as not, the process was as valued as the outcome. "The personal is political" was more than just a slogan; it often defined the agenda. This emphasis on process was one of the key ideological distinctions between radical feminist critiques of capitalism and the rest of the left. The women at the center of the credit union were committed to putting their ideology into their daily practice.

True egalitarianism meant eliminating hierarchies. All collectively run businesses confronted the issue of surviving in the greater capitalist world. Many viewed themselves as part of creating a parallel economy, one in which profit was not the overriding priority. Rather than selling Wonder Bread to make money, the goal was to provide a healthy alternative to Wonder Bread. The collective structure was a conscious rejection of the capitalist corporate model. As a collective business in the very capitalist realm of banking, the contrast was sharp for the credit union.

In its final newsletter summarizing their history, the founders described it this way:

> There has always been a recurring conflict at the Bay Area Feminist Federal Credit Union (BAFFCU)—the struggle between feminist philosophy and process, idealizing our common bond as women, versus being a viable business. A struggle between the process-oriented women and the product-oriented women reflected a struggle inherent in the nature and history of all credit unions. (While this conflict may have not been the real issue, it

was an apparent source of tension.) However, none of us, during BAFFCU's first years, had enough knowledge of credit union history to prevent us from reinventing the wheel yet another time.

As feminists, some of us believed we were doing something new, visionary, and beautiful, and we probably were. The trouble was, we were also trying to run a credit union, and, in our well-intentioned revolutionary arrogance, BAFFCU failed to take history into account. We wanted to use different processes to run BAFFCU but didn't know the hows and whys of traditional management in order to improve upon them; we went forth with only our good energy and woman spirit to carry us through. As a criticism, we never effectively struggled with the collection of bad loans, and when we finally woke up, the situation was completely out of hand. Bad loans = no dividend = no growth = eventual death. . . . The contradictions between the methods of thriving in a capitalist system and the methods of thriving within a feminist vision make the success of a feminist credit union impossible. We hope the women's movement as a whole will benefit from the experiences of our credit union. We will create a better world, and BAFFCU dedicates this newsletter to those women who carry on that work.[6]

Beyond the general contradiction with capitalism, the feminist collective faced other issues. Through all the variations in the credit union's staffing, the common problem was that there was too much work for the amount of paid and volunteer woman hours available. In an era that was just beginning to be computerized, just the clerical tasks alone could be daunting. Servicing existing customers and loans left little time for marketing to expand the number of contributing members. Many of its members opened five-dollar accounts but never regularly added to the savings. By the time the credit union folded, 12 percent of the members held 90 percent of the assets. The

6   From "The BAFFCU Bulletin," October 1979 (final edition). GLBTHS, WBA, main collection, series 1, subseries B, box 7, file 4.

goal of teaching its members to save and manage their money was never effectively addressed. Being overstretched in dealing with daily demands often left the broader vision murky. The rotation of responsibilities may have eliminated formal hierarchy, but it also stymied the work and made it difficult to maintain accountability. The refusal to identify leadership within the paid staff didn't mean that it wasn't there. But because it was denied, those who assumed leadership in order to move the process ahead were too often the target of criticisms. This in turn led some staff to leave, and those who stayed were often too paralyzed to be effective.

These issues of leadership, power, and accountability were certainly not unique to the Bay Area Feminist Federal Credit Union. Similar debates raged through many of the radical feminist efforts of the day, and were often their undoing. Not surprisingly, similar issues would also confront the SFWC.

CHAPTER 2

BRADY STREET DAYS

FOR SUCH A small office, the San Francisco Women's Centers (SFWC) headquarters on Brady Street was a bundle of energy for the five years that the group resided there. With the San Francisco Women's Switchboard also operating in the space, there was almost always at least one person, and often dozens, crammed into the three rooms. Having an actual office gave the SFWC a new level of credibility as well as a place to more easily involve a wide range of volunteers.

During the mid-seventies, the U.S. economy took a turn for the worse, as the cost of the Viet Nam war and an ever growing defense budget finally came due. A recession was formally declared, a result of stagnant business activity and rising unemployment rates. The first gas crisis helped drive an already inflationary rate further upward. In response to this "stagflation," wage and price freezes were enacted by President Jimmy Carter, and steps were taken to dismantle regulations in the hopes of spurring private job growth. By the end of the seventies, nonprofit subsidies were being curtailed.

Looking back, we can now see the 70s recession as a minor blip in U.S. economic growth. It was also the point at which income disparity was at its lowest ever. The decades of postwar prosperity had been shared by all classes. Progressive voices who had ridden the wave of social movements in the sixties were being elected to government offices at all levels. But that wasn't enough to stop the deregulation and tax changes that would, by the turn of the twenty-first century, result in the greatest income disparity since the early 1900s.

Indeed, a renewed right-wing political movement in the country was gaining steam. Ronald Reagan's unsuccessful presidential bid in 1976 was just a harbinger of things to come. The attack on gay civil rights in Dade County, Florida, marked the beginning of a national antigay backlash, including the 1978 Briggs Amendment to the California State Constitution, which would have outlawed gay teachers. Medicaid funding for abortion was cut, putting the reproductive rights movement back on the defensive, and the Bakke decision by the Supreme Court legitimized "reverse discrimination," undermining Affirmative Action. As individuals, members of the SFWC collective were heavily involved in several of these struggles.

In forming the SFWC, there was no attempt to adopt a particular ideological viewpoint. Beyond a vaguely defined radical feminist philosophy, the prevailing attitude was pragmatism: the bottom line was "Any effort to liberate women, whether from patriarchal assumptions or capitalist restriction, is worthwhile. What can we do to help?" Among the lesbian membership especially, there were varying degrees of separatism, with all believing that there were times and places for women to be together, without men. At the same time, the commitment to an antiracist and internationalist politic limited the degree to which the SFWC would segregate itself from the broader society.

The very character of the SFWC reflected its egalitarian feminist philosophy. Rather than attempt to assume direct leadership of the movement, the SFWC played a more supportive role. The core function of the organization was to assist the initiatives spawned by the larger movement. For example, the activities from the fall 1976, included in the SFWC newsletter (published jointly with the Switchboard and including a calendar of community events), included community resource listings, support groups (also referred to as consciousness raising and rap groups), participation on a Police Advisory Council to the San Francisco Police Department, the Staff Support Program (a sustainer pledge program, described in chapter 1), membership, and a drop-in room. A list from a brainstorming session about future issues and priorities could still stand today: program development, women and child care, educational programs, economic survival issues, outreach to other organizations, classism within feminism, sexism in education, and a speaker's bureau.

The "Violence Against Women" Conference

One set of issues that had long been important to the SFWC were those involving violence against women. Explicit and tacit acceptance of violence perpetrated against women was one of the most visible aspects of women's subordinate position in society. San Francisco Women Against Rape was an early sponsored project, as was La Casa de las Madres, providing shelter and services for battered women.

In the fall of 1975, Sally Gearheart, a professor in the Women's Studies Department at San Francisco State University (SFSU), approached women at the SFWC about the idea of convening a conference on issues of violence and women. The idea was enthusiastically received, and a call went out to find other sponsoring organizations. Six other organizations joined the SFWC and the Women's Studies Department: the Women's Center at SFSU, Black Women Organized for Action, Lesbians Organized, La Casa de las Madres, the Chicana Rights Project of the Mexican American Legal Defense and Education Fund, and the Golden Gate chapter of NOW. Few of the sponsoring organizations had much in the way of extra money, so what most brought to the effort was staff and volunteer time. In the case of SFWC, several members of the core group as well as many others in the SFWC circle were very active in the conference.

By the spring of 1976, a coordinating committee met weekly and involved several dozen women. Many other volunteers worked on specific components of the conference, such as workshops, a book on poetry (Poetry from Violence, published after the conference), a weekday march and rally planned for prior to the conference to call public attention to the issue (this was eventually abandoned due to other demands), and an evening cultural program. By the end of the process, over two hundred women had been involved in the organizing effort. Nor did the process end with the conference. Committees continued to meet well into 1977 to handle the follow-up from the conference.

The focus of the conference was "Violence Against Women," and the organizing committee took a very broad view of violence, not limiting the content to physical or sexual assault issues. Its stated goals were "to identify physical / social / political / economic / cultural / psychological acts/crimes against women; to identify and explore violence among women, to explore ways to eliminate the acts of violence and conditions leading to them, to identify conditions that perpetuate violence, and to develop concrete ways women can organize and mobilize to combat crimes of violence."[7] The politics of the sponsoring organizations ranged from reformist to revolutionary, but all identified as feminist.

For Women Only

It was decided fairly early in the organizing that the conference would only be open to women and girls. This position was first challenged and upheld in regard to the participation of a transvestite. A decade later this decision would have launched a passionate debate, but in the mid-1970s the transsexual gender lines were murky at best. In fact, the notes from the conference indicate that the decision was moot because in fact the transvestite in question was a female and therefore not excluded from participation, leaving me to wonder what the note taker meant with her use of the term "transvestite."

The first major challenge to the females-only policy came during the summer. The conference was initially set to be held in the fall of 1976 at San Francisco State University. Some early press work led to an article in the San Francisco Chronicle. It was a short article, but

---

7   From "Violence Against Women" conference program. GLBTHS, WBA, main collection, series 1, subseries A, box 5, file 19.

one thing it did report on was the women-only nature of the conference. This in turn led to a phone and letter campaign to SFSU administrators blasting the exclusion of men as discriminatory.

Civil rights legislation that had been enacted ten years earlier to guarantee women's equal access to education was now being used as an obstacle to women organizing. It wasn't clear who, if anyone, orchestrated the campaign, but it is an indication of the hostility the women's movement continued to face in society. One theory about the source of the disgruntlement was that it came from students in the Police Science program at SFSU, who saw the conference as a way to become familiar with issues they would likely be dealing with once they became part of law enforcement. Diane Jones, who started her nearly twenty years of activism with The Women's Building while working on this conference, recalls:

The conference had been organized, I think, for September, at San Francisco State, and I think a month or six weeks prior to the event, San Francisco State pulled out its sponsorship because they found out it was intended to be a women only event, and they said it was a violation—I believe it was part of title VII—to have a women's only event. So we had no place.

Rather than change the character of the conference, the organizers chose to find a new location. This was no easy task: they had to find a space appropriate for both workshops and general assemblies, a place that was affordable and available on short notice, and a place that was willing to allow a women-only event. After much scrambling, a location was patched together using Grace Cathedral and Cogswell College, a trade school, which were two blocks apart. It meant pushing the conference back 2 months, to December 4 and 5. But both institutions subsidized the use of their space, helping to keep conference expenses low. Diane, who was on the site committee, made the following comments regarding the new location:

There were some specific reasons why both of those entities, which wouldn't necessarily be open to this type of event, were willing and interested. Both of these men [the rector of Grace Cathedral and the dean of Cogswell College], on some level were willing to do it almost for the wrong reasons: they believed different genders had different needs and different needs to organize separately. So just as they objected to feminists' critique of men-only spaces, etc., they believed in and supported the idea.

And they also, both of these men, understood from their own life experience and intellectually the issue of violence against women. And that's what we were really attempting to do. And they really also, I think personally, were supportive of the concept of grassroots organizing in consciousness raising. Which was a lot of how the event was. Our definition of violence against women was quite broad and included many, many facets, including economic and emotional in addition to rape and domestic violence, incest, and pornography, etc. They were both interested in that.

They had no idea really (laugh) what they were doing. I think they thought they were going to be interacting with more of a social services type of event. Instead there were 1,300 women coming from all over Northern California!

Though the sponsors included women of color organizations, and women of color did work on the project, the majority of the organizers were white. The sponsoring groups that had paid staff were mainly white, including their staff. Once the organizing was off the ground, there arose a concern about the color composition, both within the organizing committees and in attendance at the conference itself. Outreach was focused on local organizations of women of color, with mixed results. One of the groups contacted in this process was the Third World Women's Alliance. This initial contact went no further, though some Alliance members did attend the conference. But in a few years a second connection with the group would prove much more significant for the SFWC (see chapter 7.)

Another step taken to keep the conference accessible was to make registration free. As the date approached and the ensuing buzz in the community made a sell-out seem likely, several hundred registration forms were set aside to ensure the participation of any woman of color who arrived at the last minute. Again, the results were mixed. Of the 1,300 conference participants, only about 10% were women of color, certainly lower than in society and in the state of California. But the conference was more multiracial than many other gatherings in the women's movement of the time.

The decision to keep registration free also meant looking for other ways to pay the conference expenses. A grant proposal was developed and sent to several foundations. This was a time when women's issues were rarely deemed worthy of foundation support. Even the local progressive foundation Vanguard rejected the proposal. However, a proposal to the California Council for Humanity in Public Policy (CCHPP) fared better. This federally funded foundation was willing to grant funds specifically to record the conference and make the tapes available, plus it would match donations received from individuals at eighty-five cents to the dollar, coming to approximately $8,000, depending on how many other donations were secured.

In the communication between the conference organizers and the CCHPP staff, the fact that men would be excluded from the conference was somehow glossed over, until it came time to sign the contracts in October. As a federally funded entity, the CCHPP was unable to support a project that had a blanket discrimination. But the grant officer was willing to accept a compromise that would open up some of the conference and leave other parts restricted.

It was already mid-October, and bills were starting to come due. The thought of losing the grant money was yet another blow. At the weekly organizing meeting, the women agonized over their choices. Taking the money meant giving in on a principle that had already taken a sacrifice to maintain. It would also mean losing the support of some of the sponsoring and endorsing organizations, including SFSU's Women's Center, San Francisco Women Against Rape, and La

Casa de las Madres. On the other hand, the conference was already in the red, and turning down the money would mean diverting so much energy to last-minute fundraising that the very success of the conference could be jeopardized. The coordinating committee, with about eighteen women present, voted very reluctantly to accept a compromise that would allow men to attend the general assembly and evening cultural program, while keeping the workshops closed to men.

Within hours, this decision spread like wildfire (even without the Internet) among scores of women involved, sparking a storm of debate. Three days later an emergency meeting of the coordinating committee was convened to reconsider the decision. This second meeting was attended by some thirty women. After a spirited and at times tense discussion, the group voted overwhelmingly (with two abstentions and one no) to refuse the CCHPP funds and to pursue other fundraising efforts. One participant felt so strongly that the event should be women-only that she offered to sign over her entire paycheck to help pay for conference expenses. At that meeting, and over the next few weeks, many of the organizers dipped into their own pockets. The money necessary to pay the pending bills was raised internally. In the end, the CCHPP did give $4,100 to pay for the video and audio taping of the conference, which would be made available to anyone.

The Conference

The conference was an overwhelming success. By mid-November, over eight hundred women had pre-registered, with another hundred registrations in the mail. Ultimately, 1,300 women attended, most from the Bay Area but some coming from elsewhere around the country. Speakers at the opening general session were Sally Gearhart, Margaret Sloan, and Kathy Barry, with poetry by Judy Grahn. The Saturday evening program included poetry by Allie Light, Lynn Lonidier, Ruth Hughey, and Beverly Bahlen, a dance performance by Stepping Out Dance Collective and music from Women of the Frente Music Collective. Over two dozen workshops were offered, with a wide variety of topics reflecting the varying views of feminism: Parental Stress and Child Abuse; Medical Violence; Violence to Women in the Media; Third World Women and Violence; Violence of Economic Oppression, Poverty, and Class; Violence of Intercourse; and Violence to Women on the Job, as well as workshops on rape, battered women of various ages, and shelter networks.

In addition, over one hundred children of the participants were cared for, overwhelming the organizers. The inadequacy of the child care was one of the biggest complaints about the weekend. Promises had been made to provide a structured program for the children, but the organizers were unable to deliver. The sheer number of children would have overwhelmed even experienced teachers. The young women in charge had no such experience to draw from, most not even having children of their own. With children running amok and participants needing to move back and forth between the two locations of the conference, many mothers were uncomfortable leaving their children and weren't able to fully engage in the conference.

Poetry gathered in the course of the organizing was published in a book, Poetry of Violence, financed by advanced sales. Over the six months following the conference, audio and video tapes were prepared and kept at Brady Street, available to anyone interested in them. In the nineties, an effort was made to gather materials on the conference for the archives, but no copies of these tapes were located.

The energy from the conference was a boost to several organizing efforts. La Casa del las Madres and San Francisco Women Against Rape, which existed prior to the conference, got a significant boosts in volunteer support. The Women's Alcohol Coalition (later to become the Women's Alcohol Center) and Women Against Violence in Pornography and the Media were formed out of workshops and the networking done at the conference.

Caring for the Mother Organization

In late 1976, with a couple of very busy years behind them, the group stepped back to re-evaluate the purpose and character of the organization. With so many members completely immersed in the final stages of the conference on violence, the distinct role of the SFWC was in danger of being lost. A Planning Committee was formed to evaluate the current state of the organization and develop its future direction. The exhaustion of organizing the violence conference took its toll on the planning process, and there was very low participation after the initial meeting. A sense of urgency, and frustration, about keeping the organization alive was growing. Fortunately, with the new year more women were drawn back into the committee, and it was able to grapple with a number of issues.

The Planning Committee paid some attention to internal issues. The size and complexity of the budget had increased to the point that it was time to upgrade the financial systems. A new accountant was found to help with planning and provide oversight and a new book-keeping system was installed. New VISTA positions were created, the character of the work was more clearly defined and applications from women of color were actively pursued.

Tiana Arruda recalls:
I was a volunteer of the Women's Switchboard, I think in 1975, and then I applied for a position opening at the Women's Centers in 1976, I think in the spring. I didn't get hired and then in the fall they had another opening and I got hired to be part of the staff. . . . At that time Roma Guy and Jean Crosby were on staff. Then Jeanette Lazam was hired at the same time I was. We were the first two women of color on staff. I'm Latina and she was Filipina. I remember that Roma gave up a part of her salary to be able to hire both of us. In those days, collectives were really willing to share their resources. And I remember very clearly that they wanted Jeanette for some of her experience with community

and movement, in the Asian community, and they wanted me for other reasons, you know, in the Latino community. And so [Roma] split some of her money in order for the Women's Center to afford to hire both of us.

A five-thousand-dollar grant from the Skaggs Foundation came in April 1977. The funding for VISTA volunteers was also continued, and they were able to get new funding from the Comprehensive Employment and Training Act (CETA) for additional short-term employment. This gave the organization some financial stability for the next year.

Another issue the Planning Committee looked at was the distinction between internal projects and "sponsored projects." The violence conference was a sponsored project that had become so all-consuming that the organization's internal work had suffered. Yet no one wanted to stop sponsoring new groups or short-term projects. The SFWC's role as a fiscal sponsor had been at the core of its identity from its inception.[8]

In these early years, until a major reform in the law in 1986, IRS oversight was minimal. So aside from staying away from electoral candidates, there were few restrictions on what could be taken on. Within each project, there was pretty much complete autonomy for the groups to pursue their own goals. The type of assistance the SFWC offered varied from providing tax-deductible status and nonprofit postage rates to putting significant labor into efforts. The financial reports for these years tells the story: in 1973, 51 percent of its $3,700 annual expense was granted directly to sponsored projects; by 1975 and 1976, that percentage had risen to 61 percent of a budget ten times larger.

There were no explicit changes in the program as a result of the Planning Committee's evaluation, but there was a slight change in

---

8   Over its first three decades, the SFWC would be the fiscal sponsor for well over one hundred organizing efforts. Some went on to acquire their own non-profit status, others functioned for years as small, mostly volunteer efforts, and others were short-term projects, such as a conference.

emphasis. The original impulse for the SFWC had been to sponsor new organizations, but by 1977 this was seen as only one aspect of the SFWC. One of the clarifications made in 1977 was that the organization would no longer play a central role in running the sponsored projects. Rather, the projects were to be self-run, as most in fact were. Projects in which SFWC was more centrally involved, like the women and violence conference, were to be viewed as direct projects of the SFWC, with a plan for how each project would fit in with other existing projects without overwhelming them.

Among these other projects were the rap groups. Consciousness-raising groups had been a staple organizing tool of the women's movement since the sixties. At issue now was how to shift the character of the rap groups as the movement changed, and as societal attitudes were shifting. While there was still some demand for support groups for women coming to awareness of their oppressed position, the limits of these groups were also becoming clear.

One of the concerns raised during the recent conference was how to move beyond speaking of personal experiences to focusing the energy on organizing. A few of the conference workshops moved to this second level; as mentioned earlier, organizing for the La Casa de las Madres got a significant boost from the conference, and another group, Women Against Violence in Pornography and the Media, was also formed out of the conference. But most conference workshops stayed at the level of identifying the problem, and most of the SFWC rap groups also continued to operate on this level.

Another issue was that most of the women currently served by these groups were white and middle class. The SFWC's experiences in organizing with the violence conference coalition had underscored the importance of finding a way to broaden its base among women of color. Various new models for the rap groups were considered, all looking to emphasize their educational component.

The structure adopted in March 1976 had included representatives from the rap groups in the decision making process. Various women involved in leading the groups were involved the collective, but by and large the women participating in the groups did not feel any particular allegiance to the SFWC. Efforts to change the character of the groups went on through the year, but by 1978 the rap groups had for the most part faded away.

The desire to have an educational component to the organization also led to one of the more exciting events in the spring of 1977, the Feminist Forum Series. The first forum, held in April 1977, was a great success. The turnout was greater than anticipated, generating great enthusiasm for ongoing dialogues. A debate between strands of feminism, the forum featured Charlotte Bunch, editor of Quest, a feminist quarterly; Margaret Sloan, founder of National Black Feminists and on staff at the Berkeley Women's Center; Jeanette Lazam, from Oakland's A Woman's Place Bookstore and an International Hotel activist; Dorinda Moreno, poet and member of Concilio Mujeres; and Susan Heller, from the San Francisco Commission on the Status of Women. The moderator was Sally Gearhart, writer and instructor at SFSU's Women's Studies Department. Though Margaret was held up out of town and missed the program, the rest engaged in a lively debate.

This first forum also turned out to be the high point of the series, as only a few more were held and these had lower attendance and less energy. Increased attention was put into using the newsletter as an educational tool, covering such issues as welfare policy, the International Hotel fight to save low-income housing, and the effort to defend Affirmative Action. The writing and production of the newsletter was one of the important means by which individuals could volunteer with the SFWC, as it was a fairly labor-intensive project that was undertaken monthly. Local women-focused newspapers were just starting, so for many women the newsletter's calendar of events was an important source of information. Later, papers like Plexus and Coming Up (now Bay Times), would take over the calendar function.

Outgrowing Brady Street

The final issue taken up by the Planning Committee was cramped office space. In the final stages and aftermath of the violence conference, the inadequate nature of the office at 63 Brady Street came to the fore. There were problems with the facilities—no heat, a shortage of electrical outlets—and there was too much demand on the space. It was used for meetings, office work, drop-in / bulletin board space, the Women's Switchboard, and Options for Women Over 40. Renovation, at SFWC's own expense, could help with upgrading the heat and electricity, but the amount of space was not changeable. By February 1977, the collective agreed it was time to locate to new office space and a committee was formed to start the search

The decision to look for a new home came together with an impulse that had arisen among the women involved in organizing the conference on violence. The frustrating experience of losing the conference site and the difficulty of finding a new one made very vivid Virginia Woolf's plea for a room of her own. In 1977, as women decompressed from the conference organizing, the idea of women owning their own space, free to do with it as they pleased, started to float though the community. After several frustrating months looking at potential offices that were either too expensive or too small and run down to be an improvement over Brady Street, the committee expanded its vision and started talking about women owning their own room. The fantasy was shared with other women, and by the middle of 1977, the committee was transformed into a new sponsored project: the Women's Building project. The idea was broadcast through the community, and the Women's Building Project was born.

Roma Guy was particularly interested in this project but also knew that it was a big undertaking that would take new skills. She located a program that could teach invaluable skills, but rather than use the limited resources of the Women's Centers she decided to raise the money herself. Responding to a challenge from a friend, she announced her plan to bicycle across Canada. She challenged her friends to pledge a penny per mile for the marathon ride. Billed as "Roma Rides for the Revolution", few thought she would successfully complete the 3,000 mile ride. She started out from Vancouver in the fall of 1977 headed east. It wasn't fast or easy, but she made it to the east coast, raising enough money to pay for the fundraising program. The ride was over, but the marathon effort to buy and operate a building was just underway.

Despite the earlier attempts to distinguish direct programs from sponsored projects, the character of this project was not clear. It began as an internal committee looking for an office and involved a number of core SFWC members. But it soon expanded to involve other women, who stepped forward specifically to work on the idea of women buying a building. Over the next year, the project would absorb tremendous resources, both from the SFWC and from the community at large. By the time the purchase of Dovre Hall was nearing completion, this lack of clarity would lead to significant tension within the staff and core collective.

CHAPTER **3**

THE WOMEN'S BUILDING PROJECT

SUPERFICIALLY AT LEAST, The Women's Building Project was just another in a series of sponsored projects. But in fact it was very different. Over the years, numerous organizations initially sponsored by the San Francisco Women's Centers (SFWC) had evolved into their own distinct institutions. Occasionally, women involved in the core of the SFWC left to become more involved with newly formed organizations, but the strength of its core was never damaged. To the contrary, its role in helping to jump-start new organizations was what kept the SFWC rejuvenated on a regular basis.

At least twice before in its short life, the SFWC had thrown a substantial amount of its own resources into launching new projects. In the case of the credit union (see chapter 1), the Centers worked with women from three other organizations to charter and establish the project, and thereafter the credit union relied on its own resources to hire a staff. As related previously, the credit union went through several of its own crises in its five-year life, and as a legal charter member the SFWC stepped forward to participate in resolving the problems and eventually closing it down. This work, though undoubtedly stressful to the individuals involved, did not seriously strain the functioning of the SFWC's collective.

The other project that drew substantial resources from the SFWC was the 1976 conference on women and violence. This was also a coalition effort, involving half a dozen other organizations and numerous individuals. It was also for a specific event with an end date. Including the follow-up work of publishing the book of poetry and preparing the video and audio tapes, it was an eighteen-month project. In the short run, it was an exhausting campaign for virtually all involved, including the core of the SFWC. In the longer term, however, the effort expanded and diversified the community base of the SFWC. Once the collective had rested and regrouped through the work of the Planning Committee, the SFWC entered into a stable couple of years. It was during this period of relative stability that the project to buy a building for the women's community began.

As it turned out, the project to buy a building came to be the defining characteristic of the SFWC in the decades to come. In fact, had the SFWC not purchased the Building in 1979, it is very likely that the organization would have collapsed before the end of the 1980s. Had the women waited much longer to make the decision to buy, they would have run into rapidly rising real estate prices that probably would have been beyond the budget of a group already struggling to pay a few hundred dollars per month in rent.

Owning the building often seemed like more of a liability than an asset, but it would also be a commitment that couldn't be easily walked away from. As such it became the anchor that kept the SFWC alive. The Building became the focus of many struggles, from the conflict with the Dovre Club to significant staffing and other internal difficulties. Through these struggles, the SFWC learned to use the building as an asset and as a political tool, and the Building was the locus for the maturation of many women in the movement.

A Challenge to Consensus

At the outset, the organizing efforts required to buy a building gave a significant boost to the SFWC. Between the coalition of San Francisco groups and individuals that came together to actually look for and purchase a building and the ties created with organizations around the greater Bay Area with the Mile-a-Thon fundraising event, the public visibility of the SFWC reached an all-time high.

Yet from the beginning, there was not a consensus within the core collective in support of the building project. Some of the opposition stemmed from the collective's organizational limitations, with some women arguing that the SFWC didn't have the human and financial resources to take on such a big project. Jean Crosby, active since the first days of the Centers, was one of the main voices of caution. This conclusion was supported by the work of a consultant, Nan Parks, who was hired to evaluate the feasibility of undertaking such a substantial liability. Her final recommendation was that purchasing any building was a risk with a high chance of failure, that failure would destroy the SFWC, and that thus the risk should not be taken.

Others in the collective opposed buying a building for political reasons. One line of reasoning argued that the resources it would consume would be better used in support of direct organizing. Another concern raised was the specter of the SFWC becoming "another YWCA," focused only on direct services for individuals and losing its role as part of a political movement. Differences of opinion struck right to the heart of the SFWC collective, with Roma Guy charging off to lead the building campaign, while her lover and a founder of the SFWC, Jean Crosby, opposed the idea.

The Women's Building Project committees didn't address these issues, as their sole purpose was to pursue the purchase of a building. But within the core of the SFWC, there were bitter debates over these questions. By the end of 1978, the project would overwhelm the SFWC's collective nearly to the point of collapse. I'll return to this in the next chapter, but first it's important to know what went into The Women's Building Project.

Gearing Up

The effort to locate a building to purchase for the use by the Bay Area women's community was under way by mid-1977, along with the initial efforts to raise the substantial funds necessary to make the dream a reality. The following article published in the December 1977 SFWC newsletter describes the process up to that point:

WHAT? AH, A WOMEN'S BUILDING

Once upon a time there was San Francisco Women's Centers, located at 63 Brady Street. Many of you visited with us. It was cozy and wonderfully alive. Over the years it became a center for more and more activity, and that energy has spread to many places in SF and in our personal lives.

If you have been to SFWC in the last year and a half you probably know that it is no longer cozy. There is no place to talk, read, write, or make a phone call; often the rooms are unavailable and very often they are too small. So in the spring of 1977 some women began to fantasize about moving into a larger building which would accommodate more than two women's organizations and which could provide a "performance" area.

Then the fantasy became a vision. And questions and realities were researched and played with. Does a building exist which we can afford, which is accessible by public transportation, be wheelchair accessible, and is relatively safe at night??? Will the community support it? Will it become a political monster? Can we raise the money to buy/lease? Can SFWC survive financially if it takes such a time-consuming coordination project so soon after the Conference on Violence Against Women? ETC., ETC., ETC.

The talking, researching, reflecting, and looking at lots of buildings led us to the present possibility: there is a building at 160 South Van Ness (between Mission and 13th); it is 15,200 sq. ft., two floors, and it sells for $300,000.

Buying this building has been researched and supported by a core of about 25 women, most representing organizations which would like to rent space and some women who are interested in the performance area and the women's building concept. The current organizations interested are: SFWC, SF Women's Switchboard, Lesbians Organizing, Feminist Writers Guild, SF Women's Speaker's Network, Insight Exchange, Women's Press Project, Every Women's Art Building, Full Moon Coffeehouse, SF Women Against Rape, and Mothertongue Theater. We will not have a "full-house" until we explore more completely the interest of disabled women and Third World women.

Lots of energy, imagination, and money is necessary to realize this possibility. Benefits are already being organized. The Feminist Film Series is scheduled for each Sunday in March and April. Mark your new year's calendar now for every Sunday afternoon. Many, many tax deductible dollars and pledges to the Building Fund are needed. The first hurdle is a $60,000 down payment to buy the building. When this $$$, plus $3,000 for closing costs, plus committed renters, plus political unity has been achieved, 160 South Van Ness will be another "room of our own" in San Francisco.

Does this idea make you feel good? It is a huge, super-exciting challenge for 1978—and on into forever. If this work would be an energizer for you, come organize, donate, research, and we will found a women's building in SF—all women are welcomed.

There is an open general meeting every Thursday at 6:30 at SFWC. If you want to donate money or know someone who might, let us know or write the check to SFWC and attach a note that says "Building Fund." Suggestions, opinions, questions are important to all of us now, so write, attend a meeting, call. We need to know what you believe can and should be possible for women in SF.[9]

As it turned out, the location at 160 South Van Ness was not to be because the group was unable to come up with the five thousand dollars needed to keep the property off the market. But it didn't stop the women. For many, just the experience of looking at and imagining that potential space built a momentum that was not to be derailed. The Film Series benefits were already in place, with five programs. The first, held at McKenna Theatre at San Francisco State University, featured films about notable women, including Colette, Night's Darkness, a Day's Sail (about Virginia Woolf), Anne Sexton, Rainbow Black (about Sarah Webster Fabio), and Gwendowlyn Brooks. The rest of film series was held at the Roxie Theater, a collectively run independent theater on 16th Street near Mission. Each set of films had a theme, with the second and third focused on local female film-makers, the fourth on films about women activists, and the final set focused on women artists. Titles included Allie Light's Possum Trot, outtakes from Word Is Out, Angela Davis, Portrait of a Revolutionary, and Frida Kahlo.

Individual donations were beginning to pour in, and dozens of women and organizations were involved in the project. The SFWC sought high-profile endorsers to give more legitimacy to the project and to bolster foundation grant proposals. Proclamations in support of the prospective Women's Building came from the National Organization for Women, Supervisor Carol Ruth Silver, Mission Cultural Center, and Advocates for Women.

Organizations that made tentative or firm commitments to rent space in a new building continued to grow, including the Coalition for the Medical Rights of Women, Union Wage, the Women's

---

9   SFWC newsletter, December 1977. GLBTHS, WBA, main collection, series 1, subseries A, box 4, file 3.

Alcohol Coalition, Women Against Violence in Pornography and the Media, Black Women Organized for Action, the Lesbian Law Project, the Organization of Women Architects, and the Older Women's Project.

The Women's Building Project set up a number of subcommittees to move the work forward. The Negotiations Committee, headed by SFWC staff member Roma Guy, worked on the financial planning and bookkeeping, applying for loans, coordinating contributions, and working on contracts and licensing issues. The Publicity Committee, led by Tracy Gary, worked to publicize the effort to purchase a building and various efforts to raise the funds needed. A Space Committee, led by Michel Ferrier, conducted outreach to potential renters and tenants, assessing their needs to help determine how space in a building could best be configured. Another committee, led by Lynn Lonidier, focused on the performance space potential of a building, assessing what was needed and which groups might use it. A Fundraising Committee, led by Alana Schindler, sought funding from foundations and coordinated a direct mail appeal and other efforts to secure donations from individuals. The hope was to complement this effort with the work of an ongoing Benefits Committee, which would pursue the production of benefit programs to raise funds, but after the spring film series, this committee never got off the ground.

There was another major benefit effort under way, however. A committee led by Nan Schlosberg and Tracy Gary was coordinating a Mile-a-Thon benefit. This huge undertaking was organized to achieve two goals: raising money and developing political support from scores of women's organizations from around the Bay Area. It was 1978, and this was still a relatively new idea for raising money: individuals gathered pledges from family, friends, and co-workers for the miles walked or biked (or hours danced, or frames bowled).

WOMEN ON THE MOVE!

THE SECOND ANNUAL MILE-A-THON
to Benefit Bay Area Nonprofit Organizations

Saturday, October 27, 1979

MUSIC CONCOURSE 8:30 am REGISTRATION GOLDEN GATE PARK

We need workers, walkers and movers. Help us by sponsoring a friend, raising sponsors yourself.
Come and enjoy the day. For more information or sponsor sheet, call 963-9110 or 431-1180. JOIN US ON THE MOVE!

This Mile-a-Thon, to be held on a fifteen-mile course laid out in Golden Gate Park, would come to involve over one hundred organizations. The format called for each organization involved to raise pledges through their own base, with the proceeds split 50-50 between the organization and the Women's Building Project (less 10 percent, which went to the SFWC as the nonprofit fiscal agent for the event). All of the logistics and publicity costs were taken care of by the Women's Building Project; all the participating organizations had to do was collect the pledges and show up to walk or run. The route laid out was wheelchair accessible, and a shorter alternative route was prepared in case of rain. Child care was also provided; learning from the "Violence Against Women" conference, far more resources went into ensuring a good quality program for the children in attendance.

Overhead costs of this massive event were kept low by using volunteer labor to organize the event. In the final months, Diane Jones, a core volunteer of the SFWC, worked full time as a coordinator, and paid collective members of the SFWC helped fill in the gaps, especially when it came to handling the dozens of small donations. Ultimately, $54,000 was raised by the event, $27,000 going toward the purchase of the building and the rest going back to the sponsoring organizations.

Some organizations, including the Women's Switchboard, the Women's Speaker Bureau, the Marin Rape Crisis Center, Options for Women Over 40, Women's Way (San Rafael), Women Against Violence in Pornography and the Media, Lesbian Schoolworkers, and the Mid-Peninsula Project Against Domestic Violence, were able to raise between $500 and $1,600 for their projects. Many others raised a couple hundred dollars, including Les Nichelletes (a performance group), San Francisco Women Against Rape, Synergy School, La Casa de las Madres, the Jeanne Jullian Defense Committee, Women in the Wilderness, St. Davis Childcare, the Berkeley Women's Center, and Women Organized for Employment. Some organizations raised less than $100; payouts started as low at $2.25 to the Sonora Women's Center, $3.38 to the Society of Women Engineers, and $6.75 to Union Wage and People's Media Collective. But even organizations that raised only small amounts of money were drawn into the community base of the Women's Building Project.

The Building

During the first months of 1978, the group looked at a few buildings that were on the market and somewhere in their price range, including several mortuaries. They also began scouting out buildings that might be a fit but weren't currently for sale. By the time of the Mile-a-Thon in October 1978, the collective had fixed on Dovre Hall, a building at 3543 18th Street. It was not currently for sale, but a realtor working with the group suggested it as a likely possibility. They approached the owners, a group called Sons of Norway, about their willingness to sell. The Norwegian immigrant base of the organization had been fully as-similated into U.S. society, and the Building's role as a social meeting ground for the community was all but gone. The building had only a few tenants, the most significant of which was the Dovre Club, an Irish pub located in the northeast corner of the ground floor. Built in 1910 and renovated in the 1930s, the four-story building was located in the heart of the Mission District. A fact sheet put together by the Women's Building Project in August 1978 described the following attributes:

- an 800-seat performance hall, with a stage and fairly good acoustics [an assessment that many would later come to dis-agree with]
- a 300-seat hall with an institutional kitchen attached
- a ground-floor bar (the Dovre Club), whose lease would be up for negotiation late in 1979
- numerous large carpeted rooms, ranging from 1,000 to 2,000 square feet each and totaling 5,000-6,000 square feet
- a smaller board meeting room
- an elevator, making all four floors wheelchair accessible[10]

The main disadvantage identified was the lack of office space, which would have to be carved out of some of the large rooms.

---

10 Women's Building of the Bay Area Fact Sheet. GLBTHS, WBA, main collection, series 1, subseries C, box 7, file 7.

In addition to the logistics of buying the building, the women also began discussing how the new Women's Building would operate. The major components of the new structure would consist of the staff (building management, fundraising, publicist, outreach to potential renters, bookkeeper, and consultants regarding legal and accounting issues), renters/tenants, and performance space users. A council of nine to eleven women representing these three components would make all policy decisions regarding the building (e.g., space usage, financial planning, etc.).

In the meantime, the collective of women involved in the various committees of the project took responsibility for decisions. At a meeting on July 27, 1978, it was agreed that the decision-making body for the next six months would be a group of women who each made a commitment for the next six months to work at least five hours per week, attend a weekly meeting on Thursday nights to make decisions, and assume a major task responsibility within one (or more) of the functioning subcommittees.

This process involved several dozen women who took on the core of the work, with all decisions made by consensus. All meetings were open to any woman, and dozens of others cycled in and out of the meetings.[11] A participating organization could choose to be part of the decision-making group and send a representative.

An early challenge to the consensus process was the question of whether the Building would rent to male-only and mixed groups. The proposal was that permanent renters (e.g., tenants[12]) would be women-only groups and organizations. Of the twenty-one women present for this discussion, held at the same July meeting that established the criteria for the decision-making body, fifteen voted yes, one voted no, and five abstained. The abstentions came for various reasons—lack of information, no strong feelings but a desire to see the meeting move on, and a feeling of being rushed without enough information. The

11 At a reunion held in the early 1990s, several hundred women identified themselves as being part of the founders' group.
12 Note that this term was not used in most of the notes, perhaps because of the power dynamic implied by posing the tenant/owner dichotomy.

no vote came from a woman who liked the idea of a woman's building but also wanted to support other struggles, for Third World rights, disabled rights, etc., and feared that an exclusionary rental principle would undermine this support. The woman who voted no agreed not to stop the consensus process with her vote. Instead, she asked that the group take up the issue of how it would support mixed groups that had similar social change goals.

As the group put its focus on Dovre Hall, other conflicts arose regarding the space itself. One of the groups very involved in the project from the beginning was the Full Moon Coffee House collective. They operated a coffee shop and bookstore on 18th Street, staffing the establishment with a volunteer collective until they lost their lease in 1978. Even before losing their lease, the group was committed to operating out of a building run by and for women. Several collective members were very involved in the Women's Building Project, and their enterprise was considered a core tenant.

However, the investigation into purchasing the Dovre building revealed that the San Francisco Planning Commission would most likely rule out a full-scale retail enterprise. Several of the weekly meetings considered ways to get around the restriction, but in the end the purchase effort went forward, leaving the needs of the coffee house unmet. Not long after, the Full Moon Coffee House collective dissolved.

The Dovre Club

The loss of one of the groups viewed as a core tenant may have gotten more attention had the timing been a little different. Just as the decision was reached to live with the commission's restrictions on retail, the issue of one of the current building tenants, the Dovre Club, came to the fore. The Dovre Club was an Irish bar located in the northeast corner of the building. It had its own entrance at the corner of Lapidge and 18th, and the only indoor connection between it and the rest of the Building was through the basement.

As the investigation into purchasing Dovre Hall advanced, the word of a pending purchase soon got back to Paddy Nolan, owner of the Dovre Club. A bar had operated in this part of the Building since the thirties remodel, acquiring a clientele that included prominent politicians and influential businessmen. In 1966, Nolan had bought the liquor license, renamed the bar the Dovre Club, and carried on the business as an Irish pub. By 1978, when the SFWC first contacted the Sons of Norway about the possible sale of the Building, the Dovre Club had accumulated its own venerable legacy. As a supporter of Irish independence and the Irish Republican Army (IRA), Nolan also welcomed pro-IRA activists to use the pub as a meeting ground. With other politicians and businessmen as its clientele as well, the Dovre Club had considerable political clout in a city dominated by machine-style politics. Who you knew was as important, if not more important, than the validity of the issue at stake.

At an August 17, 1978, meeting of the Women's Building Project, a rumor was reported that Nolan had indicated an interest in selling his liquor license to the Building. Up to this point, there had been no discussion at all about the existence of a bar in the Building. The sobriety movement that would sweep the 1980s was in its infancy, but the consensus among the organizers was that no one wanted the Building itself to operate a bar. No position was taken on the more general future of the Dovre Club as a continuing tenant, but the general attitude was unlikely to be embracing of an Irish pub. If word of the meeting's discussion got back to Nolan, as it likely did, it was undoubtedly threatening. The rumor itself may have been planted by Nolan just to get a reading on what was up with this bunch of radical feminists, mostly lesbian, who were planning to turn the Building into a women's community center.

Nolan turned to friend and patron John Maher to try to stop the purchase. Maher was from a long-established San Francisco family, a member of the Democratic Party Central Committee, founder of Delancey Street, and later to be elected to the San Francisco Board of Supervisors. Another ally called in for assistance was Jack Davis, a gay man just making his mark as a political consultant / campaign manager.

Maher contacted the Women's Building Project organizers with the claim that Nolan had a verbal agreement giving him first option to buy if the Sons of Norway sold the property. This claim was denied by Al Nelson of the Sons of Norway, but Maher's threat was to sue and tie the SFWC up in court, effectively holding up the purchase process until it collapsed. The payoff for this extortion was an offer of support and an unspecified "five-figure" donation toward the purchase in exchange for a long-term lease on the bar.

In addition to the legal attack, Nolan's supporters also had the clout to exert other attacks that could threaten the viability of the Women's Building. As the owner of a building, the SFWC took on whole new levels of responsibility (and liability) to meet public codes. With ties to the fire department and other city agencies that enforced laws regarding public buildings, Nolan had friends who could make operating the Building difficult and expensive.

In light of the political realities, the organizing committee agreed to sign a ten-year lease with Nolan. Twenty years later, when the SFWC was evicting the bar, memories of the actual agreement would vary (See chapter 10 for more on the eviction story.) Some contend that a verbal promise was made that Nolan could stay for his lifetime. Others contend that the SFWC promised that the Dovre Club could remain as long as the SFWC owned the Building. Others believed the collective made a deal with Nolan to accommodate current political realities with the expectation that someday, the Dovre Club would be gone and the space reclaimed as part of The Women's Building.

In any case, the political and legal challenges to the purchase were dropped. Some donations were collected by the Dovre Club for the Building Fund, but not at the level promised during the lease negotiations. Nor did assuring Nolan that he would be keeping his bar stop his hostility toward the new owners, even after the sale went through.

Shortly after the purchase, a fire was set in the lobby of the Building.

Damage was minimal (the fire was contained in a trash can), and no suspects were ever charged. Nonetheless, suspicions ran high that an employee of the Dovre Club had set the blaze. A number of bomb threats were also made, though no bombs were ever found, nor any evidence as to the source of the calls. The idea of a bunch of women owning a building riled more than a few feathers, and these threats could have originated with any number of people, operating from a variety of motives.

One incident in the fall of 1979 was very clearly linked to the hostility of the Dovre Club and its patrons. Inside the newly opened Women's Building, a program was about to be held. The large number of attendees, overwhelmingly female, were waiting in a line outside, snaking its way down the sidewalk past the bar.

From inside the bar, a group of men encouraged their female companions to go out and heckle and harass the women standing in line. They did. Epithets flew through the air: "Dykes go home!" "All you need is a man!" or "Too ugly to get a man!" Women in line shouted back, exhorting the women to get their own lives and break free of male domination. Women's Building staff tried to defuse the situation, moving the line into the Building as quickly as possible and urging those still in line to ignore the bar patrons. This wasn't the first time such harassment had come from inside the bar, usually targeting women in ones or twos as they came to the Building. But the numbers on the street this evening sent tensions to a new high. The San Francisco Police Department was called, but it was slow to respond.

As the tail end of the line came by, one of the women from the bar drew out a small knife and brandished it at the crowd. Roma Guy was there, and as she urged the woman and her friends to go back into the bar, she felt the blow of a fist to her stomach. Unaware at first that the hand held a knife, Roma stepped back. The woman with the knife realized in horror what she had done, exclaiming "I didn't mean to. I'm a Catholic and I really believe!" She dropped the knife and collapsed on the sidewalk. Though Roma had been the one attacked, it was she who ended up reaching out to comfort her attacker.

Fortunately, the small blade had barely penetrated Roma's skin through her coat. Apologies were offered by all the women (including Roma, for reasons unclear in retrospect except as an automatic female reaction to conflict.) By the time the police finally arrived, the women from the bar had left for home, without their male companions, who had become suddenly silent inside the bar. The line of women were all inside, attending the program they had come for.

No legal charges resulted from this incident, but several days later, Roma paid a visit to Paddy Nolan. She made it clear that this kind of behavior by his employees and patrons was unacceptable, no matter what his political ties were. He agreed, and while quiet grumbling continued for a while, the open harassment stopped.

For the next sixteen years, an uneasy peace was kept. There were occasional delays in rent payments, but Nolan's rent was always paid eventually. The lease converted to a month-to-month after it expired in 1989. While the Dovre Club shared the below-market rental rates with other tenants, it was never treated as part of The Women's Building community. Its separate entrance set it physically apart from other tenants. On rare occasions, women from offices in the Building went in for a drink or a game of pool, but there was no regular mixing. Over the years, when the staff encountered building-wide issues that were shared with tenants (e.g., security problems, construction work, or coordinated events) the Dovre Club was never part of the mix. Throughout the 80s, this wasn't a problem and was probably the preferred state of relations for both Nolan and the Building staff.

Signing on the Dotted Line

One thing that aided in pushing back the political challenge Nolan posed was that, in addition to the outreach for the Mile-a-Thon, the group had also sought additional high-profile endorsers to give more legitimacy to the project. This process was undertaken at first because such support was important for the success of foundation proposals, but the Dovre Club experience was a good lesson in the importance of building political alliances. In addition to earlier endorsements, in the year after the purchase several other prominent politicians also signed on to endorse the search for foundation support: Mayor Dianne Feinstein, supervisors Harry Britt and Louise Renne, and California Assembly President Willie Brown.

Overshadowing any organizational, ideological, or political conflicts, money was the biggest obstacle facing the Women's Building Project. After a little back and forth, the Sons of Norway agreed to a price of $535,000 and a down payment of $125,000. A $5,000 deposit was made in June of 1978. An additional $5,000 was put down after the group checked that various city codes and licensing and fire regulation requirements would not present obstacles to converting the Building from its current use.

Now there was a six-month escrow period in which to raise the remaining $115,000 for the down payment, plus an estimated $35,000 for closing costs and initial start-up expenses. In June, the women had about $30,000 on hand, leaving $130,000 to be raised by January 1979. The down payment was the just the first hurdle; still unanswered was the issue of getting bank financing for the rest of the purchase price. A monthly mortgage of several thousand was a huge jump from a rent of $200/month, and bank loans to women, let alone grassroots feminist organizations, were far and few between. However, the organizing committee wasn't letting such practical considerations stand in the way.

Gradually, the Building Fund grew. By year's end, close to $100,000 had been raised and the group had negotiated a three-month delay in closing the escrow. The Sons of Norway agreed to carry the note, meaning that the group did not need to find a bank willing to finance a $400,000 mortgage. So with a new deadline of March 31, the project needed $30,000 to make the down payment, and another $35,000 to cover closing costs and at least a few months of the $3,600/month mortgage payment.

Table 1 lists net income to the Building Fund from various appeals and benefits from June 1978 through March 1979.

Table 1: Building Fund Income
June 1978 to March 1979

SOURCE	AMOUNT
Initial anonymous major gift	$25,000
Mile-a-Thon	$27,000
Direct mail and small gifts	$20,500
Larger donations	$12,000
Benefit event proceeds	$14,500
Foundation grants	$30,000
TOTAL	$128,000

In March 1979, when the group was preparing to meet to make the final "go / no go" decision on buying, the balance had grown to about $130,000, enough to complete the purchase but with little left to hire staff or do any work on the building itself. However, there was one grant proposal pending that had good prospects, and just as the women convened, word arrived that a grant for $31,000 had come in from the Hewlett Foundation. Three smaller grants would be received in June and July: $3,000 from Vanguard, $5,000 from Joint Foundation Support, and $3,000 from the Performing Arts Council. Despite the relatively small amounts, this $11,000 would be critical to surviving the first year.

By the time of the final meeting in March 1979, there was no derailing the purchase process. With the final grant pushing them over their $160,000 goal, and with all the work that had been done to that point, nothing short of a major earthquake would have stopped the purchase, and that event was still ten years away.

But there were other challenges ahead. While the Women's Building Project had been barreling full-steam ahead, the organization at the center of this project, the San Francisco Women's Centers, had nearly collapsed. And much of the conflict had to do, in various ways, with the building project itself.

THEATRICAL INTERLUDE: ACT I

MANY PERSONAL STORIES and dramas were part of the process of buying and moving into the building. To bring these experiences to life, a play was developed based on oral histories of the women involved. *She Rises Like a Building to the Sky* had several Bay Area readings and a workshop production at The Marsh with the support of Tale Spinners and Miracle Theater. Full productions of *She Rises* were presented at San Francisco State University and Arizona State University. This play is reproduced here to give readers a flavor of the drama of the times without singling out specific women and their personal stories. The characters in the play are composites of the dozens of women involved at different points in the purchasing and operating of the building. It basically covers events in 1978–80, though for dramatic purposes some of the timing of events was changed.

SHE RISES LIKE A BUILDING TO THE SKY

A play inspired by
the San Francisco Women's Building

by
Mercilee M. Jenkins
Lyrics by Mark Kennedy and Mercilee Jenkins

A group of feminists who run a small women's center in San Francisco in the late 1970's purchase "a building of their own." They hold meetings, raise money and fall in and out of love with each other, while dealing with the notorious bar downstairs. The hothouse nature of community activism is captured by a small ensemble playing multiple and often contradictory roles. Original music and remixed 70s Women's music accent the passions, with struggles and accomplishments of women who love each other enough to change the world.

CAST OF CHARACTERS

The text is inspired by oral histories of women who created the San Francisco Women's Building (WB). Character names are fictitious.

ANNA, working class white, early 30's, founder of the Women's Building (WB)

LOUISE, from Texas, working class white, late 20's, one of founding members of San Francisco Women's Centers and Anna's partner.

RAE, middle class African American, mid-thirties, recently returned from the Peace Corp in Africa where she was lovers with ANNA.

DEBRA, inherited wealth white, from New York, early 30's, fund raiser for W B, in a relationship with SUSAN

SUSAN, middle class white, was married, early 30's, fund raiser for WB, in a relationship with DEBRA.

TESSA, Puerto Rican, late 20's early 30's, raised in New Jersey, comes to work at the WB. Falls in love with PAULA.

JANE, native San Franciscan, mid-30"s, organizational consultant hired to determine the feasibility of purchasing the WB. Becomes involved with Debra.

PAULA, white, middle class, Californian, 20's, very attractive. Falls in love with TESSA.

GEORGE, an older homeless man who has Tourette's syndrome and plays the an instrument or sings and lives outside the women's building

BEN, Paula's boyfriend and regular at the Dovre Club

WARD BINKLE, bar patron & columnist for local paper.

WOMAN #1 and WOMAN #2, bar patrons
BARTENDER
ELENA, WB collective member from El Salvador
MEMBERS 1 and 2 are all members of the women's community who attend different meetings throughout the play.
AUDIENCE MEMBER, Erotic Art Show
MUNI OPERATOR
TAXI DRIVER

PLACE: The play takes place primarily in the Women's Building, a three story building with a bar on the first floor, located in the Mission district of San Francisco.
TIME: The time is early 1979 to 1981.

SCENE OUTLINE

Act I: The Vision

Scene 1: Real Estate for the Revolution
Scene 2: Homecoming
Scene 3: The Meetings
Scene 4: Fund Raising
Scene 5: Welcome to the Hood
Scene 6: Community Meeting
Scene 7: Mileathon
Scene 8: Meeting Double Time
Scene 9: A Toast to the Women's Building

Act II: Naming Ourselves

Scene 1: The Switchboard
Scene 2: Goddesses Descending
Scene 3: Erotic Art Show
Scene 4: Getting There
Scene 5: Paula Plays Pool
Scene 6: The Two Collectives
Scene 7: Police Women
Scene 8: On Top of the World
Scene 9: The Fire

Transcription note: Some speeches in the play are taken verbatim from actual transcripts and others are written in this form to simulate actual speech. Slash marks (//) indicated overlapping speech. Equal signs (=) indicate one speaker is finishing another speaker's phrase or sentence without missing a beat. Caret (^) indicates a rising inflection by the speaker.

ACT I

Scene 1
Real Estate For The Revolution, San Francisco, 1979

(As the scene opens we hear a few bars of trumpet or saxophone solo or singing by GEORGE, a homeless man who has Tourette's syndrome and often communicates through his music. GEORGE is sitting by the entrance of Dovre Hall. ANNA and LOUISE enter.)

ANNA: Do you think anyone is going to come?

LOUISE: They'll come. You put the notice in the newsletter and they've come to see the other ones. *(pause)* This is it?

ANNA: Yeah, but that last one may have scared them off.

LOUISE: Oh, the mortuary?

ANNA: Well, some of the best buildings we've looked at happen to be mortuaries, I mean that are in our price range.

LOUISE: Like we have a price range. You seem to forget we're a small feminist collective that can barely make the rent on two rooms. We can't afford this.

ANNA: Yeah, but isn't it great? I was just driving by when I saw it. It wasn't even for sale. Belongs to the Sons of Norway, but they're willing to sell it to us because they want it to stay a community center. And that's just what it could be: The Women's Building of the Bay Area.

(DEBRA and SUSAN enter and exchange greetings with ANNA and LOUISE)

SUSAN: Is this it?

DEBRA: At least it's not a mortuary?

SUSAN: Thank the Goddess. That last one still had the bloody rags around.

ALL: (making faces) Oooowh.

SUSAN: Bad karma.

ANNA: Still you can't get a better building for the price.

GEORGE: Hey, nice la-la-dies, got any spare change today? *(Holds out a cup and mumbles swear words under his breath)*

LOUISE: I wish.

ANNA: Here you go.

(ANNA & DEBRA put some coins in his cup, as SUSAN searches in vain for any loose change in her bag)

DEBRA: *(To SUSAN)* I've got it honey.

SUSAN: And we'd like to be called women.

GEORGE: Shit, goddamn motherfuck, 'cuse me, sure, sure, whatever rings your chimes. Th-thank you, nice yyyoung women.

ANNA: Look at the brick work. Unusual for San Francisco.

LOUISE: Yeah, should be great in an earthquake. Why do we need bricks and mortar?

ANNA: And there's commercial rental space on the corner.

DEBRA: That funky old bar?

ANNA: It's a colorful Irish bar. *(Whispered aside)* IRA tendencies I've heard *(Return to normal voice)* Of course, we could always not renew their lease and do whatever we like with it. We'd be the owners.

LOUISE: Get rid of an Irish bar in San Francisco?

ANNA: Come on. Let's go in.

LOUISE: Dream on.

ANNA: The President said we could just go in and look around. Welcome to Dovre Hall.

(ALL enter except GEORGE)

GEORGE: *(To audience)* Well, in the bebebeginning, nobody thought it was a good idea, shit, goddamn, motherfuckin', were they crazy? Women had trouble getting credit cards or buying a house on their own, let alone a big-ass building.

ANNA: Watch your step. It's kinda dark in here.

GEORGE: *(To audience)* Shit, see, see, people in progressive politics aren't much into real estate in 1979, huh. *(cursing under his breath)*.

ANNA: Look at all this space. Four floors and a full basement.

DEBRA: It's big alright, but is it a good investment for us?

SUSAN: Wow! Anna has vision. I have to give her that. To think we could buy a place like this.

LOUISE: *(Pulls SUSAN aside)* Susan, I'm worried. I think this is crazy. What are we going to do with all this space? I mean I love her, but this is going too far. We can't manage all this.

SUSAN: *(To LOUISE)* I don't know. I think it's kinda out there but I like that. She's an artist when it comes to organizing people and getting things done, you know.

ANNA: *(Pulling DEBRA aside)* We'll rent it out and have tenants, Debra. We could put the Switchboard right here in the entranceway. Then in here is the auditorium with an adjoining room with a long serving bar and a wet bar. We could put on plays and music events with a little work.

DEBRA: Looks like a lot of work to me. When was the last remodel? In the fifties?

ANNA: Just needs a paint job.

LOUISE: *(To SUSAN)* Do we really want to be landlords?

SUSAN: I don't know. Let's see the rest. It's so dark. Debra where are you?

DEBRA: In the ballroom with Anna. Sounds like a Clue game.

ANNA: No, this is the auditorium. The ballroom's upstairs. Come on.

DEBRA: Who owns this place?

ANNA: Sons of Norway. Come on. On the second floor, there's a cafeteria with a full kitchen,

LOUISE: And what do they do in here?

SUSAN: Weird secret male rites, I guess. Look all the windows are covered.

ANNA: This room would be great for *(to LOUISE)* community meetings or *(to SUSAN)* poetry readings or *(to DEBRA)* fund raising meetings.

DEBRA: *(teasing SUSAN)* Or séances?

ANNA: Lot's of space to do whatever you like. Then on the third floor there's the ballroom. Great for parties...

(ANNA takes LOUISE as a partner and starts ballroom dancing. DEBRA and SUSAN join in)

DEBRA: We could have tea dances in the ballroom.

SUSAN: There probably are ghosts around here, you know, you shouldn't joke about it.

LOUISE: Or strange lesbian rites.

(As dancing around they notice the thrones)

ALL: This place has thrones?! *(ANNA and DEBRA immediately go sit in them leaving their partners)*

LOUISE: *(sarcastic)* Why, they'll come in handy for collective meetings. *(ANNA and DEBRA immediately get up)*

(Making their way up to the top floor)

DEBRA: How much is this going to cost, Anna?

LOUISE: Yes, let's get down to the facts and figures.

ANNA: It's a great deal for the amount of space we'd be getting. Real estate prices are going up. This might be our last chance.

ALL: How much?

ANNA: Let's just go up to the top floor first. Look it's all open and every wall has windows.

DEBRA: *(Out of breath)* Doesn't the elevator work?

ANNA: Sometimes. The art gallery could be on the top floor. Or the Offices of the Women's Centers.

LOUISE: *(Sarcastic)* Oh yes, we should have the penthouse (to ANNA), after all if we're going to spend LOTS of money and you two already claimed the thrones, let's really imitate the patriarchy.

ANNA: We can rotate leadership. This would be a place for all of us where we could hold political rallies. Take radical action. And you can help us get financing, right Debra?

DEBRA: I certainly can try, although I doubt the banks will be terrible impressed by us as a group they'd want to lend money to.

ANNA: Wouldn't a library be nice up here?

SUSAN: *(Looking out the window)* Look, that man's still out there.

ANNA: He usually is, but he's part of the neighborhood. What we're all about. Just imagine. This could be the offices of Women Against Rape and so many of the other organizations we helped start. With all of us here, this could be a place where women could feel safe.

SUSAN: Couldn't we turn the bar into a women's café? That could help raise money to support the building and we could do // performances there.

DEBRA: *(Overlaps with SUSAN)* You could perform // your poetry there.

SUSAN: *(Overlaps with ANNA)* //Yes.

ANNA: Yes,// and how about a childcare center? That could help the community and raise money too. Don't you see, this could be a community center for all people.

SUSAN: Except men.

ANNA: Some men. Come on. We can do this.

ALL: How much?

ANNA: Only $525,000.

ALL: *(Gasp)* What?!

LOUISE: You have to be kidding me? What are we gonna use for money?

ANNA: But it would be ours and nobody could tell us what to do.

LOUISE, DEBRA: We can't do this.

SUSAN: Well, maybe we can. Why should men get all the buildings? We should get at least one.

(song) VIVA LA REAL ESTATE

(Chorus is sung alternating lines. The first and third lines are sung by ANNA. SUSAN joins her after first chorus. The second and fourth lines are sung by LOUISE and DEBRA. GEORGE joins in on last chorus on both sides.)

(chorus)
We can do this
No we can't do this
We can do this
No we can't do this
Anna got me into this

(can be sung by group or individual)
A place where women could be safe
from violent men and fear and hate
The revolution is here
It's not too late
Viva la real estate

Were taking over one building
at a time. Block by block
it's our paradigm
We don't need to smash it
We can buy the state
It's not too late
Viva la real estate

We won't give up without a fight
Things are slipping to the right

Reagan as President?
Feinstein is Mayor.
But it's not too late
Viva la real estate.

(Bridge)
SUSAN
I've been dreaming 'bout a building
I can see it in my sleep. But I always
fall in love with things
Then they break my heart
So as soon as we get
this place, I'm leaving.

(chorus repeated)

(SUSAN and DEBRA exit)
GEORGE: I hear that!

Scene 2
The Homecoming

LOUISE: We've got to get back for the meeting.

ANNA: So let's take the elevator. It'll be faster. *(ANNA pushes the button and we hear the elevator start up)*

LOUISE: You trust this thing?

ANNA: Yeah, I have a good feeling about this building.

LOUISE: Doesn't look like it's been used much lately.

(The elevator doors open and ANNA & LOUISE get in)

ANNA: But can't you see the possibilities?

LOUISE: You wanna know what I really see?

ANNA: *(ANNA put her arms around LOUISE)* Yes, I do.

(The elevator stops, doors don't open)

LOUISE: O.K., now what?
(ANNA presses the button for the first floor but nothing happens)

ANNA: We're stuck. *(Pushes the emergency button and bell starts and then stops)*

LOUISE: Oh, great. I bet everybody's gone. *(yelling)* Hello! Anybody here? *(normal voice)* Now what are we going to do?

ANNA: Don't worry, the President of the group is supposed to meet me here to get the key back and he'll know what to do.

LOUISE: When is that?

ANNA: In a few minutes, so let's sit down and relax and conserve oxygen.

(They are quiet for a few seconds)

GEORGE: *(To AUDIANCE)* I I co-could help'm out, shit, motherfuck ah. But they probably need the time together. Yeah *(mumbles swear words under his breath)*

ANNA: You were gonna tell me what you think about this.

LOUISE: I'm worried.

ANNA: O.K., tell me why.

LOUISE: Isn't it obvious? We're a small feminist organization that has done a lot by helping other feminist organizations get started as sponsored projects. We're not in the business of running buildings.

ANNA: But that's what this is. Another sponsored project.

LOUISE: But it's too big for us to sponsor.

ANNA: We'll do this just like we've done everything else. We'll involve other people.

LOUISE: And then there's the small matter of the cost.

ANNA: We'll fund raise. Susan and Debra are really good at that.

LOUISE: Well, then why ask me if you've got it all figured out?

ANNA: Because I want you behind this. I want you to work with me on this.

LOUISE: Maybe I've just been around too long and I'm afraid of change, but look how far we've come? Ten years ago Women's Centers was a slip of paper in my purse with the non-profit number on it. Now at least we have offices and we're not operating out of someone's living room.

ANNA: That's right and we can go farther.

LOUISE: I don't know.

ANNA: Just like you and I can go farther. *(kisses LOUISE)*

LOUISE: What do you mean?

ANNA: Living together.

LOUISE: Don't start that again when I'm trapped in here.

ANNA: You always say we should spend more time together.

LOUISE: This is the longest conversation we've had in a while without being interrupted.

ANNA: See, if we live together, we won't have to get stuck in an elevator to be alone.

LOUISE: You are too much, really. You'll use anything to make your case, won't you?

ANNA: Absolutely. I just think there comes a time in a relationship when it's natural to want to live together. Otherwise it's just make believe.

LOUISE: No it's not. I can be committed to you without us living together. Besides, I like living in my commune.

ANNA: And what else?

LOUISE: I thought we were doing things differently. We don't have to live together. When Barbara and I moved in together we ended up breaking up.

ANNA: O.K. now we're getting somewhere. You're afraid if we move in together we'll break up.

LOUISE: I didn't say that. It's just that I like to have my own space.

ANNA: So do I. We can do that and live together.

LOUISE: I don't know. *(joking)* You take up a lot of space.

ANNA: *(laughing)* I do not. *(pause)* Besides as a feminist I think that's a good thing.

LOUISE: O.K., which is it?

ANNA: Any way, it's just nice to wake up in the morning and know where your left shoe is.

(They kiss and start to make out))
(RAE goes past GEORGE)

RAE: Hello, is anyone here?

LOUISE: Yes, we're stuck in the elevator.

ANNA: Hey, can you get some help?

(RAE hits the button and the door flies open. Following lines are rapid and overlapping)

RAE: Anna, I found//you.

ANNA: Rae! //What are you doing here? *(Not sure whether she should hug RAE, but she does)*

RAE: Looking for you. Are you //O.K.?

LOUISE: Hi, // I'm Louise.

ANNA: Yes, sorry this is Louise. This is Rae.

RAE: Hi. You should get this thing fixed!

ANNA: We would if we owned the place.

LOUISE: See this is the problem with buying a building. You're the landlord. You have to fix things.

RAE: I hope it's O.K. that I came. I just got back and found out you'd be here, so I thought I'd surprise you.

LOUISE: Surprise.

ANNA: Yeah, I am surprised. *(Silence)*

LOUISE: We were just going to a meeting at Brady Street; you know the women's centers office.

RAE: Oh, no I guess I don't know because I've been away in the // peace corps.

ANNA: peace corps.//

LOUISE: peace corps.// So I heard. *(stays by ANNA'S side)*

RAE: I just wanted you to know I was back and to see how you were doing.

ANNA: //I'm great.

LOUISE: She's very busy.//

ANNA: What do you think of the place?

RAE: I don't know. It's big and dark.

LOUISE: You know, we've already had this conversation, so I think I'm gonna start back. You want me to tell'm you're coming?

ANNA: Yeah, I'll be right there.
(LOUISE exits)

RAE: Does it seem like three years?

ANNA: I don't know. In some ways.

RAE: I wanted us to have a chance to talk – I practiced everything I was gonna say, but now I don't know how to say it.

(ANNA starts down the stairs and RAE follows)

ANNA: Can't you just imagine, the switchboard down here and a drop in center for women and offices for women's organizations everywhere?

RAE: I missed you.

ANNA: *(looking around)* Everybody could have a room of their own. *(looking at RAE)* I didn't want to leave. You know how many times I delayed leaving.

RAE: I know.

ANNA: You didn't answer my letters, so I thought…

RAE: I couldn't deal with all my feelings after you left.

ANNA: I mean we've got a lot of work to do, but I think this could really be something.

RAE: *(meaning them, not the building)* So do I.

ANNA: We need a place of our own where nobody can tell us what to do.

RAE: I realize now I just didn't know what to do. Anna, I know that our relationship ended but it was never really...

ANNA: finished. I know. *(framed in the doorway)*

RAE: *(coming toward ANNA)* And I think we need to do that because otherwise we'll never know whether we're really supposed to be together.

ANNA: I just can't do that right now. I've got other – my life has changed, just like yours has.

RAE: I can't help wondering.

ANNA: Please don't, I'm here now trying to make this happen. If you wanna be a part of it, that's great. If not, then I need to get to my meeting.

RAE: I'm sorry. I don't know what I was thinking.

ANNA: That you could just come back here and sweep me off my feet?

RAE: I could try.
(ANNA and RAE kiss.)

ANNA: I gotta go. *(ANNA exits)*

RAE: Hey, wait up. I'm coming. *(RAE exits)*

(pass GEORGE)

Scene 3
The Meetings

(Scene shifts back to Brady Street. LOUISE enters. SUSAN, DEBRA, and MEMBER are there working)

LOUISE: *(To SUSAN)* I guess I knew sooner or later she'd come back, but maybe she won't stay long. Why did she come back?

SUSAN: Maybe she thought Anna would be waiting for her.

LOUISE: After three years?

DEBRA: That's something we've got to learn to deal with. I mean how to be lovers and friends and still work together.

SUSAN: Good luck.

DEBRA: I think we should be free to do what we want, as long as it doesn't hurt anyone else.

SUSAN: And how do you manage that?

DEBRA: I've heard of this thing called fair fighting. It's supposed to really work.

(ANNA & RAE enters as SUSAN is speaking)

SUSAN: Yeah, like non-monogamy is supposed to really work. Oh, hi Anna.

ANNA: Hi everybody. This is Rae, my ah – we met in the //Peace Corps.

SUSAN, DEBRA, LOUISE: *(said simultaneously with ANNA)* Peace Corps.

ANNA: Yeah, this is Susan and Debra.

SUSAN & DEBRA: Hi.

ANNA: You already met Louise.

LOUISE: Yeah, so what do you think of non-monogamy, Rae?

RAE: Well, I don't know. I was told I should take Carol Migden's work-shop on how to have open relationships *(laughing)*. My friend went because she wanted to have open relationships because all the white women were doin' it but African American women weren't doin' it, so she said let me go to a white woman and check this out. And it was Carol Migden and she went out and had three relationships and it was <u>hot</u>. *(pauses and sees others aren't reacting)* So I personally think you can love more than one person at one time, if you're open and honest about it.

ANNA: I'm the eldest child of eight living children and I remember having a conversation with my mother one day. And I was trying to prove to my mother, I mean, I was one of those obnoxious teenagers, or that was one of my moments. I was trying to prove to her that she loved some of us better than others. That it was impossible for her as a mother to love us all equally. And, you know, she didn't have the concept to say I love you all differently. But I learned from her that yeah, it is possible. I mean...it has to be part of human nature that you can love people differently, equally. So the idea of nonmonogamy is a valid one to me. Whether I can live it or not, that's another story.

ALL: Amen.

(The meeting begins)

SUSAN: So we've hired a consultant to determine the feasibility of buying Dovre Hall.

(JANE enters with easel and flip charts and does fast paced financial rap. DEBRA and JANE are flirting)

DEBRA: *(clarifying)* So you're saying our mortgage for the proposed building will be $3600 a month?

JANE: That's correct, Debra. You're catching on. You must have some background in finance or real estate.

DEBRA: I know a little. I just bought my own home.

JANE: Congratulations, you're a property owner.

LOUISE: Right now, as the bookkeeper, I can tell you that Women's Centers pays $200 a month and you know we've had to go around collecting that from our friends and relatives sometimes when we were short, probably from some of you in this room.

(Some laughter and recognition)

DEBRA: Essentially, we're a $50,000 organization and we're trying to buy a $500,000 building.

JANE: Well said, Debra. So let's look at the financials. *(Talks fast and uses grease pencil and easel paper which by the end should have arrows going in all directions)* If we look five years out at what your income stream and your expenses are going to be, we can see that

on the expense side there's the mortgage, insurance, taxes, maintenance, renovation, repairs like the elevator, supplies—toilet paper,
soap, feminine hygiene products—

DEBRA: *(jokingly)* We can't afford that.

JANE: Just checking to see if you're with me. And then on the income
generating side we have tenants—your basic feminists organizations
and sponsored projects, none too well off, rentals, such as weddings…

SUSAN *(others join in except Jane, groan, and then overlapping):* Oh,
no, not that, please.

JANE: And dances which, of course, require security and clean up.
Let's see memberships—that's all of you,

(Some clapping and cheering)

JANE: Grants which we hope will be coming in soon, and donations,
such as Debra's.

(More clapping and cheering)

JANE: Then there's the first mortgage and if we take a second and then
negatively amortize, we're looking at a balloon payment of $150,000
in five years with interest rates going up.

ALL: *(Gasp, look incredulous)*

JANE: I have to add that I do think it's unlikely that any lending institution will give Women's Centers a loan of this size.

DEBRA: They might, if we raise some money first.

RAE: Have you thought of something like a – what do they call it? – a walkathon,

ANNA: No, but that's a good idea. Get lots of women's organizations involved.

*(song)*VIVA LA REAL ESTATE
(Refrain with RAE and DEBRA joining ANNA on the "can do" side and LOUISE and JANE singing the "can't do" lines)

We can do this
No we can't do this
We can do this
No we can't do this
Anna got me into this

Scene 4
Fund Raising

(Split scene involving the mileathon. DEBRA is explaining to potential sponsors on the phone how it works as SUSAN and JANE are keeping tallies while watching DEBRA. On the other side of the stage, RAE is doing the same thing with LOUISE and ANNA looking on. Could have clipboards in hand or a big chart on the wall)

DEBRA: *(On the phone)* That's right. If your organization signs up to participate in the mileathon, half of the money will go to you and half will go to the Women's Building. *Continues conversation in background)*
JANE: *(To SUSAN admiringly)* Debra's really good at this.

RAE: Yes, you'll be raising money for your organization as well as the Women's Building.

ANNA: *(To LOUISE)* It's amazing how many organizations Rae has signed up.

LOUISE: *(adding up numbers and not seeming that impressed)* Unhuh.

DEBRA: Yeah, we're hoping every organization will bring as many walkers, I mean participants as they can. We certainly want disabled people. I mean if you have any.

SUSAN: *(To JANE)* Well, she's improving all the time.

DEBRA: That's why we're calling it a mileathon rather than a walkathon.

RAE: That's great. So I'll put you down for 15 participants.

ANNA: I wish I could do that.

JANE: She has incredible fund raising skills. *(To SUSAN)* How long did you say you two have been together?

LOUISE: *(To ANNA)* How long were you two together?

DEBRA: *(Hangs up phone)* Well, San Francisco Women's Health Center just joined up.

SUSAN: How many groups have we got now?

DEBRA: Almost sixty groups.

RAE: Make that sixty one. I just signed up A Women's Place Bookstore.

ALL: ALRIGHT

DEBRA: Let's see, if they each bring between 5 and 25 people that's ...

JANE: *(Answers before SUSAN has a chance in order to impress DEBRA)* between 300 and 1500 people.

RAE: Right. And they each get 5 people to pledge $10 we'll have...

JANE: *(Again beats SUSAN to the punch)* ah *(working it out)* between $15,000 and $75,000.

DEBRA: God, you're great with numbers.

LOUISE: Gee, and we only need $50,000 for the down payment.

JANE: Just doin' my job.

ANNA: *(To LOUISE)* But don't you see. It is really possible. We can do it.

DEBRA: I better keep calling. This has got to work. *(DEBRA gets on the phone again)*

RAE: Me too. *(RAE get back on the phone)*

ANNA: This is going to work, I know it. Louise, do you have the figures from yesterday?

LOUISE: No, but I suppose I could go get'm. *(exits)*
ANNA: Great, thanks. (stays with RAE)

(Shift focus to DEBRA, SUSAN & JANE only)

SUSAN: Do you think we've gotten too materialistic since we started doing this?

JANE: Hey, it's a capitalist society, so you need capital to make change, social change I mean.

SUSAN: *(sarcastic)* As opposed to spare change.

JANE: Exactly. How's that grant coming?

(SUSAN begins typing.)

DEBRA: *(To JANE at first and then more out to AUDIANCE)* We've been in partnership ... and doing fundraising together ... Basically the money for the building needs to be raised and we share a love affair with the building. So we've probably sent out ten proposals. Susan types about 120 words a minute. She's just unbelievably fast, and so-you know, we come home, our lives are totally focused on work. There's complete integration between our personal lives and the work thing. So – people have ideas and Susan types everything up and makes it sound like we are all geniuses. I mean, Anna can't even type. At least I can type, but not like that. And she does it in this way— she sits there and, she chews gum (sound of chewing) and kind of sits at the typewriter and looks at you and types like this – just like a secretary would. But having no affect whatsoever – she's typing what you say and she reconcocts it. No computers, and so it's really an effort to reconcoct the whole thing. But the effect of Susan with her little shoes and her little foot always going like this *(tapping sound)* and looking at you and kind of – you know it's hysterical because she is, she has this fantastic brain – you know – but she looks like a secretary.

SUSAN: Right, thank you. You know, I really envy women who don't know how to type.

(Shift focus to RAE and ANNA only for rest of scene. They seem very drawn to each other despite what they are saying)

ANNA: Rae, the mileathon is going great. We're not only raising money but building community. Thanks to you.

RAE: And Debra and Susan and everyone else.

ANNA: I know, but it was your idea, so thank you. Thank you for this.

RAE: You have this way of getting other people to help you make your dreams come true.

ANNA: Not always. *(pause)* I never really got a chance to talk to you about Louise and me.

RAE: That was pretty obvious.

ANNA: Yeah, I guess so. *(pause)* Sometimes I wish we were back in the Peace Corps. Things were simpler then.

RAE: What are you saying?

ANNA: Do you think we can do this?

RAE: Are you talking about the Building or you, me and Louise?

ANNA: I don't know.

RAE: Look, I want to be a part of all this and respect your relationship with Louise. And that's what I'm doing. I know that may be old-fashioned but no use dwelling on the past, like you said.

ANNA: I don't know if I was right about that. I'm not always right about everything, as everybody knows by now.

RAE: Since when?

ANNA: Never mind. You can read my fan mail sometime. *(pause)* Speaking of which, do you still have my letters? The ones I wrote when we were together in Africa? I was wanting to make copies because they're like my diary of the place, you know. I never was good at keeping a diary.

RAE: I don't have them anymore.

ANNA: Not with you, but you have them in storage or something?

RAE: I don't have them anymore. I – it never occurred to me, you would want them back.

ANNA: Not to keep. I'll give'm back. I want you to have them.

RAE: I burned them. Had a little ritual bon fire when I got back. Kind of a healing, moving on thing.

ANNA: All of them?

RAE: What did you expect me to do? You made a choice. I'm trying to go on with my life and with us as friends. That's what you want, right?

ANNA: Yes, I guess. I never thought you'd not have them. *(pause)* I'm sorry. I'm just making this harder. I do want us to be friends. I should go. I have to go to Dovre Hall for the fund raiser. I'll see you there?

RAE: Yeah, I'll see you later, friend.

ANNA: Rae, do you think we're crazy? I mean, doing this, not this *(referring to them)*, buying a building?

RAE: Yes.

ANNA: I have my doubts// too sometimes, I

RAE: *(interrupts her)* But I think we should do it anyway.

ANNA: O.K., good. Yeah, I do too. I'm sorry. I should go. Oh, fuck the past.

(ANNA exits)

Scene 5
Welcome to the Hood

(TESSA is standing in line to get into what will become the Women's Building. ANNA and LOUISE are passing out flyers. GEORGE at his post. The door to the bar is open, with patrons, watching the line)

ANNA: Hello. Welcome. We'll be opening the doors in a few minutes for the dance.

LOUISE: Thank you for your patience.

ANNA: *(passing out flyers to line)* Come to the community meeting about creating a women's building for ourselves.
LOUISE: *(ANNA gives LOUISE some flyers to pass out)* You're all invited. We want to know what you think.

GEORGE: I'll tell you what I think, fuck off..

TESSA: *(Standing in the line)* You wanna buy this old building?

ANNA: Yeah, 'cause we need a place of our own, for all women.

TESSA: "A room of one's own." a la Virginia Woolf?

ANNA: Yeah, only bigger. You know about the San Francisco Women's Centers? We have that little place on Brady Street.

TESSA: Oh yeah, where the Women's Switch board is. (*Aside to audience as if someone in line*) I've been there. Mostly Anglo women though. (*Sarcastic*) Welcome to the Women's Movement.

BINKLE: Go on tell'm you don't want them here.

WOMAN #1: (*shouts from doorway*) We don't want you here, you lesbians, I mean dykes, right?

BARTENDER: Yeah, go ahead. Tell the fuckin' dykes to get lost.

WOMAN #2: Yeah, get lost you fuckin' dykes. (*laughing*)

ANNA: (*To Louise*) Can you believe that? Talk about the contradictions of sexism standing in front of us. It's too much. We're really needed here.

LOUISE: You think I should call the police?

ANNA: No as long as they stay in the bar, we're O.K. Are they ready yet in there?

LOUISE: No, nothing works. There's like two plugs in that auditorium.

BINKLE: That's right, man. We don't want your kind.

WOMAN #1: We don't want your kind.

BARTENDER: Your fuckin' kind.

WOMAN #2: *(overlaps with MAN #1)* Your fuckin' kind, yeah that's better. *(laughs)*

TESSA: *(To WOMEN in bar, but not too loudly)* Come over here and say that.

ANNA: *(To TESSA)* Please excuse our neighbors. They're drunk.

TESSA: O.K., O.K., no problema.

(WOMEN #1 & 2 stagger out of bar and towards ANNA and the line)

WOMAN #1: You fucking dyke, what are you doing here, go home."

WOMAN #2: Yeah, go home. You don't belong here.

ANNA: Look, just go back to the bar.

WOMAN #2: No, you just go back to where you came from.

WOMAN #1: Buy a building in a nice fancy neighborhood. Not here.

ANNA: We don't want any trouble.
WOMAN #2: Then leave now and never come back.

WOMAN #1: We don't want you around our children.

WOMAN #2: You're sick,

WOMAN #1: frustrated, need a good fuck. *(Pulls a knife)* Well, we want you the fuck out of here.

(WOMAN #1 lunges at ANNA with the knife to scare her, but unintentionally cuts her. ANNA realizes she has been cut and falls down on

the step at the main entrance. LOUISE rushes to help ANNA followed by TESSA. The following speeches are all very rapid and overlapping)

LOUISE: Call the police, somebody. *(To ANNA)* Are you O.K.? Let me see where you are hurt.

ANNA: I'm O.K., I'm O.K. I think. I don't know.

LOUISE: Let me see. *(Moves ANNA'S hand which is holding her stomach and sees blood)* You're bleeding.

GEORGE: Help, somebody

WOMAN #1: Oh, my god. Mary forgive me. *(crosses herself and drops knife then collapses next to ANNA and is grabbing ahold of ANNA)*

WOMAN #2: Ahhh, oh my goodness!" *(picks up knife and pockets it)*

WOMAN #1: Oh, I'm so sorry. *(Starts to cry)* I didn't mean to do it.

TESSA: Just step back both of you. Give her some room.

*(Hear **police sirens** getting louder)*

WOMAN #1: Oh, my god.

WOMAN #2: We're so drunk, we didn't know.

WOMAN #1 & 2: We're so sorry.

WOMAN #1: I didn't mean to do it. I'm a Catholic and I really believe.

(From the bar)

BINKLE: Man, this is great.

BATENDER Didn't think the girls would go all the way, fuckin' A. Come back girls, we'll buy you a drink.

BINKLE: Shit yeah, you deserve it. *(laughing)*

*(**Police sirens** fade away. LOUISE and TESSA are helping ANNA inside. The WOMEN move away toward the bar)*

WOMAN #2: *(To WOMAN #1)* You O.K.?

WOMAN #1: Yeah, yeah. Is she O.K.?

WOMAN #2: Yeah, sure, you just grazed her. *(Puts her arm around her)* The police didn't even come. Come on I'll buy you a drink. *(Laughing WOMAN #1 and #2 go back into the bar.)*

LOUISE: *(to ANNA)* I told you this wasn't a good idea.

(Scene shifts to the Auditorium. SUSAN is seated at a typewriter wearing a World War I pilot's leather helmet and goggles. She begins typing wildly and performing the following poem as a performance art piece. Others become the audience)

SUSAN: *(Title of poem)* A MAYAN IS A KIND OF OFFICE WORKER

> Mayans have entered the City of the Moles
> through a mousehole in the side of stone
> and are reassembling the possession of parades
> of movies of sundown over our eyes.
>
> Background bakes; sun sinks in. A writer is
> an office worker, under ground. A Mayan is

a kind of chocolate butterfly you won't like.
The brain is the best organ music in town.

When the Mayan goes looking for her heart—
thought, imagination, ideas see out from
cinemas of love against corduroys of clerks.
Mayan Walt Whitman hung up his strange shoulder

alongside brains' folded bumbershoots.
Mayan writings of Paul Goodman, Susan Sontag,
Hannah Arendt, Bertrand Russell, I.F. Stone
are world alive. (How did they live their lives?)

Keystone of the shoulderblade is a working head.
Why is wisdom Mayan? A Mayan stays sane
by interpreting Moles in terms of Mayans,
by being Mayan all the time.

A Mole remains an office worker. A Mayan is a
kind of chocolate butterfly savored to the taste
of writings on the tongue: why wisdom is Mayan.
The sexiest organ of the body is the brain.[13]

(SUSAN exits.)

TESSA: *(to the audience)* So that was my introduction to the Women's Building before it was even the Women's Building. I figured I'd better go to the next meeting and find out what was up.

---

13   Poem written by Lynn Lonidier and the performance reflects a description of one of her performances.

Scene 6
Community Meeting at the Building

ANNA: *(To TESSA on way to the meeting)* I'm going in there and put it right on the line. *(As if talking to the bar owner)* You know, we're gonna buy this building. You have to get your patrons and your personnel under control an' ta da duh dah dah. An' you know dykes are dykes and' whatever, whatever it's over. And I'm going to let people know in the supervisor's office and the Mayor's office too. And if we don't get the permits we need, etc., I'll know who's behind it and I'll be back to see you. So we're gonna have to work something out.

(Shift to bigger meeting with COMMUNITY MEMBERS in Dovre Hall. SUSAN is facilitating. By now core members are getting tired and grumpy)

SUSAN: To begin the meeting let's just take one minute, just one minute to center ourselves, to collect our energy. Take a couple of big deep breaths, deep in your belly, lean back, take a BIG deep breath. And while you're doing that, I want you to think about why you came to this meeting *(shhush sound)*. Why you came to this meeting. Take some big deep breaths, keep your eyes open or closed. Whatever feels better. Why you came to this meeting and what you hope to get out of this meeting *(talking in background)*. What do you want to see happen at this meeting. And then one more thing. What you can do to make that happen. Couple more big deep breaths. What you can do to make that happen tonight.

MEMBER 1: I didn't get my January newsletter.

MEMBER 2: *(Raises her hand)* Me either.

LOUISE: There wasn't one.

MEMBER 2: *(Aside to MEMBER 1)* They had to close down for two weeks because everybody was sick or about to have a nervous breakdown over this building thing.

MEMBER 1: I mean, I'm not one to complain, but I did pay my membership dues. I have never been involved with the movement before. I just want my money's worth.

SUSAN: *(To MEMBER 1)* O.K., thank you, *(taking a deep breath)* We'll get back to that later. Anna?

ANNA: Thank you, so we want to know what you think. Does the membership feel the Building is a priority as opposed to other uses of our time and funds.

LOUISE: We don't want to be just 10 or 20 women doing this pie in the sky thing.

ANNA: You don't, we don't have to have all the answers tonight, but we need to discuss this and find out how you feel.

(MEMBER 2 raises her hand)

SUSAN: Yes, go ahead.

MEMBER 2: Well, I've been around in progressive politics for a while and a Women's Building just for women's activities, well that sounds to me like "sitting ducks" you know, centralized in that way, one explosion and that's the end of the building. The end of the activities and so forth. I hate to say this but I think it's kind of a stupid idea.

MEMBER 1: If I might just say something here, I think we have to ask ourselves why do we want a women's building? You know, if we're going to raise $100,00 or $50,000, it really should go to Women Against Rape or the battered women's shelter and we should pay for their rent and not take on the whole responsibility of buying a building and running it and all of those kinds of things. Where are our priorities?

(DEBRA raises her hand)

SUSAN: Debra?

DEBRA: When I first came to San Francisco, I looked up the word "Women" in the phone book and luckily I found the Women's Centers, a very unique organization dedicated to birthing other women's organizations, such as Las Casa de las Madres for battered women which might not be here today without Women's Centers. And I have to admit I had my doubts at first about whether we could do this or should do this – buy a whole damn building. But even before I came here, when I was in New York, I dreamed about having a women's community center that would be an artistic cultural center along with a community organizing center. And I'm willing to make a commitment to that dream and make it happen here. No matter what anybody says. I think we can do it and I told the committee privately, but now I want to make it more public, that I'm willing to take a second mortgage on my house to make it happen. I'm willing to put up what's most valuable to me to make this dream come true.

(modest response)

MEMBER 1: Yeah, that sounds great, but do we have the resources to do this and is this what we want to do with the resources we have. I mean, be property owners and landlords?

MEMBER 2: In terms of the Women's Building, well I – it sounds like the question you're asking is our priorities. What's gonna get dropped? What are we gonna lose that we already have, you know, and I for one don't want to lose the energy that's gone into community organizing. Ah, you know, if everyone who's on the Women's Centers staff wants to do the Women's Building and not community organizing, then that's a real problem. Unless everyone thinks that the Women's Building is community organizing, of course it is// but its not the only...

ALL: *(interrupt, so overlaps)* It is. *(ALL start taking at once)*

MEMBER 2: community organizing. And that's that's why it's real complicated and hard to respond to...

SUSAN: O.K., That's real good and thank you, and I see that you want the floor and I want to see who else does, so that I can try and bring in some other hands who have not yet spoken.

RAE: Well, I just think something is being suspended, but not lost, in anticipation of something to come.

LOUISE: I just want us to really know what were getting ourselves into.

TESSA: I've been listening to everyone talk for a long time which is good because I'm new here and I don't know very much about all this. But I hear a conflict and I don't see how it can be resolved. I mean do you want a building or don't you? What does that mean? I don't know, but things won't be the same that's for sure. I've been to Brady Street and it didn't interest me too much. It's small and cramped and I'm not sure it's meant for me, Tessa, a Puerto Rican from Jersey with a Masters Degree in psychology and a dyke who can't go home again, so where do I belong? I don't know. I want to be a part of this social change and justice we are talking about, but I'm not sure how it can work, but I like this neighborhood. It reminds me a little of home. I look out the window and I see faces that look like mine.

ANNA: Tessa is right. We want a place where all women feel welcome and we want it now. You all are bringing up very important points that we have to address, that's why we want to hear from you, but I think the real bottom line is our political commitment, not our finances. And I think it has to be now or never the way real estate prices are going. This is our chance to give ourselves a permanent home and make a lasting contribution to future generations of women and girls. We know how quickly social change can be reversed. I see that happening right now with the Bakke decision, the battle for abortion rights, the murder trials of women who kill their abusers in self-defense, the assassination of Milk and Moscone, the Dan White verdict. I could go on and on, but I think you get my point.

(nods of agreement by all)

SUSAN: *(frustrated)* Well, I can see we're half way through our agenda and our time is almost up. So let's take a break. We will be giving tours of the building after this.

(ALL start to disperse. DEBRA walks away talking to SUSAN privately)

DEBRA: O.K. I know, there is a class arrogance that comes with being wealthy, and in that class arrogance you are an utter idealist who believes you can do anything.

SUSAN: That's what I love about you.

DEBRA: But I think the thing I hate is that Anna, this working class white woman, has everybody listening to her like she's a fucking goddess and the minute I open my mouth I'm shot to death because I'm from a wealthy privileged family. We're all making it up and she just sounds like, you know, she knows what she's talking about.

Scene 7
Mileathon

(Crowd noises-cheering, excitement, whistles. TESSA, DEBRA, SUSAN, PAULA, ANNA, RAE are all walking in the mileathon and talking to each other as they shift positions standing next to each other GEOREGE cheering)

ANNA: O.K., it's really happening now. I can feel it. We're gonna do it.

RAE: I can't believe the turn out. We're gonna beat our projections.

ANNA: That's right. I knew we could do it. And whoever said the Women's Movement is dead has got to be crazy. This is beautiful.

RAE: And now people know who we are.

ANNA: Yeah, Rae, that's right. They do.

(DEBRA & SUSAN walk up to ANNA & RAE)

DEBRA: This is amazing. You realize how much money we've raised?

SUSAN: I'm sure Jane could tell you. Where is she?

DEBRA: I don't know. Must be around here somewhere. But it must be over $50,000

(TESSA walks up and interrupts)

TESSA: Hey, has anyone seen Paula?

SUSAN: Who's that?

ANNA: A new volunteer. Yeah, I saw her jogging up ahead.

TESSA: She wants to be the Arts coordinator, so I thought I'd talk to her about that grant.

ANNA: Now? You are conscientious.

RAE: And she does look good in running clothes, but hey, I hear she's straight.

TESSA: I never believe those kinds of rumors.

(TESSA moves on looking for PAULA. DEBRA starts talking with RAE. SUSAN moves over to talk with ANNA. SUSAN and ANNA's speech often overlaps)

SUSAN: Anna, Anna I've been meaning to ask you what you thought of the poem?

ANNA: What an incredible performance=

SUSAN: =Yeah, freaked a few people out=

ANNA: = loved it, but ...

SUSAN: Oh, yeah? What did you like about it?

ANNA: I *(slight pause)* loved the images, like the chocolate butterfly=

SUSAN: ="you won't like."

ANNA: And that line, how does that go? Oh yeah, "The sexiest organ of the body is the brain."

SUSAN: That's you.

ANNA: Me?!

SUSAN: This poem is about you. Don't you get it? Everybody has a crush on you because of that brain of yours, but the trouble is also that brain of yours. It never stops. You're a workaholic. You don't take the time to notice what's going on with the people around you.

ANNA: I know you're probably right=

SUSAN: =I am. Do you wanna be a Mayan or a mole?

ANNA: Those are my choices?

SUSAN: Yeah. Do you want to break the mold or be a mole? You've got to stay Mayan all the time. Don't lose your vision in the details.

ANNA: That's easy to say, but the details get the job done. The trouble with you, Susan, is that you're too much of a poet, a romantic about the Women's Movement and politics and social change. That's why you always get hurt.

SUSAN: This isn't about me, although you're right. Do you think Debra is attracted to Jane? Look she's talking to her right now.

ANNA: Susan!

SUSAN: Never mind, don't answer that. I'm trying to tell you something about you. Look what you're doing to Louise and Rae.

ANNA: What! I've been completely honest with both of them.

SUSAN: But have you been honest with yourself?

ANNA: What do you mean?

SUSAN: I mean, "go looking for your heart." God, I hate explaining my work.

ANNA: I am in a committed relationship with Louise.

SUSAN: I may live in a fantasy world, but you try and remake the world and sometimes it doesn't work, especially when it comes to relationships.

ANNA: That's not true.

SUSAN: Just because you call it a "committed relationship" doesn't mean it will last forever. Look at me. *(SUSAN moves on)*

ANNA: What are you saying? Susan wait...

(Shift to TESSA who has caught up with PAULA)

PAULA: Oh, I just love this. All these women. It's just like the Women on Wheels concert. Women are so beautiful. I just love women, even if I am straight. I don't care.

TESSA: That makes two of us.

PAULA: What?

(RAE moves up to talk with ANNA; DEBRA catches up with SUSAN)

RAE: Ah we haven't had much chance to talk in awhile about anything personal, so maybe this isn't the best time, but...

ANNA: Go ahead. Everybody else seems to be using this opportunity to talk to me.

RAE: O.K., it's just that well...

(Shift focus to DEBRA and SUSAN)
DEBRA: How long did you say this walk was?

SUSAN: Fifteen miles. But I'm sure Jane could figure it out for you in inches.

DEBRA: Who's idea was that? I never agreed to that. I thought we did everything by consensus.

(Shift back to ANNA and RAE)

RAE: I'd better go ahead quick before anyone else comes by, since you do know everybody.

ANNA: Am I gonna like this? Don't tell me you're leaving?

RAE: No, but I do have a surprise for you. *(pause)* I'm going to have a baby.

ANNA: A baby!

RAE: You know I've always talked about it, but I finally found a donor.

ANNA: Oh? Good I... *(RAE and ANNA: hug)*

RAE: Actually, I've already been inseminated. And I just heard. And I wanted to tell you first.

ANNA: Rae, that's very exciting. I've been so busy with the building, I didn't even realize...

RAE: I know. You said you never wanted to be a parent anyway, so it's probably all for the best.

ANNA: Yeah, I guess so...

RAE: Looks like I'm having a baby and you're having a building.

ANNA: Yeah or we're all having both.

RAE: Oh yeah?

ANNA: Just another sponsored project brought to you by the San Francisco Women's Centers.

RAE: They'll probably take about the same commitment.

ANNA: Goddess, I hope you're wrong.

(Sound of rally come up, maybe somebody on a bullhorn or a cheer)

Scene 8
Meeting Double Time

(Truncated speeded up meeting)

SUSAN: *(seems a little distracted and upset)* Let's take a moment now that we're all here to give ourselves credit for being here. We'll just do a quick check-in: one thing you'd like to share with us that happened this week.

MEMBER 1: My cat left me for another woman.

ANNA: I've been to too many meetings so I have no life.

ALL: Ditto

RAE: I quit my job to do political organizing and now I'm broke.

PAULA: I've got the straight woman in the Movement Blues.

LOUISE: I need a vacation.

ALL: Ditto.

SUSAN: I think my girlfriend is in love with another woman.

LOUISE: Ditto.

TESSA: I wonder what I'm doing here.

ALL: Ditto

SUSAN: O.K., thank you. So looks like we're all in about the same space. Now let's continue our discussion about the Building.

LOUISE: Can we afford it?

PAULA: Maybe we can't afford not to.

ALL: money, money, money

TESSA: We just raised $50,000.

PAULA: If we don't take ourselves seriously, who else will?

LOUISE: How will we get a bank loan?

(refrain from VIVA LA ESTATE but ALL on the "can do" side, except LOUISE. Then meeting continues in real time with ANNA and LOUISE fighting in front of the others who silently watch)

We can do this
No we can't do this
We can do this
No we can't do this
Anna got me into this

ANNA: You can't think like a bookkeeper if you want to make social change.

LOUISE: I think like a bookkeeper?! You don't <u>think</u>, that's the problem. Who's gonna run this place?

ANNA: We'll form a Building Collective.

LOUISE: Just what we need, another collective.

ANNA: Tell me why you still don't think it's a good idea.

LOUISE: I just want you to realize the risk we're taking. This is 1979. The 60's are over. Milk and Moscone are dead. Ronald Reagan 'll probably be our next President.

ANNA: So what does that mean we should do?

LOUISE: Conserve our resources. Be aware we're not going to have the support we once did. People are already saying the Women's Movement is dead.

ANNA: Is that what you think?

LOUISE: No I don't, but I don't like being declared dead and I know that means something. They wish we were dead and they think they can make us go away.

ANNA: That's why we need a building, so they can't make us go away.

LOUISE: I don't want you to answer my objections. I want you to listen to me before it's too late. We can't do this.

ANNA: Louise, I think everything that you're saying is important. You're telling me what I need to know to make this work.

LOUISE: *(stands up)* You are so stubborn, goddamn it. I know you're going ahead no matter what I say. The Women's Centers is about to go under from just meeting about this—building, while we try to do everything else we're supposed to do like sponsor new projects, administer our current projects, answer phones, get out the newsletter. We could lose everything we've worked for.

ANNA: We could lose everything, if we don't get this building. Now that we've raised most of the down payment, let's just see if we can get a bank loan.

(DEBRA enters excitedly)

DEBRA: We just found out that The Sons of Norway are willing to be holders of the note. We won't have to go to the bank.

SUSAN: The Sons of Norway and their president, who is this Norwegian prince sitting on his throne.

LOUISE: In fact, we have no money, we have no time to really do this, so basically we're talking smoke and mirrors.

DEBRA: I have these Norwegian relatives. I can put on my Norwegian accent: "Vell, it's soo goood to be here in San Francisco.

SUSAN: *(in similar Norwegian accent)* "We, the Sons of Norway, give to you, the daughters of a new revolution, our beautiful home."

ANNA: Our revolution no longer has to take place in the streets. We are homeless no more.

(ANNA and DEBRA hug. SUSAN stays where she is.)

You have to be willing to dream if you want to change the world.

(Meeting breaks down as everyone talking in excitedly in sub-groups and no one is listening to LOUISE)

LOUISE: Never take a job as the bookkeeper for the revolution. Believe me they won't thank you for it. They'll say don't rain on our parade, don't oppress us with your numbers, don't buy into the power structure, don't murder our dreams. *(exit)*

Scene 9
A Toast to the Women's Building

(ANNA, LOUISE, DEBRA, TESSA, SUSAN and RAE are celebrating in the corner bar. BEN is drinking at the bar. BINKLE is typing his column which is intercut with their conversation. GEORGE drinking beer in paper bag outside)

ANNA: Should we do this?

ALL: Yes.

RAE: To the Women's Building of the Bay Area.

(ALL toast)

BINKLE: *(reads aloud his column)* Hoisting a glass to our new inmates in this great enterprise called San Francisco. She's ever changing but still retains her beauty, even amidst the feminist fashions of the day, such as unshaven legs and armpits.

BEN: Yeah, may it be a short-lived fashion. *(They laugh)*

ANNA: I liked it when we all joined hands in a circle and made a two year commitment to the building.

DEBRA: It was very emotional, all those women saying, yeah this is great, let's do it, even if it seems impossible.

RAE: There was such a spirit of cooperation and willingness to dare to do this…

LOUISE: Well, I think the reaction was more mixed.

TESSA: Raise your hands if you're willing to commit three to five hours a week to make this happen.

SUSAN: *(seems a bit drunk)* I mean if you're not already putting in 60 hours a week.

ALL: *(laughing and raising glasses)* YEAH
(ANNA, LOUISE, RAE, DEBRA and TESSA are talking in the background)

DEBRA: *(To SUSAN)* Honey, are you O.K.? Be careful. You don't usually drink very much.

SUSAN: No, you be careful. Where's Jane?

DEBRA: I don't know. Please stop asking me that.

BINKLE: This indeed has been a boys club, albeit with a devoted female following. Will these women last? I doubt it. I can't say I was for it, as you know, but I will endeavor to be a gracious neighbor to the ladies, until proven otherwise.

BEN: Yeah, one of 'm is my girlfriend.

BINKLE: Is that a fact? Bartender, another drink for this young lad.

LOUISE: Now we just have to make it work.

TESSA: I can't believe we finally made a decision.

DEBRA: I must admit it was a little frightening when we actually had to sign on the dotted line.

LOUISE: You know, the decision was probably made without a decision. To stop the momentum would have been a major effort.

RAE: It was happening, this ball rolling down the hill gathering moss and=

ALL: =getting bigger and bigger.

BARTENDER: Everything O.K. over there, ladies?
(ALL laugh)

ANNA: We have our work cut out for us.
(ALL clink glasses and freeze)

ALL: SONG: SHE RISES
Well she rises, yes she rises
Well she rises, you know she rises up
Well she rises every morning and she smiles to greet the day,
Yes, she rises like a building to the sky.
How high, how high, to the sky.

So get your hammer, get your nails
grab your paint brush and your pail
put on your overalls and your hard hat
we're getting ready to put out the welcome mat.

END OF ACT I

CHAPTER 4

SAN FRANCISCO WOMEN'S CENTERS IN TRANSITION

AS 1978 ROLLED on, a great deal of the energy of the San Francisco Women's Centers (SFWC) was taken up by the Women's Building Project efforts. The Mile-a-Thon raised money for the organization, both through its own collected pledges and from a 10 percent fee charged as the fiscal sponsor of the event, and things were on track for the purchase, yet other aspects of the Centers' mission were floundering.

The crisis reached a head in October 1978, when the core staff "fired" itself. A cash flow problem had already depleted the organization's ability to meet even its minimal payroll, and since that September, Jeanette Lazam, Roma Guy, and Jean Crosby had been laid off. Though all continued their activism on behalf of SFWC or its projects, Tiana Arruda was now the sole paid staff member.

Although these financial problems helped lay bare the SFWC's problems, there were deeper layers of disunity, affecting not only the paid staff but all the core volunteers. In October, a two-week moratorium for the collective was declared, and the SFWC was closed for the first time since moving into the Brady Street offices. The Women's Switchboard and Options for Women Over 40 were also housed at Brady Street, so the doors weren't literally closed, but the absence of SFWC staff was noted with considerable alarm by it supporters.

There were many points of disagreement and many sources of tension within the collective, but there was also a relatively long collective history and a shared commitment to search for common ground. After the brief hiatus, the full collective came back together and identified three broad points of unity to present to their membership and other supporters. The first was the public acknowledgement that there was a lack of unity within the current collective. The second was that the community still needed the SFWC (this despite the lack of clear unity about the essence of the SFWC.) The third agreement was that these differences could not be sorted out without input from the broad community base of the SFWC.

The first written airing of the crises was an article by Marge Nelson, coordinator of Options for Women Over Forty, for their newsletter in late 1978. It was reprinted in the February 1979 issue of the SFWC Newsletter:

OPTIONS for Women Over Forty is a sponsored project of SFWC. It was she (SFWC) who gave us birth, arranged a CETA contract for four salaries, donated an office, a phone and many staff hours of concerned support and guidance.

Now SFWC is undergoing a difficult, painful time of re-evaluation, transition, and change, brought to a head by a crisis among the staff over lack of agreement on goals and by severe, unrelenting financial pressure.

Since SFWC has been in existence, she has given birth to twenty-two sponsored projects. That's a lot of children and a lot of energy going into our community that has not necessarily been returned to the mother center. Most of us know what that trip is about. SFWC has organized countless fundraisers for its projects and few for herself. She is currently devoting over fifty staff hours per week to the new Women's Building, Dovre Hall. Notes come in to SFWC that read "Gook luck in your crisis" with a check made out to the Women's Building Fund. It is marvelous that people are giving support to this project, and to all others, OPTIONS included, but clearly something is missing.

Like the martyr that many mothers play, SFWC has tended to put herself in the background, asking only a 5 percent return from her sponsored projects and devoting high energy to the newest baby.

However, when this goes on for too long, the mother begins to lose a sense of herself, of her own center. For SFWC, this state became a reality with the realization that the staff were in disagreement over many issues. There was no longer a clear sense of goals—of her own centeredness.

This condition has been sorely aggravated by long-standing financial problems: a large debt, low salaries, and constant worry over meeting program and overhead expenses. To ease the strain, several of the staff went off the payroll, but are still working as "volunteers." Clearly this is not the labor policy we want to encourage, and yet it takes about 270 hours of work per week to keep SFWC operating.

Such a state cannot be ignored. If Women's Centers is to endure, she needs clear direction as to her goals, and enough money to support a full staff at living wages.

In order to begin to deal with the crisis, the friends of SFWC and staff have organized a Transition Steering Committee. OPTIONS is donating twenty hours of staff time to this committee and its work. We want our readers to know why we feel this is important.

First, there is the fairly obvious fact that we would not exist it if were not for the SFWC. Perhaps even more important is the fact that because they do exist, we are able to begin a little farther along the road than if we had to start from scratch. Because of our head start, we are able to emphasize our outreach to Third World women, working class women, poor women—all groups that are often not served by new organizations in the women's movement. In a society dominated by the white middle class, new organizations—unless they specifically focus on Third World and working class groups—will tend to attract only white middle class. That's how it works.

Ever since coming to work at OPTIONS, I have had a clear sense of how much of our energy feeds off the base provided us by the SFWC. We hear directly about what's going on in the women's community and among many anti-racist groups. Because of the energy going into securing the Women's Building, we do not have to worry about where we will be housed. We will be part of a growing, vital new center along with many different women's groups.

SFWC grew out of the mass movements of the 60s and early 70s. The coming together of many movements produced an upheaval that affected our lives profoundly. Now these movements have dispersed or quieted down. There is a growing right-wing effort to take away all that we have gained.

As movements fade, people are pulled in many different directions. Symbols that once seemed so simple, so persuading, grow dim. Where once they gave meaning to all of the complexities and contradictions of our lives, they now only seem to forsake us and leave us with only the complexities and contradictions. Without a unifying cause, personal differences become more visible and much more threatening. Without the excitement of a viable movement, it gets a little harder to be "up" for working long hours for little pay.

Yet if we do understand history, we know that it is precisely at times such as these that we must work to keep our movement and the organizations it has created alive and visible. SFWC is an important organizing arm of the women's movement in our community. If she dies, a crucial base of our support will be gone. I'm not sure how well we can get along without her.

Like a mother who's exhausted, Women's Center is going through a transition crisis. She needs time for self-evaluation, reflection, and rest. As children often do, some have become frightened that mother is lying down. Will she ever get up?

She will. Transitions and crises can be terrifying. But we can emerge from them with new strength and clarity, if only we will believe in ourselves. When that faith gets a little shaky, we need a lot of help from our friends.

We at OPTIONS hope that you will add your support of SFWC to ours. Send in a donation and maybe a note of encouragement. As older women give strength and support to younger women who have "mothered" us, we can begin to close the gap between us. And we shall be doubly enriched, for our lives will grow in meaning as the women's movement gathers women of all ages and colors and classes into its fold.[14]

There was an immediate and gratifying response to the call for assistance, as over two dozen women stepped forward to help get the SFWC back on her feet.

Internal Challenges

True to the tradition of being "nice" at all costs, the notes from the

---

14 SFWC Newsletter, February 1979. GLBTHS, WBA, main collection, series 1, subseries A, box 3, file 8.

dozens of meetings held during this transition make only vague references to the depths and character of the conflicts among the staff. But the notes do make it clear that at the center of all the problems was the spontaneous and fluid character of the organization and its subsequent structure. Though periodic evaluations of past work and relations were done, there had been no extensive long-range planning for the future. Rather, work plans and priorities were generated by the movement, and the role of the SFWC was to assist in this. It saw itself as both as a community organizer assisting grassroots efforts and as a public foundation that helped to raise funds for these efforts.

There is much to be said for an organization that subsumes its own interests to the demands of the broader movement. At the same time, failing to recognize and address the organization's own needs is, in the long term, a prescription for collapse. For the SFWC, lack of clear strategic goals and plans for achieving them made it difficult to assess the proper role of leadership and establish clear lines of authority and accountability.

Further, the level of activism around women's issues was changing. This paralleled the increasing shift in tactics to court and legislative battles and provision of direct services, and away from mass challenges to broad policy issues and general societal/cultural values. That meant relying more on the individual work of lawyers and lobbyists and less on street actions that involved as many people as possible. Throughout its first years of existence, the SFWC was in the main responding to the demands of the movement. It probably wasn't clear at the time, but this period was coming to an end. Increasingly, it would be up to the core collective, not the movement as a whole, to decide which projects to take on, increasing their political power as an organization.

Even as demands on the core collective were going up, another undeniable factor in the crisis was the burnout issue. The Women's Building Project was generating and consuming large amounts of woman power, but the same cannot be said regarding other projects. The monthly newsletter was a labor-intensive effort, as was maintaining regular drop-in hours and keeping up with bookkeeping and other administrative details. The Switchboard was also struggling to maintain a sufficient volunteer base to maintain full hours. At the beginning of 1979, the Bay Area Feminist Federal Credit Union (see chapter 1) still appeared to be stable, was employing several of the active members of the Women's Centers, and was one of the organizations slated to move into the Building in April 1979. Yet it too would soon unravel, with the loss of several key volunteer and paid staff positions. The large base of Options for Women Over Forty was indicative of the aging character of women's movement activists. Fewer women in their twenties were stepping forward to play active roles, not just at SFWC but throughout the women's movement and around other progressive causes.

Indeed, as the grassroots base of the right was growing, the progressive social movement spawned by the 60s was shrinking in numbers of activists. Some of the values of the 60s were beginning to be reflected in broader social morality, and pressure to mobilize was lessening. Pockets of mass mobilization occurred, particularly in the lesbian/gay movement—the first national lesbian/gay march attracted some 100,000 people to Washington, D.C., in 1979, and Gay Pride marches were being organized in many cities. But in many cases, fresh bodies were not stepping forward to fill the ranks as veterans burned out or stepped back to deal with delayed family and career issues.

The need to lay off paid SFWC staff also highlighted the race issue; the paid staff before the crisis consisted of one Asian, one Latina, and two white women. At least since the 1976 violence conference, the SFWC had been grappling with how to involve more women of color in its core. They had "hired" other women of color, but these women actually worked for various organizations sponsored by the SFWC—the credit union in its first year, Options for Women Over 40, La Casa de las Madres—but Jeanette and Tiana were the first women of color to work directly for the SFWC. Jeanette had been increasingly drawn into Filipino community politics, through the struggle to save the International Hotel and opposition to the Marcos dictatorship in the Philippines. She joined the KDP (Union of Democratic Filipinos), a revolutionary, cadre-style group, and was left with little time for the SFWC, especially after she was laid off in September and had to find other ways to make an income. The result was a step back in terms of the racial diversity of the core. Though Tiana, the other woman of color on paid staff, remained throughout the transition period, she felt isolated as the only woman of color active in the core collective and as the only paid staff for several months. At a January 1979 meeting, her comments about the process were summarized in the notes this way: "[Tiana] continues to work without direction, feels isolated and alone in spite of support from individuals. Wants direction from the Transition Team. Still has questions about continuing to work for SFWC because of the insecurity and directionless of the job. Fears that SFWC may be worse now than before Transition."[15]

Another tension at play in the collective was a sexual/familial dynamic. Throughout the 1970s, lesbians had made up a substantial majority of the active participants of the SFWC, and coupling and uncoupling was a common occurrence. No doubt this at times caused a tension or awkwardness to meetings, but in the main the group had succeeded in rising above personal relations to carry out its work. In fact, the SFWC probably overall benefited from the social role the organization played, as some lesbians became active not just to exercise their civic responsibility but also to be in the company of other like-minded lesbians.

Jean and Roma had been lovers for several years and were at that time living together. They also had opposing views on the Women's Building Project. Roma was motivated by a visionary ideal and was one of the driving forces behind the effort. Jean, on the other hand, handled the business end of the Women's Centers and brought an accountant's more conservative vantage on the risk involved in such a purchase.

---

15 SFWC meeting notes, January, 1979. GLBTHS, WBA, main collection, series 1, subseries C, box 7, file 16.

To further complicate the dynamics, another active collective member, Diane Jones, had been Roma's lover years earlier, when they were both in the Peace Corps in Africa. Diane had arrived in San Francisco in 1976 and become active in organizing the violence conference. In support of the building project, she was one of the key coordinators of the Mile-a-Thon fundraising effort. In these first few years, Diane and Roma held back from a romantic relationship. When Diane chose to bear a child (Annie, whose birth coincided with the 1979 purchase of the Building), her co parent was Linda Jupiter, a member of the SFWC who was very involved in the credit union. The active circle of "aunts" included Jean and Tiana, but not Roma. Nonetheless, the sexual attraction between Roma and Diane remained, and would a few years later lead to yet another shift in the couples within the SFWC collective.

External Events

The crisis within the SFWC wasn't unfolding in a vacuum. There were also several events in 1978 that impacted virtually every sector of the progressive movement in the Bay Area. 1978 was the year that the California gay and lesbian community was fighting the Briggs Amendment, a statewide measure that would have codified discrimination against lesbians and gays in employment. Under the leadership of Phyliss Schlafly, the conservative movement had been successful in passing similar measures in numerous cities and counties around the country.

The measure was defeated by more than a million votes at the November polls, as was a similar measure in Seattle, Washington. These wins finally stalled this tactic of the right wing, at least for the time being.[16] Regardless of how active the individual women of the SFWC were in this campaign, the intensity of the debate over the

---

16 As important as these victories were, the rightward swing in U.S. politics was already well under way. It would soon lead to Ronald Reagan's election in November 1980 (though ironically his opposition to the Briggs Amendment contributed to its defeat).

summer and fall months and the exhilaration of victory energized everyone.

Unfortunately, the high of winning even a defensive victory was short lived. Two other events in November 1978 also rocked the San Francisco progressive community. On November 18, followers of People's Temple leader Jim Jones shot and killed U.S. Representative Leo Ryan and members of his team investigating allegations of abuse at their Guyana compound. At the same time, 913 members of the church were killed or committed suicide, including Jones.

Through the 1970s Jim Jones had been a respected religious authority in San Francisco. He began playing a role in city politics in 1970 when his church set up a fund for the families of slain police officers. He was an ordained minister in the Disciples of Christ, a mainstream denomination, and led a congregation of up to eight thousand members, mostly poor African Americans. His church provided social programs, jobs, and health care. He gave funds to the NAACP, the Ecumenical Peace Institute, and various social programs, like a senior citizen escort service.

Jones' ability to raise money and turn out thousands of volunteers to get out the vote or rally for issues or candidates made him many friends among the politically powerful. His allies included the Burton family, Willie Brown, and George Moscone. In 1976, Mayor Moscone appointed Jones to the San Francisco Housing Authority. In 1977, accusations of fake healings, sexual exploitation, and coercive fundraising were raised by former congregation members. This began to undermine the minister's standing and led to his move, along with one thousand of his members, to Guyana in 1978.

Even though the cultish character of the People's Temple had become clearer since then, the violent events of late 1978 were a shocking reality check to many throughout the Bay Area. Then, just nine days after Ryan's murder, on November 27, former San Francisco Supervisor Dan White assassinated Mayor George Moscone and openly gay Supervisor Harvey Milk. Even setting aside the longer-term political consequences of Dianne Feinstein becoming the new mayor, the death of Milk was seen as an assault on the increasingly visible and politically powerful gay/lesbian movement and community, including the San Francisco Women's Centers. As one of the sponsors of the candlelight march held in the wake of the assassinations, the SFWC took responsibility for providing medical services at the rally. Diane Jones recalls that several African American women collapsed under the stress of the previous ten days and needed transport to the hospital. While none of these events directly affected the SFWC transition, they were close enough to home to throw pallor over the group's deliberations.

The Transition Team

Nowadays, organizations commonly look to consultants to lead them through a strategic planning process. But twenty-five years ago, this was not an option. To sort out the issues, the SFWC instead relied on the work of a group of dedicated women, all with their own varied stakes in the organization.

In November 1978, a Transition Team was convened, initially for a two-week period of discussion and meetings. The participants in the transition team included Lynn Lonidier, Roma Guy, Laura, Marge Nelson, Diane Jones, Barbara Starkey, Rebecca Sandridge, Jean Crosby, Jeanne Adelman Mahoney, Gretchen, Nanala, Tiana Arruda, Debra, Alana, Barbara Harwood, Elizabeth, Pat Durham, Ana, Nan Schlosberg, Tracy Gary, Marya Grambs, Linda Jupiter, Ann, Snake, Pan Haskins, Nissa, Ruth, Joyce, Mara. Unfortunately, the records do not include the full names and affiliations of all the women who participated in this process. Within this group were three who had been the paid staff: Roma, Jean, and Tiana. The rest of the participants were either involved in Options for Women Over 40, the Switchboard, or the Women's Building Project, or they were long-time active members of the SFWC.

The planned two weeks of discussion and planning stretched to nearly four months, involving two dozen women and numerous subcommittees meeting to hash out specific details. In many ways, it was a murky process that was replicating some the problems that had brought the SFWC to this point in the first place: there was no clearly stated and agreed upon strategic vision to guide the daily decisions made mainly by the core paid and unpaid staff.

Not all of the notes from this process have been preserved, but there were at least twenty different meetings in the period between November 6 and March 1, each involving from four to twenty women, plus at least one larger community meeting. Nor was the group's only task to be strategic planning—the daily operation of the Women's Centers itself was at stake. The "closing" of the doors in October was always viewed as temporary, and the first order of business of the Transition Team was to determine the bare minimum of tasks to be done and find the woman power to make them happen.

The first meeting of the full Transition Team was convened on November 6. The women came up with a list of twelve "priority" issues, with three singled out as the most important to settle: account-ability, planning, and funding. The other issues represented a list of current or potential activities of the SFWC: the newsletter, sponsored projects, educational projects, coalition work, community organizing, publishing/printing, resource center, child care center, and commu-nity worker/advocate. This hodgepodge list is a fair representation of the thinking of the time: all over the place. However, the crisis in hu-man and financial resources would force the Transition Team to focus on the core issues, defining what the SFWC did, who would do it, and how it would be done.

Remember, these same four months were also a critical time for the purchase of The Women's Building. For the most part, the transi-tion team was not addressing the issues involved with the purchase; the issue only arose when the Transition Team addressed which as-pects of the SFWC would change with the purchase of the Building, in particular its role as a community center/drop in/resources center. However, the prevailing assumption was that the building would be purchased, and some of the women involved in the Transition Team were heavily involved in the building project and believed its success was tied to the survival of San Francisco Women's Centers. At the time, none thought that the Building would be the anchor that ensured a future for the San Francisco Women's Centers.

Even during the transition itself, there was confusion as to what, exactly, was in transition. For some it was about moving from the old SFWC, which was on hold, to a newly functional SFWC. To others, it was about the transition to being part of the new Women's Building. The Transition Team never took on this issue in a full way, and within a few years of the move to the Building it would take another crisis to resolve the issue of the relationship between the Building and the SFWC.

The full group of some two dozen women met several times over the ensuing months, but many of the discussions and proposals were generated in various subcommittees. A small group on Accountability/Power was charged with defining the two words, their relationship, and how they were to function within the SFWC. This was seen both as a short-term issue of sorting out the current dysfunction within the collective and as a broader question of how the Women's Centers would function in the future. Out of the discussion of this small group came an Affirmative Action Committee, charged with developing future hiring policies and strengthening the organization's commitment to diversity.

Another small group, called "the Little Committee," was charged with looking at the SFWC's current responsibilities and coming up with a few options for how to fulfill these responsibilities during the transition period. Though the initial charge of this committee was for the transition period, many of its discussions and recommendations fed into broader discussion of the future character and structure of the SFWC.

Two committees met to deal with money issues. One was a fundraising committee, with the goal of raising $30,000 to get the SFWC through the immediate crunch and have a cushion for the future. One of the complexities was raising this money for the SFWC just as the Building campaign was raising five times that amount for the purchase of Dovre Hall. Because the Building Project was a sponsored project of the SFWC, 5 to 10 percent of the Building fund was due to the SFWC for administrative fees, but this was part of the organization's regularly projected income and was not easing the cash flow crunch. Another finance committee was convened to deal with catching up on record keeping, producing financial statements, and handling the process of hiring someone to take on the ongoing bookkeeping tasks.

Outcomes

Despite the limitations in both the process and the outcomes, the Transition Team was successful in keeping the SFWC alive. The doors at Brady Street were reopened after only two weeks, and enough money came in to keep minimal staffing in place. By the end of the process, five broad functions of the SFWC were identified: (1) its role as a physical center, including drop-in services, office space, phones, resource files, etc., (2) membership development, including the newsletter, public relations, and other publicity efforts, (3) fundraising, both for itself and to support organizing efforts, (4) community organizing and sponsored projects, with the former initiated by the SFWC or in direct collaboration / coalition with other groups, and the latter brought to SFWC by other organizers / communities, and (5) finance/administration as a nonprofit.

The team designed a decision-making structure and described the new character and makeup of the SFWC Board of Directors. Four concepts framed the structure: (1) each of the five functions would be developed and implemented by a committee, with each committee coordinated by at least one core staff member and open to any member of the SFWC, (2) workers would control the decision making, (3) community members would have advisory roles, and (4) a paper board would be named to comply with state and foundation requirements. "Workers" were defined as both paid and nonpaid individuals who took responsibility for specific tasks or functions of the SFWC, working a minimum of ten hours a week (not counting the weekly meeting), or who coordinated one of the five functional areas of the organization. Each committee could involve anyone willing and able to contribute to its work, with its members defining their role as a committee and developing its own work plan, to be reported back to the weekly workers' committee by a committee coordinator.

The general idea was that a central group would coordinate these separate committees and set general direction and policy. But though there was a general consensus that those undertaking the work should have control of the decision making, there was not an agreement on how this would exactly work. Would all the committee members be part of this decision-making body, or would it consist of representatives from those committees? How much autonomy would the functional committees have? These questions were left to be resolved as the work unfolded.

There was also a commitment to community feedback, acquired through membership meetings and other advisory capacities. The need for a formal board, in order to meet legal requirements and to assist in fundraising efforts, was acknowledged, but with the caveat that as a board it would have no real power—that power would continue to reside in the group's committee structure. In the wake of this process, a new Board of Directors was identified, drawing on the women involved in the transition process: Tiana Arruda, Jean Crosby, Tracy Gary, Jeanne Adelman Mahoney, Jean Livingston, Marge Nelson, Roma Guy, Rebecca Sandridge, and Nan Schlosberg.

A formal affirmative action policy was thoroughly discussed and adopted, particularly in reference to hiring but also as a more general ideological statement. The commitment to involving women of color was easier said than done, however. The salaries offered for the bookkeeper position and other paid collective members were low, and it was a struggle to find anyone able and willing to fill the positions.

By the time the Transition Team was wrapping up its process, the decision to buy Dovre Hall and transform it into The Women's Building was done, and just as the SFWC was adopting its new structure and looking for new staff, it was time to move in, and for a new collective to be built that would operate the Building.

CHAPTER 5

SETTLING INTO THE BUILDING

EVEN AS THE Transition Team was winding up its work, the purchase of the Building was finalized. The move was initially planned for April 1979. This turned out to be an idealistic goal, as the enormity of the task of opening a building began to sink in. Most of April and May were spent preparing the space for the move—phone lines had to be put in, doors were replaced or in some cases put in or widened to ensure accessibility, and old carpets were pulled up. Repairs and improvements, like installing lighted exit signs, had to be made to bring the Building into full compliance with fire codes. The April date came and went, but move-in day did finally arrive on June 4, 1979.

None of the existing tenants of the Building were evicted after the sale. The Building's office space was far from full, and many of its room were large gathering rooms—most with bars of their own dating from the Building's days as a German and then Norwegian community center. Just taking over and organizing the space that was already available was a huge task, especially for a group moving from a small, three-room office. The Women's Building Project of the Bay Area, functioning as a sponsored project of San Francisco Women's Centers (SFWC), was the recognized owner and operator of the Building. No steps were ever taken to apply for separate nonprofit status, and in the eyes of the state, the SFWC was the Building's owner, accountable for any liabilities.

Over the next year or two, as old tenants left and new office space was carved out of larger rooms, the Building was slowly taken over by women's organizations and services. Early tenants were SFWC, the Bay Area Feminist Federal Credit Union, Options for Women Over 40, Coalition for the Medical Rights of Women, Concilio Mujeres, San Francisco Women Against Rape, Women Against Violence in Pornography and the Media, Vida Gallery, Lilith Theater, and Women's Speaker Network.

The San Francisco Women's Switchboard moved from the Brady Street office into The Women's Building as well. Over the years, the Switchboard had relied principally on telephones to provide information and referral numbers. Though it was not primarily a hotline, those staffing the phone lines were often involved in counseling callers. Sharing offices with the SFWC at the Brady Street office had given the Switchboard more direct contact with women, but its main identity was as a telephone switchboard. The women of the Switchboard chose a location on the fourth floor of the new building, where they could have more privacy for their phone conversations. Being on the fourth floor did give them privacy, but it also isolated them from the hubbub and energy that was growing throughout the rest of the Building. Affected by the dramatic decline in volunteerism of those years, the Switchboard folded within a year of moving to the Building. This left a gap, as there was now no obvious place for women in need to turn. Throughout the 1980s, women looking for help often made their first call to The Women's Building, and whoever happened to answer the phone suddenly found themselves in a counseling situation.

The SFWC was more interested in providing an information-and-referral program that women could directly access. Visiting the drop-in center in person would expose women to much more than the specific information they might have been looking for. But deciding where to place such a drop-in center was easier said than done. It made no sense to locate it on the fourth floor. The first floor made the most sense, but no ready space was available there. Instead, the drop-in center was initially set up on the second floor, combined with the reception function.

Individuals from many of the tenant organizations had been involved since 1978 in the process of purchasing the Building, and they moved in with a vested interest. The vision was to bring the coalition spirit that went into the purchase into the actual operation of the building itself. In that context, a Building Council was established, involving representatives of all of the tenants, to meet on a monthly basis. The council was envisioned as the body that would develop long-term plans for the Building, settle general policy questions, and approve major facility changes. The daily work of running the Building was to be done by a Worker's Committee, which would meet weekly to coordinate the work of subcommittees.

Had it been five years earlier, when the flow of activism was stronger and there was more woman power to carry on the work, this model may have worked. But the situation had in fact changed. The Building Council did meet from time to time during the first year, but the reality is that each of the tenant organizations faced its own struggle to keep its project alive. There was little time available to focus on the details of running a building.

The purchase of The Women's Building turned out to be one of the last major collective efforts by radical elements of the San Francisco women's movement. Without the individuals who threw their all into it and the organizational support of a wide array of organizations, the core collective of the SFWC would never have been able to put together the down payment or had the political will to take such a big risk. At least to some degree, the decision to take that risk was based on an assessment of the movement that bought it. But that assessment was no longer accurate; the seventies were coming to an end in more ways than one, and the country was at the dawn of a new political era.

There were certainly signs that the future contours of the movement would look different: the increasing bellicosity of the religious right's assault on lesbian/gay rights and abortion rights was having an effect on national politics, leading to Reagan's election in 1980; the Moscone/Milk assassinations led a lot of people to reevaluate their political beliefs, alliances, and reasons for activism; the socialist/communist left endured continual splintering and growing irrelevance, increasingly unable to move beyond the 60s (or the 50s for some organizations). The vision of the Building had been to provide a base of operations for the women's movement and other progressive movements that had thousands of people responding to the call for political activism, a place to launch organizing projects into a variety of communities. But now that the flow of activism was dwindling, the Building came to serve more as a haven for activists and existing organizations. Increasingly at odds with dominant political culture, people gathered at events at The Women's Building in order to find a sense of community and gather the inspiration to carry on. That's not to say that organizing in communities stopped during the eighties, and at times the San Francisco Women's Centers and The Women's Building played important roles in supporting projects. But the movement was now on the defensive, trying to hold onto past gains and fighting over scarce resources.

Money and Volunteers

One obvious challenge confronting the women was the shortage of capital. A massive grassroots effort had gone into raising the initial down payment, and very little was left over to ensure the operation of the Building, let alone for any major upgrades to the real estate. Most business students know that a business that is opened without funds for the start-up costs and to cover a couple years of deficit is probably doomed to failure. The consultant that recommended against the purchase had seen this as the most significant flaw in the plan.

Sure enough, the shortage of money was a problem right from the start, with an extremely tight cash flow. The weight of the liabilities was so heavy that it was hard to see the Building as an asset. Between June and December 1979, about $25,000 in grants came to The Women's Building, not quite enough to cover seven months of the $3,600 monthly mortgage payment. That left rental income and other donations to cover the cost of utilities, supplies, and staffing. Paying for renovations and code upgrades was another issue entirely. To this day, it is hard to convince charitable foundations that giving money to operate a facility promotes social change.

The purchase went forward because the women involved were convinced that the lack of financial capital could be compensated for by community involvement. But once the purchase was made, the immediate goal was accomplished and many moved on to something else. The effort to operate a building wasn't as glamorous as raising the money to buy one, nor did it demand the same skills. Unlike the seventies, when a new wave of volunteers always seemed to step forward for new projects, in 1979 only a few women stepped forward to carry on with The Women's Building Project.

A core SFWC collective remained. In 1979, this collective included Tiana Arruda, Roma Guy, Nan Schlosberg, Diane Jones, Jean Crosby, Gretchen Walsh (who left in early 1979), Tracy Gary, Laura, Marya Grambs, Lynn Lonidier, Kim, Barbara Starkey, Linda, and Dorinda Moreno.

It became clear by the end of the first year that the Building Council was not going to be effective in running the Building. Tenants were brought together on occasions as a Tenant's Council, but it was more about sharing information than setting policy. The Worker's Committee evolved into a staff collective, some paid, others not, for the Women's Building Project. Participants in this collective during the first year included Tiana, Dorinda Moreno, Ali Marrera, Carmen Vasquez, and Flavia Maucci. Though not formally on the staff collective, other women who were part of the SFWC collective also helped out with the work of running the Building.

The shift in political culture wasn't the only contributor to the decline in numbers of volunteers. The economy was also changing. Years of inflation meant that by the 1980s many young people couldn't afford to volunteer their time, even if they wanted to. College tuition and rent were both rising, so part-time work and low wages were no longer enough to live on. At the same time, the federal funds that had often helped pay subsidies for political organizers were drying up, making it even harder for small progressive efforts to pay their staff a living wage.[17]

The result of these political and economic changes was a declining pool of volunteer labor. Burnout among radical activists isn't a new thing, but through the sixties and seventies there had always been new people stepping forward to fill in the ranks. By 1980, the number of new young people stepping into activism had plummeted to a small trickle. And many organizing efforts were competing for those who did appear, whether they were new to politics or just new to the Bay Area. Among these few, there weren't many for whom the tedium of running a building was attractive.

Many activists did come through the Building as paid staff members. The low pay meant that there was some level of political commitment to the project, but it also meant that the turnover rate was high, particularly as women learned skills that could earn them better wages elsewhere. Or women moved on to work for another cause also desperate for woman power. The reason that The Women's Building did make it through its first years was that there was a stable core of activists and a periphery of supporting actors—some paid, others not—that enabled the Building to remain open and functioning in accordance with its original vision of serving the radical/progressive communities during the 1980s.

Fortunately, no one knew how inhospitable the coming decade would be for progressive grassroots efforts. Once the down payment was made to the Sons of Norway, with a $500,000 balloon payment due in ten years, the die was cast. There was a commitment to keep the Building open at any cost.

---

17 Throughout the eighties, many a small nonprofit that had become dependent on federal or state funds would fold. The San Francisco Women's Centers had used public funds, most often on behalf of specific sponsored projects, but the general budget of the SFWC and of The Women's Building never relied heavily on public grants. Its diversified sources of support, including a strong individual donor base, enabled it to weather the shifts in federal budget priorities during the Reagan years better than many organizations.

Women of Color and The Women's Building

Involving women of color in all aspects of the Building's operation was a high priority for the collective. For years, the SFWC had
been struggling with the issue of racism and the composition of its
active membership. Women of color were involved during most periods, but the principal and most visible leadership came from white
women. By 1979, long experience had shown that without women
of color in leadership positions from the start of an organizing effort,
it was very difficult, if not impossible, to build a truly multiracial organization. Despite the central role that women of color have played
during the entire life of the San Francisco Women's Centers, throughout the eighties The Women's Building was still viewed with distrust
as a "white woman's" organization by many looking from a distance.

At least part of the reason for this was spillover from a common
perception of the women's movement as a whole as basically a white
movement, both in terms of its composition and the issues it addressed. There may also have been a racist presumption that only
white people would have enough resources to own a building. In fact,
however, most of the women who worked directly for The Women's
Building during its first couple of years were women of color. Carmen
Vazquez remembers her time on staff at The Women's Building in the
early 1980s:

> I was at the Building on staff, and during that time the major-
> ity of all the women who worked at The Women's Building were
> women of color. And a good many of them were Central American
> women. We had [name unclear] from Peru and Graciela and Alicia
> and Flavia from Argentina. Tiana and [name unclear] from Brazil
> and myself and Ali Marrero [are] Puerto Rican. During a good part
> of that time there was still Jay Casselberry and Jacque Dupree. BG
> was never on the staff of the building, but she was a tenant — she
> was first on the Tenants' Council then she had her office upstairs
> and so she was always somehow involved. And then Happy Hyder

became involved with the Gallery, and so there was a real core of women of color from working-class backgrounds or middle-class backgrounds in Central American countries but with a very radicalized political upbringing that was very different from anything here. So those are the people that are running the place. You better believe that the kind of programs and meetings and people that this place was going to be open to is going to be more than the marginalized radical white feminist group. Of course, it also meant that there was a lot of political conflict.

Despite this multiracial composition, throughout the eighties, many women of color viewed the Building as a white organization. Regina Gabrielle, hired in 1986 to develop lesbian programming for The Women's Building, describes this dynamic:

I brought a network of lesbians of color to the building, and women who were not necessarily open to the building. They knew of the building, they had gone to maybe some events at the building, but they were pretty much alienated by The Women's Building. Because the building is a white women's organization. "It's those crazy white lesbians." … Certainly in 1986, lesbians of color felt marginalized and alienated and discriminated against, even though the building had lesbians of color, women of color involved in its collective, on its paper tiger board. … That's always a theme. I think the women's movement in general will always have to deal with racism.…

For the women of color that did work there and were involved … they were somehow white-identified. That we are white-identified, so infuriating, because it invalidates women of color who are involved. In any organization, it invalidates their existence and their contributions. Women of color, and especially lesbians of color, have made the building really a very, very special and unique place.

The one thing that was a constant of life at The Women's Building was political conflict. Race and racism were factors in nearly every situation, but there were other issues that aroused passions as well. Some of the conflict was with external forces, but in the first couple of years considerable conflict was internal to the collectives that owned and operated the Building: the San Francisco Women's Centers and the Women's Building Project. There was a built-in power dynamic over money, given that the SFWC "owned" the Building in the eyes of the state and the bank, while the Women's Building Project collective was responsible for operating it.

This conflict began with racial overtones. The SFWC was pre-dominately white and lesbian, with a mixture of working-class and middle-class women. Many in this collective had been working together for some time—since before the Building was purchased—and they had long personal histories as well. The Women's Building staff collective, on the other band, was just being established specifical-ly to operate the Building. This collective was comprised mainly of women of color, most from working-class backgrounds, with a mix-ture of lesbian and straight women. No matter what the intentions of any of the parties were, the fact is that women of color were regularly going, hat in hand, to ask for money to carry out the work of the Building from a group of white women, who then turned around and nagged to get reports on how the money was spent.

Fortunately, at the core of the SFWC were several white women with a good handle on the dynamics arising from racial differences. The experiences of Roma and Diane in the Peace Corps in Africa, and Jean's experience at Glide Church were to serve them well. Since the mid-seventies and the violence conference, the SFWC collective had actively tried to address issues of racism in their work. The very composition of The Women's Building staff was a reflection of their commitment to the leadership of women of color, even as it made racial dynamics impossible to sidestep.

Within months of moving into the Building, the tension reached a crisis. The first building coordinator to be hired was Dorinda Moreno, a straight Latina. She had been part of the SFWC collective, but with this position she moved fully into The Women's Building collective. She soon took offense at the frequent requests from the SFWC staff to account for various expenditures. By the fall of 1979, the two collectives were having serious conflicts. A weekend retreat was held at a cabin in Willets, three hours north of San Francisco, in an effort to defuse the tension and build a new sense of collectivity. In the short term, the gathering was a success.

Not long after, Dorinda left the staff, and with the passage of time a new level of trust began to develop. But underlying problems were not resolved. A structure that separated The Women's Building from the SFWC remained in place, even though there was significant overlap in personnel between the two collectives. Nor was Dorinda's position as building coordinator specifically filled. Instead, her responsibilities were spread out among the remaining collective members.

The Building and the SFWC

The functions of The Women's Building were somewhat different than those of the SFWC, but there were also some commonalities, particularly the role as a community center. Though this was central to the impetus and vision of the SFWC, it was The Women's Building that provided the physical structure that brings a community center together. The worker's collective, and a variety of subcommittees formed to carry out specific projects and tasks, spent a great deal of time dealing with the physical facility. Consensus was still the goal for final decisions, though the limitations were acknowledged. Rarely, if ever, did a small minority block a decision.

Given its own history, the SFWC collective thought it very important that there be an organizational distinction between themselves and the Women's Building Project. The Women's Building collective had been set up in 1979 with the goal of becoming its own independent nonprofit organization. The SFWC was to sponsor it only for a couple years while it got its feet on the ground and built up its financial base.

But by 1980, it was clear that such financial stability was still a long way off. Rental income from tenants (including the SFWC) and one-time events was barely enough to cover the mortgage and utilities. It took additional fund-raising events, like the Run in the Park and the Women's Crafts Fair, to pay at least a few salaries. Basic renovation and building maintenance were dependent on grant money or other windfalls. Nearly all money was funneled through the Building's fiscal sponsor, the SFWC, which was confronting its own money problems.

In terms of the actual people involved, there was a lot of overlap. Many of the tenant organizations had at one time been a sponsored project of the SFWC. Most of the women active in the operation of the Building were also active in one (or more) of the organizations housed at the Building. Conversely, most members of the SFWC collective were spending most of their time on issues related to the Building.

The SFWC continued to respond to requests for fiscal sponsorship and endorsements, but it wasn't really involved in any new political efforts as an organization. The newsletter production overlapped with work around the Building, as promoting its space and the activities of its tenants and renters was a central element of the newsletter's content. A women's arts and crafts fair that had outgrown the women's bookstore, Old Wives Tales, was taken on with the political goal of empowering women artists, but with equally important goals of bringing the community to the Building and raising money for its operation.

Although the SFWC was a corporate entity with a half-million-dollar asset and an annual operating budget over $100,000, there was nothing corporate in how it functioned. As with many volunteer-based groups, decisions were most commonly made by the women involved in the issue at hand, whether they were paid or volunteer staff of the SFWC, paid staff of The Women's Building, or someone working with one of the tenant organizations. There were no clear organizational charts, and job descriptions, if any, were often very fluid.

In the mind of the broader community, little distinction was made between The Women's Building and the SFWC. Even for those inside the Building, tenants as well as the collective members, lines of responsibility were very blurred. The racial dynamics between the two collectives persisted as an undercurrent. The proposal to merge the collectives, in effect collapsing The Women's Building collective back into the SFWC collective, came from Carmen Vazquez.

Reuniting the Two Collectives

A Puerto Rican lesbian transplant from New York, Carmen first came to the Building collective for a part-time job teaching Spanish. At the urging of Jay Casselberry and Jacque Dupree, members of The Women's Building collective, she then applied for a paid part-time position with the SFWC. In this capacity, she was the representative to the Building/Tenants Council and worked closely with the Worker's Committee that oversaw the operation of the Building. From her position working with both collectives, she recognized that merging the two groups could resolve an organizational source of tension. With an outside facilitator from the Third World Women's Alliance, the two collectives held a series of meetings and agreed to merge, with the group to be known as San Francisco Women's Centers/The Women's Building. In the years since, the main public identity has been "The Women's Building," and the internal shorthand most commonly used is "TWB."

While this reorganization helped stabilize the core of women that made up The Women's Building, it also meant that women of color were no longer a majority of that core, as had been the case with the Women's Building Project collective. Though the SFWC/The Women's Building collective was in fact a multiracial group, it was still often perceived as a white women's organization.

Despite the tension and occasional high drama, often sparked by mundane issues of whose turn it was to unplug the toilet or mop the floor, the women of the two groups shared some fundamental political values and goals, which helped them successfully navigate the pitfalls of multiracial collective efforts. In the face of a national political tenor that was moving toward the right, the women involved in both collectives were committed to a radical vision of the future. They continued to be motivated by broad demands, like the desire to see full reproductive health care available to all women, regardless of class and age, or fervent opposition to a foreign policy dedicated to propping up ruthless dictators. Most would have considered them-selves socialists of some sort, though by the late seventies that was a pretty fluid ideology.

While all were motivated by lofty ideals, on the practical, daily level reality was very different. The women were immersed in keep-ing the plumbing repaired and the bathrooms serviced, fighting with the elevator repair company to keep the elevator running, writing grants to the city for funds to install exit signs and fire doors, and nag-ging Paddy Nolan to pay his paltry rent for the Dovre Club. There was so much to do in just getting the Building into basic operating shape that it was hard to pursue even the narrower strategic goals of provid-ing a quality facility for use by the movement.

In the words of Graciela Perez Trevisan, who was part of the col-lective in 1981-82 and then again from 1984 to 1986:

But the daily maintenance of building was, oh my God, it was always a headache, always a headache, because we all have to be responsible. Because of money, you know. ... I remember in '84, in '85 and '86, we didn't have money to have somebody there a full day, except for the information and referral person. But that person sometimes was so busy with phone calls and people all day, that anybody was responsible for putting toilet paper in the bathrooms. The bathrooms, probably they overflowed three times a week, so anybody had to go and clean, right? So, you know the maintenance of the building was always a big issue.

The merger of the collectives in 1980 did help to streamline the work and improve communications, leading to reduced tension within the collective. Just having fewer meetings to go to made life a little easier. There was now one large collective, with over a dozen women, each putting in at least five hours per week, and many far more. But running the Building was still an overwhelming project, and now it was everyone's responsibility to keep it open. And even though the level of activism in the women's movement was shifting, there was still a community, many of whom financially supported the Building, who demanded some level of accountability.

But money and human resources were not the only obstacles the women confronted. There were also external political challenges that threatened the Building, though in some ways these served to shore up their ideological determination to carry on despite the serious financial difficulties.

A Building Under Attack

The political opposition that had attempted to block the initial purchase of the Building didn't disappear once the deed changed hands. Although the overt harassment by Dovre Club patrons had diminished, the struggle with the bar was by no means over. Relations with owner Paddy Nolan also continued to be strained. Despite the existence of a lease, The Women's Building staff had to actively push Nolan to pay the monthly rent, and on more than one occasion he fell months behind in his payments. This despite the fact that his rate was rarely raised, and was soon was well below the average commercial rates for the area. The spirit of feminism, combined with some fear of Nolan's continued political clout with City agencies, prevented the staff from pursuing a hard line in making collections, despite the often precarious cash flow situation. Ultimately, the rent was always paid, but the constant effort that it took to collect it served to undermine morale and invalidate the SFWC's role as the owner of property.

The bar wasn't the only renter to cause problems. In its first years, desperate for rental income, the Building often rented rooms to

individuals for private parties. Though the clean-up costs and maintenance demands of these private groups were often greater than those
from events sponsored by organizations, most of these events went
smoothly.

However, one Sweet Sixteen birthday party, held on November
3, 1979, did get out of hand. Even though private security had been
hired by the parents to keep order, word had gone out to the local
youth that this was the party of the night. By 11 p.m., hundreds of
youth were hanging around outside the Building, and soon they were
using fire escapes and back doors to sneak into the party. Over 250
youth took over for an hour before The Women's Building's security,
the hired private security, and the San Francisco Police Department
were able to break up the party and clear the Building. By then there
had been extensive trashing of the public areas of the Building. In the
wake of this debacle, a community meeting was held, in part to allow
the Building to apologize to its neighbors for the disruption caused by
the party and in part to work toward improved rental policies.

There were more serious attacks on the Building as well. Around
9 p.m. on Valentine's Day 1980, building security worker Judith
Birnbaum came upon a fire on the second floor, in the drop-in room.
Flyers and brochures had been intentionally piled up and set ablaze.
Judith attempted to control the blaze with a fire extinguisher (she cut
her hand while breaking the glass cover), but the fire spread quickly.
She called the fire department, and it was put out before it spread
beyond the second floor. The fire resulted in $60,000 in smoke and
water damage. The Building was closed for the night, and Judith was
the only one injured. The drop-in room was completely destroyed,
and there was significant damage to the child care room and the
office of the Third World Women's Alliance. Twenty-six windows in
the Building had been broken by the fire department as part of the
fire-fighting effort. Insurance covered some of the cost, but these were
repairs that couldn't be put on hold, meaning that other renovation
work had to be deferred. There was no proof to identify who set the
fire, nor did anyone claim credit for it as a political act. Some thought

it to be the work of a homeless woman who often spent her nights in the Building's doorway, but we'll never know the truth of the matter.

In its first few years of operation The Women's Building also received numerous bomb threats, none of which would ever be traced to anyone. No actual bombs were ever found inside the Building, but the threats could not be ignored and evacuation of the Building was required each time. This was disruptive to the work of all the tenants (except the Dovre Club, which was open in the evening hours, and most of the threats were daytime occurrences), to say nothing of the psychological impact on individuals.

On 1:40 a.m. on Wednesday, October 8, 1980, a pipe bomb was exploded in front of the entrance to The Women's Building. Because of the early morning hour of the attack, no one was inside the Building, and the bar was unaffected. Glass in the front door and nearby windows was broken, and the marquee and building tiles were damaged by the blast. Total damages were modest—under $5,000—but coming as they did on top of the fire damage, it was just one more source of financial and emotional strain.

There was no explicit threat or warning before the explosion, and no one ever claimed responsibility. The incident was investigated by the police, but with no results. So we can only speculate as to the specific target. Perhaps it was one of the tenants—such as Women Against Violence in Pornography and the Media, who were organizing a Take Back the Night march the following weekend. Most groups, including tenants, believed it was the Building itself that was the target, as a symbol of women's independence.

Bomb threats were made throughout the eighties. These threats did little to mend relations with the local police, already strained by the November 1979 party and other noise complaints lodged by neighbors. Even though The Women's Building was the target of the threats, the women were the ones calling for help and were therefore seen as the problem. In the post-9/11 era, bomb threats are recognized as terrorist acts, but in 1980 they were viewed almost as pranks. No one was ever identified in the threats, though many at the

Building had suspicions that the first threats came from patrons of the Dovre Club.

Collective member Graciela Perez Trevisan reflects on an experience from 1985:

> I remember bomb threats. I don't remember when they were, but I remember [living through] two or three bomb threats. One I do remember. It was specifically an event that we were going to have. It was organized by Jewish Women's Secular Group, and they were doing a benefit for Palestine Women's Organization, and there was a bomb threat. So, actually, it was a whole day of tension for us. We all were doing security that day, checking everyone who came in the building and asking them to sign when they came in, and when they left the building....
>
> The Women's Building has a history of attacks against it. I think that's because it was a very radical organization. A very radical public space, also, with a lot of radical women's groups and community groups meeting there. I think that the right wing is not only active now [1996], it has always been active, and conservatives too. I think that a lot of people didn't want to see The Women's Building.

As painful as the impact of the fire and the bomb threats was, they also had the effect of strengthening the collective's resolve to carry on. The fact that attacks and threats were being made was an indication of the need for something like the Building. Internal conflicts were easier to keep in perspective when an outside attack could come at any time.

Beyond the direct attacks on the Building, the women also had to deal with the general condition of life in an economic downturn, including a need for increased security. With so many different organizations housed at the Building, many relying on volunteer support, new people were regularly coming into the Building. This made it hard for anyone to be sure who was there for legitimate business, and who was looking to make an easy, quick buck picking up someone's purse or backpack or pilfering equipment from unlocked offices. It was also hard to make sure people who were working on some project at the Building were aware of security issues. New locks were installed throughout the Building, but policies about keys were unevenly maintained.

In an effort to deal with the security challenge, an alarm system was installed. Initially it was tied to the police department, but after numerous false alarms, the system was instead tied to the home of someone on the collective who lived fairly close and could come check it out before calling the police. In addition, women were hired on a part-time or intermittent basis to provide security for the Building, especially for evening events. They would cover the event and then make sure the Building was empty when it was locked up for the night.

The informal way in which women were hired on more than one occasion led to other difficulties: sometimes the security person was helping herself to other people's belongings, sometimes she was unjustly accused of stealing. Other resentments arose over perceived or real favoritism about who got more or better hours of work providing security at the Building. The isolation of the work—combining tedious tasks haphazardly assigned to security with occasional tense incidents, all at low pay—led to a very high turnover in security staff.

Identity Politics

The conflicts with the broader community didn't come only from adversaries. Political differences within the women's and lesbian/gay movement and other progressive communities also led to conflict. The seventies was a period in which many thought the revolution was just around the corner, and the focus was on changing all aspects of society. Certainly there was a lot of internal political debate, but the enemy was clear and usually agreed upon by all. By the eighties, the only revolution that seemed on the horizon was the right wing backlash, and radical and progressive politics were clearly on the defensive. Without a broad national demand to galvanize and unite various communities, the movements became fractured, and the emphasis shifted to defining and then defending one's own community. The politics of identity became a defining feature of the 1980s, lending justification to the reality of a fractured progressive politic.

Particularly in the feminist and lesbian/gay political communities, there was a resistance to the idea of hierarchy among the various identities. One positive result was an acknowledgment of and a desire to learn about various cultural heritages and social conditions, moving beyond the presumption that one voice can represent all viewpoints. On the down side, with no criteria for setting priorities, an already shrinking movement was increasingly fragmented.

The complexity of defining goals by identity is evident in one of the first major political controversies to confront The Women's Building: whether to rent to a group of policewomen. The issue was brought to the Building in 1980 by Del Martin and Phyllis Lyon, two prominent figures in the women's and lesbian movements. As founders of the Daughters of Bilitis, both had been part of the original coalition that gave birth to the SFWC in the early seventies. The organization had also been one of the charter groups of the Bay Area Feminist Federal Credit Union. By the early eighties, the Daughters of Bilitis was gone, but both Del and Phyllis were significant voices in the women's community on a variety of issues relating to lesbian rights, women's health care, and antiviolence efforts. They had been working with women police officers, both lesbian and straight, for several years when the group decided they needed a neutral meeting space, away from formal police department offices. Given that the whole idea of buying a building for the women's movement was to provide a safe meeting place, it was only natural that they would approach the Building about renting office space.

In supporting efforts to combat violence against women, many women had developed close working relations with the police department. For radicals, there was always an element of ambivalence toward these relations. In the early days, when the prevailing view was that the rape victim somehow asked to be raped and that husbands were justified in the use of violence against their wives, the police and prosecutors were the target of demands for change. As attitudes began to shift, the challenge turned to developing skills and tools to enforce laws. One tactic in changing these attitudes was to increase the number of female police officers. In the context of equal rights for women in employment, breaking into traditionally male careers like law enforcement was a legitimate demand. The formation of women's caucuses within vocations and professions predominated by men was common by the seventies, and this was seen as an important step in breaking down gender lines in employment.

For women coming from a radical perspective, support for the police, whether in terms of employment rights or in defending women from violence, meant support for an institution that was considered to be fundamentally flawed. In the broadest sense, the role of police in society was to preserve the status quo, a status quo that many saw as preserving entitlements for wealthy white men at the expense of other groups in society—people of color, the poor, and women.

In San Francisco's Mission District in the early eighties, for example, the repressive role of the police was being played out on the streets on a regular basis. Since the seventies, a large influx of immigrants from Central America had come into the United States, and many found their way to the Mission District. With the cuts in public funding for social services that characterized the Reagan years, many were unable to find work or go to school. The result was gangs of young people, predominately Latino, hanging out on the street corners with nothing much to do. They soon became a target of the San Francisco Police Department, and by the time the issue of renting to the policewomen's caucus came before the Building, there was a significant community outcry against the police department.

Even beyond the specific acts of police violence against Latino youth, for immigrant women there was a more generalized distrust of the police. In their experience in Guatemala, Honduras, and El

Salvador, police routinely and openly terrorized the public. They were just as likely to be raped by a police officer or soldier as to be assisted in any way. While white people may have seen the Mission District police violence as an aberration, for many immigrants it was considered the norm. The police, even in the United States, were not friends. Having them meeting at The Women's Building could well be enough to keep immigrant women away.

All of these dynamics played out within the collectives that ran The Women's Building. On the one hand, saying no to the policewomen seemed to fly in the face of what the Building stood for—opening doors for women in all parts of society. It offended not only the group of women police officers but also their supporters, some of whom were part of building's donor base. Not only would the Building lose a new source of rental income, but future donations from the broader community would also be jeopardized. On the other hand, saying yes would allow what many saw as the enemy into the midst of a supposedly safe place.

The collective agonized over the decision, sharing past experiences with police, both bad and good, and weighing the community impact of their decision. Ultimately the collective came to a consensus that the short-term gain of renting to the policewomen couldn't outweigh the longer-term strategic aim of building a base within the Mission District community, particularly with immigrant women.

Though this consensus had been built within the Building collective, the decision was not so well received in the broader women's community. Del and Phyllis were livid and made a very public break with the Building, and other individuals followed their lead. Just as the broader women's movement was going on the defensive and giving up more radical demands, The Women's Building had risked its future in taking a clearly radical political position. An already precarious funding base had just become narrower.

While this rental decision cut off support from some of the white and more conservative elements of the women's movement, a debate over another rental decision weakened the Building's radical credentials. At issue was the rental of meeting space to activists from lesbian and gay proponents of sadomasochism (S/M) in sexual expression.

Samois was a group of lesbians dedicated to exploring the outer ranges of sexual expression. In early 1981, they reserved space at The Women's Building to hold an event during that year's Gay Pride Weekend. Initially, no one saw any problem with the rental. But by the time the organizers called back in April to confirm the space in order to promote the event in the official Pride publications, several issues had come up. The collective asked to meet with members of Samois in order to address these issues.

The debate over S/M was movement-wide in the early 1980s. Since 1978, members of Samois had been attempting to meet with members of Women Against Violence in Pornography and the Media. They wanted a distinction drawn between misogynist pornography and consensual and, to them, liberating expressions of sexuality. Educational material was published and distributed to educate the lesbian community and challenge the predominant condemnation the group faced. Many lesbians at the time were straining against a homogenous standard of the politically correct lesbian that had grown in the early years of being an out community. Short hair, jeans, and plaid shirts had been de rigueur for nearly a decade, and heaven forbid that a woman who identified as a lesbian explore the possibility of bisexuality. Being a proponent of S/M was perhaps the most controversial challenge to political correctness in sexuality.

The Women's Building may have emerged during an era of sexual liberation and exploration, but open discussion of sexuality remained a charged issue for many. For those steeped in feminist views, sado-masochistic role play smacked of the kind of oppression most were dedicating their lives to eradicating. Now here were women asking to use the Building as a place to validate, indeed to celebrate their sexual preference. In a collective already working to accommodate differences in race and class and involving both straight and lesbian women, the issue of sadomasochistic sexuality raised new challenges.

After two meetings between members of Samois and The Women's Building collective, they agreed to let the meeting go ahead, though by this time it was too late to list the meeting place in the advanced publicity of Gay Pride events. But then, just two weeks before the event, new concerns were raised by members of the collective who hadn't been at the earlier meetings with Samois, and new conditions were proposed regarding appropriate behavior by participants at the Samois meeting. For instance, no one was to be led by a leash in public areas of the Building. A few such specific activities were to be prohibited, but there was also a general statement prohibiting any activities that would make other building patrons uncomfortable. These late conditions infuriated the women of Samois, in particular the general prohibition, which they saw as making them responsible for how others felt.

While the content of the concerns was distressing, even more distressing was the process used to communicate them. The women from Samois felt they'd put in considerable effort to address the issues of The Women's Building collective. They thought a consensus had thereby been reached, only to have it all tossed out by unilateral demands from The Women's Building. From the Building collective side, there were various opinions about how strictly the "behavioral" guidelines should be applied. After several weeks of confusion, the event went ahead as planned, with no special guidelines in place. Nor were there any problems with the event. In fact, the only issues raised about the event came from some participants, who felt that meeting in the dining hall, with others coming in and out to access the kitchen on that floor, provided insufficient privacy.

In December 1981, Samois again approached The Women's Building about holding a second meeting during the 1982 Gay Pride Weekend. They wrote a lengthy letter to The Women's Building Advisory Committee, addressing the process during the prior year and asking for a better process this time around, including a written statement as to the decision of the collective about the rental.

Graciela Perez Trevisan, an immigrant from Argentina, had just joined the staff in the fall of 1981, remembers:

> I was doing bookings, so that was at the end of '81. I got this letter from someone, asking to rent at the Building. Actually, the letter already contained another paragraph saying that if we didn't rent the building to them, they were going to make public our refusal. Now, that was, I think, around Christmas, and I was planning to go to New York. So I said "Okay, great. I won't be here for the decision." But when I came back from New York, ... nobody had made a decision, right?
>
> Certainly for something like that, it was decided to have a whole collective meeting. So I would say that it was a hard and painful meeting. We met from, I think, nine o'clock until six o'clock, the whole day, and the whole collective, you know, trying to make a decision.
>
> You know, what I have to say, that that was back in '81, right, and times have changed, and people have changed, also. I have changed, too. But I don't have any problem to say that at that moment I was one of the four people who opposed renting space to this group. The other persons were the African American woman, the Cuban woman, a Peruvian woman. ... We couldn't accept it on the basis that, you know, several of us coming from situations with extreme violence and dictatorships and police states. It brought, actually, a lot of hard feelings and emotions around torture and rape and issues that, of course, now, on an intellectual level, I was very clear that this was consensual, right? I mean, that's what S&M is about, right? Consensual.
>
> But, in any case, it's hard. And it was hard for me, individually, you know, to come to terms with S&M and with other issues, particularly, as I said, because of this situation of violence that I came from. ... It was only the four of us who were against, but the African American woman actually said that if we rented to that group, she was going to resign, and nobody wanted her to resign.

So, actually, the result was that we couldn't get consensus and then we didn't rent the space, because we couldn't get consensus. Now, as I said, that was back in '81. If I had to rent space now to an S&M group, to sex radicals, I will do it.

Given the high emotions involved, the stakes of saying yes were too high. No one would leave if the group was denied, but a yes would result in a loss to the collective. So this time, the rental was denied.

Paid staff was down to just a couple people by this time, so it would take many months for the formal, written explanation to be written and sent to Samois. Unlike the decision around the rental to the policewomen, this decision had less of a public and fiscal impact. In part this was because there was less publicity about the decision. But to the degree that it was a public decision, the debate over S/M sexuality was movement-wide, and in the early 80s, many feminists opposed it as an oppressive expression of sexuality. It was a minority that saw it as a private sexual preference to be defended.[18]

After weathering the battles over the policewomen and Samois, the collective realized the need to step back and assess just what owning a building meant to a political organization. The strategic planning process conducted in 1982 was very significant in stabilizing The Women's Building. On an ideological level, the year-long process was crucial to setting the groundwork that would keep the Building alive through the rest of the decade.

---

18 [2]This issue would come up again in the 1990s, when the National Association for Man-Boy Love (NAMBL) approached the Building about a meeting space for a conference to be held in conjunction with Pride Week. The paid staff at the time was unfamiliar with the group and did request background materials on NAMBLA's mission. They made a decision to accept the rental. Soon after, however, NAMBLA's meetings held in a public library came to the attention of the press, and with the subsequent controversy, their rental at The Women's Building was reconsidered. Again, after some contentious deliberations, the staff and board turned down the request, making them a hero in some eyes and a villain to others.

Theatrical Interlude: ACT II

Scene 1
The Switchboard

(They are still moving into the Building. The switchboard is already in operation. TESSA is volunteering at the switchboard. Occasionally you hear children's voices at a distance in the Building)

TESSA: *(Answering phone)* Hello, Women's Building of the Bay Area. Yes, the meeting to discuss names for different rooms in the building is today at 4:00. *(pause for response)* Yes, you should come with ideas about important women in history or herstory, unhuh, right, that you think we should honor.

(PAULA and LOUISE come to check out the auditorium for the Erotic Art Show. They come in and out of the space as TESSA is on the phone)

LOUISE: *(To PAULA)* I've been spending tons of time just sort of getting to know the physical space of the building and um, well, let's face it. This auditorium is a dive. Makes me think of old fashioned dyke dances in the dark.

PAULA: It's not really a vibrant happy space that people will love to come to.

LOUISE: Not to mention no lighting and a poor sound system.

TESSA: *(Picks up phone)* Buenas Dias, Women's Building of the Bay Area. What's the new building like? Well, it's new to us, but it's not that new. *(response)* Oh, I love old buildings. I love the history I feel just walking into this place. *(response)* Well, there are all these different groups all scattered around like the ah
San Francisco School of Self Defense, Concilio de Mujeres, Broomstick, WAVPM, that's Women Against Pornography and Violence in the Media, Lilith Theatre

PAULA: Well, at least we can rehearse here.

LOUISE: When the aerobics class isn't meeting.

(LOUISE and PAULA walk out of the auditorium area)

PAULA: So why do I keep hearing we're on the verge of losing the building at the same time we're making renovations?

LOUISE: Oh, that's because we seem to be going forward and moving backwards at the same time. I'll see you later. *(LOUISE exits)*

PAULA: Keep me posted.

(TESSA catches PAULA'S eye)

TESSA: So what's the play you're rehearsing?

PAULA: It's not a play. We're putting on an erotic art show and I'm organizing a poetry reading.

TESSA: Sounds good. I'd like to see that.

PAULA: Good. We'll have flyers here at the desk as soon as we can agree on anything – like how it's gonna look, what it's supposed to say.

TESSA: Collectives do work in mysterious ways. My name's Tessa.

PAULA: Paula. Good to see you again, but I gotta go.

TESSA: Your boyfriend waiting? He can come in, you know.

PAULA: He'd rather play pool next door. And how did you know I had a boyfriend? Do I look that straight?

TESSA: I volunteer at the switchboard. We know everything.

PAULA: And I used to think lesbian feminists didn't gossip.

TESSA: The personal is the political, you know.

(PAULA exits as RAE enters with baby)

PAULA: Hi, Rae. How's Lisa? *(to BABY)* Oh, you're so cute.

RAE: Not now, Paula. *(To TESSA)* Has anyone seen some kids?

(Phone rings. TESSA answers it)

TESSA: Women's Building of the Bay Area. Could you hold please?

RAE: They're escaped from childcare again. This doesn't look good for me as a new mother.

TESSA: They didn't go out the front door.

RAE: They know better than that. I just hope they haven't gone into the basement. That place gives me the creeps.

TESSA: Wait. I did hear children's voices earlier coming from upstairs.

RAE: That's probably them.

TESSA: Take the elevator and then you can walk down and find them.

RAE: No thanks, I'm not taking that elevator. See you later.

(RAE starts to exit upstairs. VOICES of children running and laughing overhead)

TESSA: Who are you voting for? At the naming meeting?

RAE: St. Theresa or whoever is the patron saint of lost children.

TESSA: Oh, I was thinking about Audre Lorde.

RAE: You can't. She's not dead yet.

TESSA: We only get to honor dead women? *(TESSA realizes she's left someone on hold)* I'm so sorry. Are you still there? We had an emergency. No we don't have gym facilities. *(hangs up)* Do they think this is the Y?

(A YOUNG WOMAN rushes in and starts talking)

YOUNG WOMAN: *(To TESSA)* I'm twenty one and I'm a lesbian and a Women's Studies major. *(To audience)* The Women's Building is this crickety old magical building down in the Mission. *(To Tessa)* I'm with the NOW group that's working toward ratifying the ERA and just, it's really for me, it's exciting because I guess it's the first time, probably since High School, that I've found something that uhm that has helped shape and define me.

(Phone rings)

TESSA: Excuse me. I have to take this call. *(Picks up phone)* Women's Building of the Bay Area.

YOUNG WOMAN: *(Shifts focus to DEBRA who has come in with some boxes)* The weather's been really warm an' sunny and I ride the bus and at the uh bus stop, there's a bench at uhm 18th street and Valencia and there's a tree near the bench and I just sit there thinking everything is really beautiful, you know. And it's really great to be able to go to poetry readings 'nd uhm organizing meetings and dances at the building.*(DEBRA puts down her boxes)*

DEBRA: My favorite thing is that the diversity of different things, that you have the weirdest, you know, the sexual transvestite, you know, ball, and the tea dance with elders happening at 4:00 on the same afternoon.

YOUNG WOMAN There are sexual transvestites here?

(LOUISE enters with plunger)

LOUISE: I'm spending all my time unplugging toilets and fighting with the elevator company. We haven't paid them for their last visit and they won't come out and fix it. And what the fuck does that have to do with being a political activist?

DEBRA: It has everything to do with being a political activist. We're here because......

YOUNG WOMAN: *(interrupts)* O.K., I'll be back later for the meeting. Bye.

TESSA: Hasta luego.

(SUSAN and ANNA enter)

DEBRA: *(surprised and uncomfortable, but trying to cover it)* Susan, hi. How are you? Are you out of the hospital now?

SUSAN: Just on a day pass.

DEBRA: Oh, good. I mean....

SUSAN: I can't talk to you right now.

ANNA: *(Guiding SUSAN up the stairs)* I'm just going to show her around, so she can see what we've been up to. Louise, why don't you come with us.

LOUISE: Sure, nothing better to do. *(Gives DEBRA plunger)*

DEBRA: Yeah, we've been painting and everything....You'll like it.

(ANNA, SUSAN and LOUISE go up to the second floor and sit on a bench at the landing. DEBRA stays downstairs, not knowing what to do next, maybe sits on her boxes)

TESSA: *(phone rings. TESSA answers but we don't hear her talking. Shift focus to SUSAN, ANNA and LOUISE)* Women's Building....

SUSAN: We're at the meeting I guess when uhh I notice that uhm my lover, Debra, is in love with Jane, the Consultant, I notice that. I actually don't really, I couldn't really say, what happened after the go-no go meeting. I mean I remember walking in here a few times... And the end of this is I have a nervous breakdown and I go into the mental hospital. And I mean you know I'm there in the mental hospital an' I get a phone call an' you say, "oh guess what that grant came through we just got a check for blah blah blah you know," it's addressed to me, you know, so it's, it's, very ironic uhm it but it was very terri(hh)ble=

ANNA: =extremely terrible=

SUSAN: =yeah

(Sounds of aerobics class starting, music and instructors voice)

ANNA: Meanwhile I'm trying to get things started and make the mort-gage and I go to see Susan 'cause it's restful for me.

LOUISE: <u>Nothing</u> is in place – no staff, no procedures. There is not the kind of money that's needed. Nothing, nothing, nothing, nothing. Plus, oh goodness, still trying to be this little collective.

ANNA: "Oh Susan it's soo nice here – people – you just ring a bell and people come //and"

SUSAN: It's hell=

ANNA: =it's like peaceful=

SUSAN: =if you're not attempting to slit your wrist every seco\\nd

ANNA: //yeahh

LOUISE: //yeahh.

ANNA: You're very sociable I mean you make an effort and...

SUSAN: Kinda still twist my hair an' tie it in knots and st\\uff for

ANNA: //right, you have a lot of symptoms.

SUSAN: Meanwhile Debra an'=

ANNA: =an' the consultant=

SUSAN: =were together. And it was my idea to hire her.

LOUISE: *(remembering this)* That's right. Oh, I'm sorry.

SUSAN: I thought our relationship was perfect s(hh)ee, and now they're together^ while I'm rotting away in this mental hospital tu-tearing my hair out you know an wh\\ile the building is

ANNA: //in the meantime, my core at the Women's Building is falling apart and we just=

SUSAN: =bought this huge building...

ANNA: "The Women's Building."

LOUISE: That's controversial in and of itself.

(Shift focus to DEBRA)

DEBRA: *(To TESSA)* I probably had five or six meetings with Jane to discuss all this stuff. And I came home one night and said, you know, I think I'm falling in love with this consultant, you know. And had no intention of doing anything about it. I mean, just needed to sort of say it. And within two days Susan had us broke, you know, had in her mind that I was leaving her and breaking up and doing this whole thing which was not where I was at all. And it was really um, un-threading for her, in a way that, you know, was kind of un, not where I was. And she was, you know, she was institutionalized within two months. And then we did break up. And um, I got involved with Jane about a month and a half later. And you know, I was terrified at what happened because I'd never been with anybody that had had you know, that had been in that space. So, um, anyway, it's hard.

(Lurching sound of elevator stopping, pounding on door and muffled voices heard)

TESSA: *(Shouting)* Someone's stuck in the elevator again.

Scene 2
Goddesses Descending

(JOAN OF ARC, preferably wearing some piece of battle armor, & FRIEDA KHALO, a flower in her hair, are stuck in the elevator on the way from heaven to the Women's Building. AUDRE LORDE is their guide)

ARC: *(to Lorde)* Can't you get this thing moving?

LORDE: Do I look like an elevator operator to you?

ARC: I'm sure, Madam, I don't know what that is. *(pressing buttons)* I just thought you might have seen one of these before. Damn. I led my people on the battlefield. I just don't know anything about mechanics.

LORDE: Well, I've seen one before, but I'm a poet, so that's not much help.

KHALO: Let me see. My husband, Diego, was no good at this kind of thing, so I had to be, but don't tell anyone.

ARC: What did you do? Something useful I hope.

KHALO: I guess that depends on what you think of art. I painted pictures, mostly of myself.

ARC: Well, I think you're gonna fit right into this new Women's Movement. I hear they are very self-obsessed.

LORDE: May be that's good for once, for women to be concerned about themselves. It will balance the world out more, you know?

ARC: *(To Khalo)* Why were you called?

KHALO: I wasn't exactly. They are not naming anything after me because they do not see me as a feminist on their terms. I come because of the mural. Someday they will create a great mural that will cover the entire building and I will help give birth to that. Mind if I smoke?

LORDE AND ARC: Yes!

LORDE: You can't smoke in here!

ARC: What is that? Are you trying to burn us all alive.

KHALO: Sorry, sorry, I forgot. What was I thinking? Forgive me. See I put it away.

ARC: This is why they will never name anything after you.

KHALO: You either because you are white, a martyr and who understands the French feminists anyway? *(to Lorde)* Poet, what is your name.

LORDE. Lorde, Audrey Lorde.

ARC: I like it. I am Arc, Joan of Arc.

KHALO: I think they will pick you.

LORDE: I must admit I like the idea of them naming a room after me, even if I'm not dead yet.

KHALO: You aren't? Then why are you talking to us?

ARC: Why not? *(to KHALO)* Don't you hear voices and have visions?

KHALO: Yes, of course, when I was alive, but now I don't see the point.

ARC: We're in their dream, not the other way around.

KHALO: Oh, I see. *(KHALO: is pleased with the idea and goes off into her own world imagining how she could help them with her painting)*

LORDE: That's right. We need you to help us dream up this place.

ARC: But just what is a women's building? I never heard of such a thing.

LORDE: Neither had they. But they wanted a permanent home where no one could kick them out or tell them what to do.

ARC: I never had a regular home but nobody tells me what to do but the Lord Jesus.

LORDE: I hear that.

ARC: Of course you do, you're standing right next to me.

LORDE: Right. It's sort of an expression. *(ARC looks at her strangely)* It's not important.

ARC: I didn't think so.

KHALO: I have it. The building has been born out of great pain and they must paint their pain on the walls, just like I had to paint my pain in self-portraits. So they must paint a giant woman giving birth.

ARC: *(Ignores KHALO)* What does it mean naming a room after you – a space. I think I'd like a monument like all the men have.

LORDE: What good is a monument? No use to anybody but the pigeons. I think a room sounds just fine. A place for people-women to gather in my name.

ARC: Well, what is this place San Francisco like? It didn't exist when I was alive.

LORDE: It's beautiful. Some people think it's heaven on earth, but it's not quite that good.

KHALO: My husband, Diego, painted a fabulous mural here in San Francisco, as a tribute to the workers. And I will help them paint one for the women.

LORDE: Lot's of interesting characters here. You'll both like it. And you'll like the building too, even though it does need some work. I did a reading there once. They mean well but I was competing with salsa music *(stops herself looking at ARC)*, a Mexican band playing downstairs, not that I don't like that kind of music-...

KHALO: Music, of course, there must be music. *(Starts to dance)*

LORDE: But I was furious at the time. Told'm too.

ARC: Is that why they picked you? To make up for this?

LORDE: Maybe and they like my poetry too.

KHALO: We'll probably be here for a while. Can we hear some?

LORDE: "In the curve scooped out and necklaced with light
Burst pearls stream down my outstretched arms to earth"[19]

KHALO: Beautiful. Thank you so much.

ARC: Yes, that's fine. Is this thing moving? Are we stuck again?

LORDE: I wouldn't be surprised. Sometimes it's just real slow. Know what I'm sayin'?

ARC: Why wouldn't I?

LORDE: Never mind.

KHALO: I can't wait to see my canvas, the walls of this building.

ARC: I am convinced. I will serve these women, but then what if they don't pick me?

LORDE: You're still part of the dream.
ARC: Ah, oui.

LORDE: Oops, we're going back up again. We forgot to pick up Harriet Tubman.

KHALO: This is so exciting.

---

19 Excerpt from Bridge through My Window, *The Collected Poems of Audre Lorde*, New York: Norton, 1997, 9.

ARC: Oops? Another expression of yours? I will never understand you Americans.

Scene 3
Erotic Art Show

(ANNA, LOUISE, and RAE enter the top floor gallery, TESSA, PAULA and AUDIENCE MEMBER area already there)

LOUISE: Do you believe we just came in through a vagina?

RAE: That's what that was?

(RAE, LOUISE and ANNA all start looking at the paintings along one imaginary wall which is facing the audience)

RAE: Can anyone tell me what is this fixation? Every woman seems to want to get a speculum and examine her cervix, photograph her private parts and then blow'm up to wall size.

LOUISE: That could be a conch shell.

ANNA: Or the inside of a flower.

RAE: Who am I with here?

TESSA: Buenos Noches, mis amigas.

LOUISE and ANNA: Hi Tessa.

RAE: Hey Tessa, what do you see in this picture?

TESSA: I *(hesitates)* I'm not sure, but listen you're just in time for the poetry reading. Paula's going to read. We're trying to get everybody together.

PAULA: You are my steam engine, baby
Roll on through
my tunnel of love
(Audience member starts hissing)
Release me from my sleep
and move mountains with your
passionate determination
I want to feel you in me.....

AUDIENCE MEMBER: *(Stands up)* Do we have to listen to this? I don't want to hear a poem about male/female intercourse which is rape as far as I'm concerned. You can read that pornography somewhere else.

PAULA: So you think it's your right to censor me. You want to treat me the way the world's treated you?

AUDIENCE MEMBER I want you to sit down and let a lesbian read her poetry. That's what I'm here for.

LOUISE: Do you think we should do something?

PAULA: I thought this was a place for all women.

TESSA: It is. Go ahead Paula. I'm a lesbian and I still what to hear you.

RAE: That's right. Let her go ahead and speak.

AUDIENCE MEMBER: I thought this was about women identifying with other women, not men. What kind of place is this?

ANNA: *(coming forward)* The Women's Building is run by a collective, the San Francisco Women's Centers. And some of us are here right now and we did not know the content of this show ahead of time. So what we will do is take a few minutes to caucus among our-selves and then we'll let you know what we decided on this question. O.K.?

PAULA: You have to have a meeting?

AUDIENCE MEMBER: O.K., I can see that. We'll wait. That's cool.

(LOUISE, ANNA, RAE and TESSA move away and stand in a circle to caucus)

ANNA: What are we going to do here? We could have a riot on our hands.

TESSA: Isn't this what we talked about in all those meetings? This building is supposed to be for all women no matter who they are— black or white or latina, gay or straight.

LOUISE: I agree, but everywhere else you go it's only straight sex that is legitimated. This is the one place where lesbians can come and feel proud of their sexuality.

RAE: Does one woman reading an erotic poem about heterosexual love making take away from that?

LOUISE: Probably to them it does.

TESSA: Paula is part of the building, she's with Lilith Theatre, one of our tenants. We need to support her.

ANNA: That's an important point. We don't want to send the message that there's only one party line at the Women's Building.

LOUISE: Yeah, like there isn't. Just joking.

TESSA: This is an open mike, all women were welcome to sign up.

RAE: That's right. There weren't any restrictions placed on it, so why should we do that now?

LOUISE: O.K., O.K., I agree. I am totally against censorship anyway.

ANNA: O.K., then we have a consensus. Let's go back in and tell them.

LOUISE: All our decisions should be this easy.

RAE: Yes, they should be.

(ANNA, RAE, LOUISE and TESSA return to art show)

ANNA: *(Stands in front of group to make announcement)* Alright, thank you for your patience. The Women's Centers Collective, who own this building, caucused and decided that since this had been declared an open mike reading with no restrictions as to topics or participants, we would not now want to keep anyone who had signed up from readings their work.

AUDIENCE MEMBER: Sell outs. It didn't take you very long to sell out now that you own property *(exits angrily)*.

PAULA: Well, you know what? I very much appreciate the collective's decision, except that I don't think it's really something you should have to meet about. You should already know the answer and anyway, I don't care to read my poetry which comes from deep inside my soul to a hostile audience. *(dramatic exit)*

ANNA: *(Coming back over to RAE, TESSA, and LOUISE)* Well, that worked out well.

RAE: At least you averted a riot.

TESSA: Right, now we can just enjoy the art.

LOUISE: Good idea. Oh my god, look at this one over here.

(ALL rush over. End of scene)

Scene 4
Getting There

(This is a split scene. SUSAN is in a phone booth talking to Muni information. DEBRA is outside the Women's Building.)

SUSAN: Could you please tell me how to get the bus to The Women's Building of the Bay area?

MUNI OPERATOR: Where would that be, Ma'am?

SUSAN: You haven't heard of it? Well, it's going to be very famous. We own it. *(pause)* Uhm, it's on 18th street., you know.

MUNI OPERATOR: No I don't, Ma'am. What are the cross streets?

SUSAN: Uh, I know, I just can't think of it right now. Damn. *(Hangs up the phone, then picks it up again)* Oh, sorry, thank you.

(Shift to outside the Women's Building with GEORGE and DEBRA)

DEBRA: I just thought that people would magically donate really nice furniture, and nice art, and you know, that millions of women artists would give their work, and make the building beautiful, and in fact people did. But the quality of the stuff has always been a little uneven. It was truly like a patchwork quilt. And initially I was this sort of uptight person about how the building should really look.

GEORGE: Goddamn, fuck'n shit.

DEBRA: Yeah. Hey, George.

GEORGE: Wh-What's up, Debra?.

DEBRA: Oh, you know who I am?

GEORGE: I'm here fuckin' everyday. I know what goes on, *(under his breath)* shit, piss, fuckin' A.

DEBRA: Great. Listen I wonder if I could buy you a cup of coffee. I need to ask you something.

(Shift to SUSAN who is trying to hail a cab)

DRIVER: Where you wanna go, lady?

SUSAN: The Women's Building of San Francisco.

DRIVER: Huh?

SUSAN: It's in The Mission and I have $20.

DRIVER: O.K. hop in, we'll find it.

SUSAN: Really? Good. *(Gets in the cab)*

(Shift to DEBRA & GEORGE outside Building)

DEBRA: George, you know, I've got people coming to the building today—funders. You know, maybe you've seen me with these people in suits, and stuff, dressed up, you know,

GEORGE: Yeah, god damm, mother fuck.. Can't miss'm.

DEBRA: Yeah, anyway, I'm showing them the building today, so they'll give us money so we can fix this place up, you know.

GEORGE: Yeah, god damm, fuck'n shit. It needs it, shit.

DEBRA: Yeah, and I need you not to say Goddamn fuck, I need you not to do that in those moments, you know, right in the front of the building. I know that this is something that you think you can't control or people say that you can't control. But I need you to try to control it.

GEORGE: Can I play the trumpet instead, shit, fuck?

DEBRA: Sure, that would be great. *(pause)* Look, I know it's not right, how things are for you. But that's part of what we're trying to change, you see?

(Shift to SUSAN & DRIVER in the cab)

DRIVER: So what is this place? The Women's Place?

SUSAN: Building

DRIVER: You have a whole building? That's very nice.

SUSAN: Why should men get all the buildings. We should get at least one. *(To self)* I've got to stop saying that. My therapist thinks I have an obsessive need to form women's organizations. I'll show her.

DRIVER: Hey, don't get mad. I'm just trying to figure out where it might be.

SUSAN: It used to be Dovre Hall. There's an Irish bar on the corner.

DRIVER: Oh, the Dovre Club. I know where that is. It's just for ladies now?

SUSAN: Not the bar, just the rest of the place. *(to self)* I'm so tired of explaining everything.

DRIVER: What's that?

SUSAN: Ah, nothing, never mind.

(Shift to DEBRA'S scene. FUNDERS arrive at the Building with exaggerated props like large briefcases or large bows around their necks or masks. GEORGE: moves to the side of the Building and gets out his trumpet)

DEBRA: Oh, good you're here. How is everyone?

(GEORGE plays a fanfare on his trumpet)

FUNDERS: *(Each says a line overlapping each other)*
Is this it?
Interesting neighborhood
Never been here before.
Certainly not gentrified.
Where did you park?
Is this it?

DEBRA: Yes, beautiful day isn't it.

FUNDERS: It's hot alright.
Phew!
Watch where you step.

DEBRA: The weather here in the Mission is so good.

(DEBRA looks over her shoulder at GEORGE who is mumbling but inaudibly, except for an occasional swear word or two) Let's just go right in, shall we? *(Ushers them into the building)*

GEORGE: *(nods)* Goddamm, fuck'n shit. Have a nice day. *(plays a fanfare)*

(SUSAN'S cab pulls up and she starts to get out but sees DEBRA and gets back in)

SUSAN: Could you just keep driving around the block until my $20 is up? I gotta think what to do.

DRIVER: Sure, lady. It's your dime. But how 'bout I park the cab and we go in and have a nice drink at the Dovre club. Might calm your nerves.

SUSAN: Oh, shut up and keep driving. I can't go in there. Anybody from the Building might be there.

Scene 5
Paula Plays Pool

The Irish bar in the corner of the Women's Building in the late afternoon, BINKLE is seated at the bar typing his weekly column for a local newspaper. Sitting next to him is his one eyed cat. BEN, a man PAULA has been dating, is playing pool. The BARTENDER is behind the bar serving drinks and talking with BINKLE.

BINKLE: You waitin' on her today?

BEN: Not necessarily.

BINKLE: *(To Bartender)* He is. I can tell.

BEN: I'm playing pool. Can't you see that?

BINKLE: I can see – how you're lookin' at that door and then the clock.

BEN: You can see all that from where you're sittin' and write your column at the same time?

BINKLE: I don't have to look.

(PAULA enters. Light floods into the dark bar from outside. BEN plays a shot. PAULA looks happy to see BEN, but walks over to the bar and orders a drink. BEN continues playing pool.)

PAULA: Corona with lime.

BEN: Make that two. *(Takes a last shot)* Wanna play a game?

PAULA: I don't mind.

BEN: Rack'm up.

(PAULA comes over to the pool table, gives BEN his beer and sets up the game as BINKLE is talking)

BINKLE: Almost everyday he comes in and waits for her. Sometimes she shows up, sometimes she doesn't.

BARTENDER: He always has what she's having.

BINKLE: I know. He upgrades from Bud.

(PAULA and BEN talk while playing pool)

BEN: Did you solve all the world's problems today?

PAULA: Worked on some of them. What did you do?

BEN: Tried not to create any problems.

PAULA: Well, you didn't succeed.

BEN: How's that?

PAULA: I'm here aren't I with you. That's a problem.

BEN: Not for me.

PAULA: I know. What do you care?

BEN: I care. Any minute those women next door could come storming over and take you back and do Lord knows what with me.

PAULA: Is that what you think lesbians are like?

BEN: When they get mad—at men.

PAULA: They've got better things to do.

BEN: And why don't you?

PAULA: I'm tired of being better.

BEN: Oh and then you're gonna come on down to me?

PAULA: Not like that. I don't know who's gonna make me crazier you or that place. *(PAULA makes a good shot)*

BEN: Damn, you lesbians can play pool.

(Shift focus to bar. BINKLE has bought the BARTENDER a drink)

BINKLE: So she's from next door.

BARTENDER: They do come in from time to time.

BINKLE: Is she?

BARTENDER: Well, I guess they all are.

BINKLE: That's what I figured.

(Shift back to pool table)

BEN: You wanna go out tomorrow night?

PAULA: What?

BEN: You know, go to the movies or something. If you can get free?

PAULA: I am a free woman.

(The door opens and TESSA enters)

TESSA: There you are. Now I know what you've been up to lately. Improving your pool game.

PAULA: You caught me.

(*BEN is waiting for PAULA to shoot. BEN takes a drink. TESSA looks at PAULA and then BEN*)

TESSA: (*Coming over to PAULA and sort of whispering*) Are you alright? You left in kind of a hurry.

PAULA: (*PAULA makes a shot*) I'm fine. I'm winning.

(*TESSA goes over to the bar and gets a drink*)

BEN: Watch out!

PAULA: What are you talking about?

BEN: You might get in trouble for playing pool with me. You know guilty of consorting with the enemy.

(*BEN goes over to the bar. PAULA looks over at TESSA and BEN. ALL freeze. The scene becomes PAULA's nightmare. PAULA is on trial*)

ANNA: Please sit down. We are only here to ask questions, not to pass judgment.

TESSA: You were seen in the company of a man. Is that correct?

PAULA: Yes.

TESSA: What is your relationship to this man?

PAULA: You know I really hate that word. Love no longer exists, only relationships which we work on, discuss, hover over, smash up, but please no passion. Everyone communicates and relates, but no longer romances, goddess forbid.

SUSAN: How would you describe it? Please, don't let us speak for you or misrepresent your feelings.

PAULA: Oh, stop identifying with me as a victim. I refuse to be. And you're in control, so why don't you just admit it, instead of acting like you're in a perpetual state of surrender.

ANNA: There's no need to be defensive. We're just trying to get things clear.

PAULA: We're friends. I like him.

TESSA: But why, when there are so many women to be friends with and love?

SUSAN: Well, of course, you know, there's conditioning, all the years of training, women are taught to focus on men. It takes time to love a woman with no rules and no game plan.

PAULA: That's just it. The women I know now burn with an intensity like mine. They are not comfortable, they want too much. They think all the time about everything—oppression, poverty, rape victims, abortion, the ERA and they write about it all incessantly.

SUSAN: But those are things you should love women for.

PAULA: I know, I do, I....

ANNA: Is this all you have to say in your defense?

TESSA: She's being honest. I think we have to give her credit for that.

ANNA: Have you had sex with this man?

PAULA: I don't think that's any of your business.

SUSAN: The personal is the political, you know.

TESSA: Maybe she's bisexual.

ANNA, SUSAN, TESSA: Oh, no!

SUSAN: That's worse. You can't be trusted. You'll always go back to men when it's convenient.

ANNA: And break some poor woman's heart.

PAULA: Like you don't break each other's hearts.

ANNA: That's different.

PAULA: Oh is it? Isn't the pain just as strong. It can be worse because you're working together, doing everything together.

SUSAN: *(To ANNA & TESSA)* That's true.

TESSA: *(To ANNA)* It's a mess sometimes.

ANNA: Excuse me, that is not what we're here to discuss. We're here to pass judgment on Paula.

PAULA: You have no right!

(TESSA comes up to pool table and addresses PAULA waking her out of her nightmare fantasy)

TESSA: Paula, Paula

PAULA: You can't tell me what to do!

TESSA: I wouldn't even try. I just thought we'd play pool. Are you O.K.?

PAULA: Oh, sorry, I was thinking about something else.

TESSA: Well, I play the winner and that looks like you. Set'm up. Want another beer? Ben's buyin'. He's O.K.

PAULA: Oh, that's great, you've been talking. I'll have another beer. *(To self)* At least one. I'm gonna need it.

(Shift focus to bar)

BINKLE: Give me another. This is gettin' complicated. I'm glad I don't have to write about this.

BARTENDER: That's good 'cause I don't think they liked what you wrote about'm last time.

BINKLE: So, nobody likes what I write about'm.

BARTENDER: You wanna take bets on who goes home with who?

BINKLE: I believe that's whom. And I'll take the girl for five bucks.

BARTENDER: You got it and I believe "woman" is the correct term, since they're over 18.

BINKLE: Well, excuse me. See how this is affecting you. Next thing you know you'll be using "Ms."

(TESSA & PAULA play pool during this conversation)

TESSA: You break. Sorry about how things turned out at the art show.

PAULA: Forget it. I'm just tired of this whole lesbian feminist separatist bullshit. We should be claiming sexual freedom for all women, not just lesbians because then they're restricting themselves too, you know? Side pocket.

TESSA: I agree completely. *(PAULA makes the shot)* Damn.

PAULA: Oh what am I spouting off about this to you for, sorry.

TESSA: It's O.K.

PAULA: It's just I wanna feel like I belong but I don't.

TESSA: You do. Nice shot.

PAULA: I don't know, some days I feel like I do, but other times I feel like the enemy. You know, white straight middle class, goddess help me.

TESSA: You really wanna know what people say about you?

PAULA: I don't know.

TESSA: That you're a knock out. Everybody wants to know, "hey what's her story?"

PAULA: Yeah, right. Well now they know.

TESSA: God damn, you're a mean pool player. They like you. I like you.

PAULA: I like you too. I appreciate that you call me and tell me what's up. Leave me little notes.

TESSA: I tell you what. Let's get out of here. I've got my car outside. Let's just go up to the top of Twin Peaks or something and look at the fog.

PAULA: Well, I don't know I...

TESSA: Unless you're busy *(looking at BEN)*

PAULA: No, It's not that.

TESSA: Is he your boyfriend?

PAULA: Is this an interrogation?

TESSA: No, no, sorry. I guess you're still mad.

PAULA: Sorry, it's kinda still fresh in my mind.

TESSA: Well, it's a beautiful night, might even be clear.

PAULA: I could use some clarity tonight. O.K., let's go. Hey Ben, I gotta get out of here get some air. It's been a weird couple of days.

(TESSA and PAULA give BEN their sticks)

TESSA: See ya, Ben

BEN: So who's gonna play pool with me?

PAULA: We'll be back.

BEN: Yeah, sure. I'll be right here holding my breath.

BINKLE: See that's how they recruit them.

BARTENDER: What?

BINKLE: Lesbians. I think they just got a new member.

Scene 6
The Two Collectives

(Scene begins. TESSA and RAE are working together getting a mailing out for the Crafts Fair in the Women's Building office)

TESSA: You think we should be going ahead with the crafts fair given what's been happening lately?

RAE: You mean the bomb threats and the actual bombing or the IRS audit, the stolen money or the in-fighting between the two Collectives?

TESSA: Yeah take your pick. I just wonder if it's safe to have all these people show up here including children under these circumstances. We don't even know who's behind this stuff.

RAE: We have a pretty good idea that it might be our IRA neighbors. But we can't let them intimidate us into leaving. That's the same old tactic that's always been used on us-all of us in one way or another.

TESSA: Yeah, I guess a lot of people are waiting for us to fail.

RAE: You got that right.

TESSA: Meanwhile, Anna's started her little recruitment thing with me about working at Women's Centers and I'm like nah, no, maybe, yes, no.

RAE: *(laughs)* Anna draws people in. She creates a place for everybody, even if it might not be exactly the place you had in mind.

TESSA: But I want to work at the Women's <u>Building</u> Collective with you and everybody else because the Women's <u>Centers</u> Collective are....

RAE: mostly white?

TESSA: Yeah and they're hiring the Women's Building Collective

RAE: who are mostly women of color.

TESSA: Yeah, so I guess the Women's Centers doesn't want to run the Building, huh?

RAE: That's right, so you have the white women who are the landlords upstairs and the Women's Building Collective downstairs cleaning the toilets and watering down the soap because we don't have enough money.

TESSA: *(sarcastic)* Yeah, that's different. So anyway, Anna has decided I should work for the Women's <u>Centers</u>, maybe to break up this split, I don't know. She keeps bugging me.

RAE: What are you gonna do?

TESSA: I just don't know if this is the right place for me. What would my compadres say?

RAE: Same thing black people say to me. "Why you in the white woman's movement, instead of with your people in the struggle?"

TESSA: Yeah, I hear that. You know this is <u>not </u>the first building that I've been involved with. United Latin American Citizens, where I used to work, they also owned the building that they had their offices in. And I wasn't very political about being gay, until this very defining moment. There was this group that had applied for space called GALA, the Gay Latino Alliance. And they were discussing this request for space and it was really horrible. I mean to listen to the homophobia in the discussion and the jokes. Finally, I couldn't stand it anymore and I got up and made some impassioned little speech. And you know people heard it, people apologized. And that was really the beginning of my being out and an advocate. And I will never go back in the closet or be silenced again.

RAE: Amen, sister. I was active in the Panthers for a while, you know, but there you gotta deal with sexism and homophobia. Here it's racism, so you have to choose. You know what I'm saying?

TESSA: I know. It's hard to find a place where you really belong, I mean, all of you, especially if you're a Puerto Rican lesbian with an education.

RAE: Or a black single mother who's a lesbian, I think.

TESSA: You are, don't worry.

RAE: You know, you and Paula may be doing more to bridge the gap between the two collectives than all the meetings we've been having. I mean the personal is the political and all that.

TESSA: What about you and Anna?

RAE: Well, I'd like to do my part to bring the two collectives together, but I haven't had much chance. But that's O.K. Right now, I'd rather focus on my daughter, Lisa, who's the most important person in my life.

TESSA: She's amazing. So much self-confidence already.

RAE: I know. Her generation is going to be different.

TESSA: They'll have the choices we fought for.

RAE: Any job they want, health care, control over their own bodies, affirmative action, the ERA.

TESSA: If the conservatives don't undo everything we've worked for.

RAE: It's harder to take back rights, once people have them. I hope I live to see the first woman President.

TESSA: May she be black..

RAE: That would really turn things around.

TESSA: Turn them upside down.

RAE: Or right side up for a change.

TESSA: That's right. Viva La Revolution. May they carry on what we've started.

RAE: *(laughing)* Are we getting high on the glue on these envelopes or what? I think we need a break.

TESSA: We're definitely overdue.

RAE: For a lot of things.

TESSA: Hey, have you seen Susan?

RAE: No, is she out now?

TESSA: I guess so. I saw her come in today but she didn't say anything. Just got right in the elevator and I haven't seen her since.

(TESSA & RAE exit)

Scene 7
Police Women

(ANNA, ELENA, RAE, LOUISE, PAULA, TESSA. Meeting in Audrey Lorde room which is a smaller space than other big meeting rooms)

ANNA: As you probably already know and that's why you're here, a woman's caucus of the police department wants to meet in the Building.

ELENA: lesbians?

RAE: Of course, who else?
(laughter)

ANNA: There is a lot of controversy and emotions around this issue and that's why we're having this open meeting, so please let's really listen to each other. This is all a part of defining who we are and I know we won't be able to satisfy everyone's vision. O.K.? So since we're in a circle and we're a smaller group tonight, I'm just going to ask people to take turns informally, so you won't have to raise your hand, but please be aware of each other's need to speak.

ELENA: My name is Elena and I'm from El Salvador and a new member of the Women's Building Collective. In my country, the police and the military are not your friend as you must know by what is happening there now. I appreciate that things may be somewhat different here than my country, although I'm not sure how different they really are-maybe by degrees. But I would not feel comfortable with the police meeting here, even if they are all women or all lesbians, it doesn't matter to me. When I see that uniform I know I am not safe and I want this building to be a safe place for me and other women as well.

LOUISE: I understand why you would be concerned, but you may not be familiar with the history here. We've been working for a long time to make the police force more representative of all communities including gays, lesbians, Hispanics, Black people, Asian, so that they would serve these communities better and not be like the repressive forces you are talking about. I mean, how else can we do it? How will anything ever change?

RAE: Look, I was involved with the Panthers and I've been hit over the head by the cops, so I may not be from Central America, but I would not get a good feeling if I passed a police man or woman in the hallway. They could be spying on us. We're a progressive organization.

PAULA: Yeah, but you're sure happy to see the police or fire department when you need'm.

RAE: That's right, but that doesn't mean we want to live with them=

LOUISE: =It's just that=

RAE: =I grew up in a military family. I know what their mentality is and I don't want them to have an office down the hall from me.

LOUISE: We've got the Mayor, the Police Chief, the Police Commissioner everyone behind this and it seems sort of, well, really ironic to me that the Women's Building isn't behind this when this is about equality for women and people of color.

TESSA: I don't think anybody here thinks that the police is a sort of progressive or even neutral organization no matter who wears the uniform. I know that the representative of the women's police group is a Latina and I respect her for the choices she has made and I hope she does make a difference, but so far that hasn't changed how people in my community, the Mission, where the building is located, are treated.

RAE AND ELENA: That's right.

TESSA: We are still stopped and harassed without provocation. In my experience, the police are always there when we don't want them, but when we call, they never come.

RAE: It's the same for African Americans, especially male. If you're in a progressive organization, the police may actively be out to get you. Look what happened to the Panthers.

PAULA: I feel like most of the staff or collective members have already made up your mind, but I just want to tell you that these are our people too. I take this as a personal betrayal. We fought hard to get the police department to accept women. Forget it. I'm never coming back to this place. What the hell are you people doing, anyway?

TESSA: Paula wait...

ELENA: Before you leave I hope there is something you will consider. I understand that this is very personal to you, but it is also to me. I am like the women from Argentina who everyday come to the square demanding what has happened to their loved ones who have been disappeared. That is what has happened to my brother. The last time we knew of him, he was being questioned by the police. Now they deny he was ever even in jail. I look at those uniforms and the guns that they wear and this is what I see. You must understand I can not change my feelings on this.

LOUISE: I'm very sorry for you and your brother, but I'm from a working class Irish family and my brother is a good cop and my father is too and I love and respect them very much and I just wish that I had had the opportunities that we are trying to give women and minorities now because my life would have been very different. I might not have ended up a bookkeeper which is a job I hate because that's what women do. *(in tears)*

ANNA: *(Reaches out for LOUISE)* I think we have all spoken from our hearts as we can see when we look at the faces around us. I know this is a very hard decision and some community members view this very differently than those of us working in the building, although not all, as you can see. But we are the ones who will see the police women when they come in for their meetings and use the organization's office. We might see them everyday and that does feel like too much. We are after all in the Mission and we want to support that community and be supported by it. That has not come easily. People have a tendency to take sides and we would be on the wrong side. And that would mean a permanent alienation that I don't believe The Building as a whole could tolerate and continue to grow and prosper.

PAULA: Well then I guess you'll be growing and prospering without some of us. *(starts to exit upset)*

LOUISE: We've all experienced being excluded so many time for being women, lesbians, whatever. It's a shame now that you feel we have to do that to each other.

TESSA: We're not excluding anyone as women, or as lesbians or anything like that, we're just excluding an organization from living with us. Don't you see?

LOUISE: No, I don't.

PAULA: I don't either. *(exits)*

RAE: Everyone is welcome anytime as who they are as individuals, but not as a member of the police force. We do not want to have that as part of the Women's Building. That's all.

LOUISE: I'm sorry you feel that way because how can I feel comfortable coming to the building, if a part of me or my life and family is not welcome.

RAE: Then that's you decision.

LOUISE: No I think that decision was made for me and I don't appreciate it. *(angry exit)*

ANNA: O.K. I think it's time to stop here. People are leaving angry and I think maybe we can talk to each other better one to one or in smaller groups at this point, and maybe at least begin to heal some of these wounds or share how we're feeling. Alright? The question of who should be here in the Women's Building is one I know we will continue to struggle with.
(ANNA exits going after LOUISE and TESSA goes after PAULA, who we now see in front of the Building with GEORGE)

PAULA: I always felt they weren't talking about me or that this wasn't a building for me. I guess what it was, was that I was equating the fact that I didn't feel like this building was for me, and the fact that I felt like it was being neglected, with the fact that if it were for me, and all that I was feeling about the physical space and how much there was and the beauty of the woodwork and the stairs, and the lighting and this, that and the other, and I was thinking, oh I would really um take care of and love this building.

GEORGE: I I love this Building too, god-god damn it.

(PAULA exits)

TESSA: Paula, wait.

(TESSA follows PAULA as RAE appears)

RAE: I tell you what happened. Nobody protected me. That's always the way. Have a confrontation with a white woman, everybody rushes to support her. Anna couldn't end that meeting fast enough and rush out to talk to Louise. Nobody came rushing up to me to see if I was alright. I guess everybody just assumes Black women can hold their own, don't need any support, 'cause we speak our minds, but if that was so easy, you think more white women could handle it.

Scene 8
On Top of the World

SUSAN *(SUSAN is on top of The Building standing on the edge of the roof)*
I can do this.
I weigh nothing now
a hundred pounds of transparent skin over bones
light as a wing
I can just spread my arms out
and fall away
down to the street
just falling effortlessly
I won't feel anything
(looks down)
I'll just fall away.

Damn, I can't do this

(SUSAN steps back and takes her glasses off and resumes position with arms outstretched)
I don't have to see anything
just fly.

(GEORGE comes up on the roof wearing SUSAN'S WWI pilot's helmet)

GEORGE: Careful little bird, you're not ready to fly.

SUSAN: *(looks at GEORGE)* Don't startle me. I'm trying to jump, but I'd like to do it myself, thank you.

GEORGE: Damn it, not without a helmet, fuckin' shit.

SUSAN: But that's my helmet.

GEORGE: Well, why don't you come and get it, then?

SUSAN: *(Stepping down from ledge to chase him and get her helmet then realizing what she's done)* Oh shit. I'm a failure at suicide too.

GEORGE: That's not necessarily a a bad thing. It means you don't really want to do it.

SUSAN: What do you know about it?

GEORGE: Not much really. I've only tried a time or two myself, *(mumbles)* shit.

SUSAN: Wait a minute, you're the homeless guy who hangs out in front of the Building swearing and playing the trumpet all the time and swearing.

GEORGE: That's me. Can I play something for you? *(Whips his trumpet out of his coat)*

SUSAN: Not right now.

GEORGE: O.K., maybe later.

SUSAN: How come you're not swearing and stuttering so much?

GEORGE: I I have my moments. And I'm on drugs.

SUSAN: How'd you get up here?

GEORGE: Same way you did.

SUSAN: I mean why?

GEORGE: Oh, I saw you driving around the block for awhile and then I saw you up here and uh I figured *(pause)* ah you might need some company.

SUSAN: So even the loony people know I'm loony.

GEORGE: We try to look out for each other.

SUSAN: We do?

GEORGE: Yeah, I'm I'm George.

SUSAN: I'm //Susan.

GEORGE: Susan//, yeah I know. *(pause)* So what brings you here, Susan, to this beautiful roof top.

SUSAN: I don't know, depressed, burned out, broken heart, romantic notions about the women's movement that's what I've been accused of, being in love with the wrong woman, being an artist, having secretarial skills.

GEORGE: Shit, you lost me on that last point.

SUSAN: Never mind. I thought the Women's Movement was the answer to all my problems. I divorced my husband so I wouldn't have to be a housewife, helpmate, secretary but here I am doing the same things for women for a lot less money and no social approval.

GEORGE: Yeah, but would you go back?

SUSAN: No, I was crazier then if you can imagine that. I believe in what we're doing. Maybe I just don't believe in myself anymore.

GEORGE: Well, everybody else believes in you. The way I hear it, there'd be no Women's Building without the money you raise. Besides, if every woman who felt the way you do, jumped off something – without wearing a helmet – the Women's Movement would be in real trouble.

SUSAN: Yeah, I guess so. But they don't need me now.

GEORGE: Shit, are you crazy? Look at this place. There's a lot to be done.

SUSAN: I was gonna jump off the Golden Gate Bridge but this seemed more poetic *(goes back to the edge)* but this doesn't seem that high and the cement...

GEORGE: *(follows her)* You see it's not about jumping. It's about flying. You know how to fly. That's what you've been doing all along.

You just forgot there for a little while when you fell down because you weren't wearing your helmet. But you're gonna be O.K. now. *(GEORGE takes off her helmet and puts it on SUSAN'S head)*

SUSAN: What makes you so sure?

GEORGE: Because you didn't jump when you had the chance. And that does not make you a failure. You know that, right?

(SUSAN nods; faintly hear sirens in the background)

You ready to go back now? Or would you prefer a police escort?

SUSAN: No, let's go. The entire women's community is probably mobilizing to look for me too.

GEORGE: *(laughs)* Probably, damn. Who'd guess you'd be up here with me.

SUSAN: I mean talk about humiliation, *(laughs)* some people commit suicide quietly.

GEORGE: Hey, it could be worse. Might might be the FBI or the CIA looking for you.

(GEORGE and SUSAN start moving to the exit)

SUSAN: Do you believe in conspiracy theories?

GEORGE: Absolutely.

SUSAN: This could be the start of a//beautiful friendship.

GEORGE: // beautiful friendship. Yeah, I saw that movie too.

(The sound of ambulances and police cars stopping very close)

SUSAN: *(goes back to the edge)* Hey, I'm the jumper. I'll be right down. Oops. I mean I'm coming down the regular way. *(Laughing)*

GEORGE: That's the spirit.

SUSAN: I'm sorry. I know it's not funny.

GEORGE: It's pretty fuckin' funny.

SUSAN: Is your medication wearing off?

(GEORGE and SUSAN start walking again toward the exit)

GEORGE: No, just felt like saying that. You wanna take the elevator?

SUSAN: Are you kidding? Not even with a helmet. I got stuck in there for half an hour which is why…

GEORGE: You're still here. Now isn't that poetic?

Scene 9
The Fire

(Sounds of sirens, fire trucks pulling up, sounds of a fire, breaking glass, voices of firefighters. Lights up on LOUISE, TESSA, PAULA, ANNA, DEBRA, and RAE standing behind a yellow tape police line)

GEORGE: I I came back to the Building that night and it was on fire. I called the Fire Department. Damn it. It pissed me off. At at first they wouldn't believe me, but then the whole neighborhood was callin' –goddam,mother fuckin' shit, smoke everywhere. I thought the whole place might go up, and before I knew it, th-there they were. Not only the fire fighters, but the whole damn collective was at the barricades. Shit.

ANNA: *(As if to a FIRE FIGHTER)* Excuse me, we need to get through here.

RAE and LOUISE: We own this building

DEBRA: Yes, we're the San Francisco Women's Centers Collective and we own this building.

TESSA: As property owners, we have the right to be here. *(to others)* I can't believe I said that.

GEORGE: Goddam mother fuck-they were great.

PAULA: Is this it? Have we lost everything?

TESSA: Paula, I thought you weren't coming back

PAULA: So did I but when I heard the sirens, I had to come down and see what was happening – all we worked for. It's not so easy to leave.

TESSA: I'm glad. Welcome back *(hugs PAULA)* to whatever is left of us.

(Move into building and start looking around, water and debris everywhere. ANNA sees that a FIRE FIGHTER is about to take down a wall and rushes over)

ANNA: Could you be careful taking down that wall. This is our building.

DEBRA: Welcome to ownership

PAULA: Any idea who did it?

GEORGE: They, they thought it might be the guys in the bar, but it wasn't cause An An Anna had made a deal with them. That old fart, the owner, could keep it as long as he lived. That was damn, damn neighborly if you ask me.

RAE: It could be arson. Looks like it started in the drop-in area with this pile of magazines.

DEBRA: I heard a neighbor say that a homeless person was seen leaving the building after it was closed.

GEORGE: NO, no it was not me – god damn mother fuck –sh-shit shelter tonight. I I usually watch the Building at night, you know. Shit, but I was at the shelter

TESSA: No one is accusing you, George.

GEORGE: I I watch this place, you know. We look out for each other, goddamn it.

ANNA: Yes, we do. That's what we do. Thank you, George

(ALL looking around at the debris)

PAULA: *(Looking at Tessa)* It's too late to go home and go back to bed *(To all)* and too early to get coffee. Should we just start shoveling debris out of the door?

DEBRA: I know this sounds crazy, but maybe somebody is doing us a favor lighting a torch to this thing, so we can rebuild it.

ANNA: Debra! For god's sake, what a thought.

DEBRA: No, seriously, then we can collect the insurance and do this right.

PAULA: She has a point. Unfortunately, the auditorium wasn't touched.

GEORGE: *(GEORGE looks around)* Goddamn, mother fuckin' mess.

DEBRA: You can say that again

ANNA: And he will.
(ALL laugh, including GEORGE)

RAE: Oh, lord, the news team's outside

DEBRA: You know, this could be good publicity for fund raising.

TESSA: An opportunity to speak to the community about what's been happening to us.

(GEORGE, DEBRA, ANNA, RAE, TESSA and PAULA come together to form a united front)

TESSA: Hello Channel Five

ALL: Welcome to the Women's Building.

(Reprise of "She Rises" song)

(THE END)

CHAPTER 6

OPERATING THE BUILDING AS POLITICAL ACTION

DURING THE DISCUSSIONS about buying a building, one of the biggest concerns was whether this was the right thing for a political group like the San Francisco Women's Centers (SFWC) to undertake. No one wanted to become another YWCA, providing direct social services to individuals. Most of the women involved with the SFWC in its early days came from a tradition of grassroots organizing. Their goal was building movements for social change, not moving into buildings. Likewise, the women who came into the core of the new Women's Building collective also had backgrounds as activists. Their long-range goal was to end the capitalist economic system, so owning property seemed like a step backward. Despite these concerns, the purchase had gone ahead and the group was now a property owner. But no one was ready to fully embrace this role. The conflicts over renting space to the policewomen and to Samois were essentially political, yet it was very difficult for the women involved to understand that owning and operating the Building was itself a political act.

The controversies over renting the Building indicated that the collective needed to focus more on its own political education. While there was a common understanding of the specific issues that concerned women, there was also a recognition that women's rights didn't exist in a vacuum. Graciela Perez Trevisan remembers her first year in the collective, in her position as bookings coordinator:

[My job in 1981 and 1982] primarily was to rent rooms in The Women's Building to women's groups and community organizations. And besides, as a collective member, we had meetings, right, to talk about development and the structure of the building, et cetera, et cetera. And I also remember that we had meetings, you know, like study group meetings. There was really an interest at that moment to expand our awareness, and those other issues that we were working for, beyond specifically the women's community. That is, moving to talk about issues that have to do with information on politics, here [in the] U.S. ...

So, you know, if you remember at that time there was the El Salvador war, Nicaragua. So these issues, political issues, were incorporated to our ... our study and our fight, which means, in the sense of The Women's Building, that we rented a space, and we had groups, as I said, from the women's community there. Very, very versatile groups—women's groups, but we also had other groups that weren't specifically women's groups, but we thought that they were political work that was important. And something else that The Women's Building tried to do at that time, and then later when I came back to The Women's Building in '85, was, we wanted to reach the Latino/Latina community, since The Women's Building was located in the heart of the Mission District. So we wanted to not only have a staff who spoke Spanish, but also to make the place more friendly and more receptive for people living in the Mission, particularly, as I said, Latinos and Latinas.

The process of internal political education was consciously begun with study sessions. The goal was to give the collective members a common starting point for decision making. Political topics for study included feminism in general, imperialism and international relations, and domestic issues, such as reproductive rights and the impact of "Reaganomics."

The process of studying and discussing these issues brought home the frustration of some collective members that The Women's Building itself wasn't directly taking on these issues in any ongoing way. Here they were dealing with how much toilet paper to buy while life for women got steadily harder and the national political climate shifted to the right. There was a strong pull on individual women to jump into various campaigns, leaving no time for the work of operating the Building. If the collective was going to keep its members, they had to learn how to give more meaning to the mundane daily work of keeping the Building open.

The Strategic Planning Process

In 1982, a Planning and Evaluation Committee was formed within The Women's Building collective to undertake an extensive survey of the Building collective's strengths and weaknesses. The phrase "strategic planning" didn't have the currency it would develop later, in the 1990s, but this was basically the aim. An outside consultant, Barbara Johnson, was hired to lead the collective through a process that ultimately took over a year to complete. Everyone in the collective was involved in at least part of this work, and in the final discussion they adopted a refined mission, structure, and general work plan that guided the group for the rest of the decade.

Original brainstorming had identified twenty-two issues and goals for The Women's Building, most of which the committee grouped into four areas of concern: (1) improving working conditions, (2) achieving self-sufficiency, (3) sustaining collectivity, and (4) understanding the Building as an asset.

Working Conditions

This concern focused on the physical and emotional climate for the entire collective. Work had been done to bring the Building up to code and make it safer for all, but general layout inside the Building wasn't ideal, and construction of some sort was often under way. Specific issues to be addressed included the physical reorganization of the administrative offices and moving the reception area down to the main entrance as a first step in renovating the lobby area.

The most critical issues in this category, however, concerned staffing: how to divide up the work between paid and unpaid collective members, and how to set wages, health benefits, and cost of living raises. The goal was to establish systems of accountability and training for collective members and other volunteers, and to pay full-time salaries to at least a few people in order to ensure the daily operation of the Building. At several points during the 1980s, the number of full-time staff was down to just two women, but usually at least three or four women, and sometimes more, were paid to work full – or half-time.

Self-sufficiency

The long-term goal was to increase the collective's economic security and to make the Building self-sufficient. The first step toward this goal was to upgrade the financial workings of the organization.

The Women's Building had some things in its favor: It was a "non-profit" in the most literal sense: every penny brought in was funneled right back into the project. Even with cost-of-living raises for staff and the addition of basic health insurance benefits, nobody was making money off the enterprise. Other than the mortgage on the Building, the group didn't carry much debt. And a basic financial accounting system was in place.

But owning a building and applying for public funding for upgrades and renovation placed new demands on the collective. In the short run, the focus of this area of work was to improve the budgeting and tracking process within The Women's Building. But in the long term, the aim was to "increase the cash flow receipts by increasing the amount of reliable rental receipts and outside funding sources."[20] Hovering always in the background was the knowledge that in 1990 the balloon payment on the mortgage would come due. Though it would take a few years before actual work in a capital campaign began, the goal was identified in 1982.

Sustaining Collectivity

In addressing the related issues of staffing and budgeting, a high premium was set on maintaining the collective essence of the organization. It was an ongoing process to (1) define who was in the collective, (2) define their responsibilities, and (3) recruit and train new members.

As stated earlier, the politics of The Women's Building collective members were clearly to the left of center. No attempts were ever made within the collective to come to a more defined unity about the evils of capitalism or which brand of socialism to support. But at the conclusion of the planning process, a new statement of the group's principles of unity was drafted to define the general outline of their political views. It was formally approved in 1984.

STATEMENT OF PURPOSE

SFWC/WB is a feminist organization. We recognize that sexism, racism, imperialism, and the hierarchy of classes are integral to the maintenance of present socio/economic systems.

We exist to facilitate and participate in the collective strength of women working together to provide a women's center where all oppressed people can freely express themselves and work to develop a free and non-oppressive society.

---

20 Planning and Evaluation Committee, Memo Re: Proposal for the Women's
     Building, February 24, 1983. GLBTHS, WBA. Collection 3, Series 1, box 1

GOALS

1. To bring a working-class perspective to the women's movement in the Bay Area so that it will address not only issues of sexism but also issues of imperialism, racism, and heterosexism.

2. To bring a feminist perspective to the broader people's struggle so that it will include issues of sexism and heterosexism.

3. The Women's Building will be owned by the San Francisco Women's Centers and will recruit women to its Directing Collective who are committed to the purpose, goals, and objectives of this organization.

4. SFWC/WB will be managed collectively, and all decisions will be made by consensus. All standing committees will make policy [and] political recommendations to the Directing Collective. The Directing Collective will make all final ownership, policy, and political decisions.

OBJECTIVES

1. To develop a marketing plan that targets those populations we exist to serve and work in coalition with.

2. To develop a fundraising strategy that will stabilize our income and create a base for self-sufficiency.
3. To develop a strategy for the balloon payment.

4. To identify, organize, and sponsor projects that reflect our goals and purposes.[21]

---

21 Planning and Evaluation Committee, Statement of Purpose, 1984. GLBTHS, WBA, main collection, series 2, subseries A, box 8, file 7.

Understanding the Building as an Asset

Although addressing the first three areas of concern helped to stabilize the organization, the key breakthrough from this planning process was coming to understand the Building as an asset and a political tool. The collective's own history already provided examples of the political nature of space: the problems confronted in organizing a women-only conference on violence and the debates over renting to the policewomen and Samois. The women were recognizing that beyond providing (or not providing) access for specific gatherings, the Building provided affordable office space that could be critical to any number of organizing campaigns. The Building could be a key asset to the movements the women wanted to support, and as such it was a real political tool.

This recognition put the responsibilities of building coordination, maintenance and security, renovation work, and marketing and bookings of rental space at the heart of the collective's work. Prior to this evaluation, 70 percent of staff time was program oriented; this now dropped to 30 percent, with 70 percent of staff time devoted to facility management and administration of the Building. Most of the paid collective positions took on these aspects of the work. The other paid position was most often a fundraiser, and this work was now undertaken with a view of the Building as an asset to be supported. Other programs were maintained, including sponsored projects, the information and referral program, and occasional newsletters.

The strategic planning of 1982 was a lengthy process that at the time seemed to detract from the women's daily work. However, it was very important in strengthening the unity of the collective and in furthering its ability to find new volunteers and staff over the next few years. The improved financial systems helped the women get the resources they needed to remodel the Building into a more useable workplace[22] There was still never enough money, but the daily sense

---

22 It was by no means an ideal site; that would take another twenty years to accomplish.

that the Building would collapse under the weight of debt was eased. A clearer sense of purpose gave the collective hope that they would make it to a better future.

Learning on the Job

Following this lengthy evaluation and planning process, The Women's Building experienced a period of relative stability that would last through much of the rest of the eighties. Not that there wasn't turmoil. Indeed, there was one crisis after another—some in response to various political struggles, others in the form of personal crises—and the ongoing cash shortage sometimes made it difficult to maintain the facility and pay staff salaries.

At the core of the collective were about a dozen women who hung in through all of the intensity. At one point, around 1984, the paid staff was down to just two people, plus women who worked on an hourly basis to provide security for the evening hours. But the dozens of hours of volunteer labor from the rest of collective members kept the Building open and operational. The only time in the 1980s that the Building wasn't open during scheduled hours was for one week following the earthquake in October 1989, while the stability of the structure was assessed by City engineers.

The continuity provided by the core of women, some of whom had been with the SFWC since its Brady Street days, enabled the group to keep its core mission of providing service to the women's movement at the forefront even while dealing with overflowing toilets. Basic job descriptions were developed, and there was a division of responsibilities within the collective. Yet in the weekly meetings of the collective, everyone had equal voice; tasks were often taken on without regard to the formal job descriptions; and certain functions were purposely rotated in order to give everyone experience and access to the same power. Though very democratic, this wasn't necessarily the most efficient process, and it was fraught with communication problems. It was one thing to identify collectivity as an important goal, but achieving it was an ongoing struggle that often fell short of the goals set in the strategic planning.

Regina Gabrielle's story of her first hiring process reflects the disorganization of the period:

My interviewing committee was Graciela Perez Trevisan and Carmen Vasquez. I think I had a couple of interviews. What was provoking was that I went for my interview and they didn't show up. Nobody showed up; there was no one there. There was no one at The Women's Building, nobody on staff that could tell me what was going on. It was really like, oh, this is funky. So really, welcome to the nonprofit world. Welcome to the collective. I said, "Okay, well, I don't know." I left a message with someone. I don't know [who]. Back then, nobody identified themselves. For all I know, it would have been a volunteer, which would have been fine. It was just so disorganized. I was a little taken aback. Then I got a call, "Oh, sorry, sorry," and [we] rescheduled, and it happened again. It happened again! Nobody showed up!

I got really angry. I got really angry, [at] whoever the poor woman was at the front desk: "I want to speak to somebody."

"Well, there's nobody here."

"Well, there's got to be somebody here. Somebody's got to run this place. What is this? This is ridiculous. Get me somebody." I just remember yelling at her, and then this woman, Holly Fincke, opened a door and came out and said "Is there something wrong?"

I was like, "Who are you?" She was someone who worked at The Women's Building. I said, "I just need to express this. I'm really angry." I just remember yelling at her and saying, "Who do you people think you are? Do you think your time is more valuable than mine? This is the second time. The first time, maybe I can have some understanding. Okay, yeah, I'll give you that. But the second time, this is ridiculous."

Holly was great. She listened, she tried to calm me, and she said that she would definitely bring it to the collective. "We have a collective" and blah, blah, blah. So I left, and I just was like, "Those people are crazy. Those women are fucking crazy."

I really think that they were really disorganized and unprofessional. I didn't think that it was racial, and I didn't think that it was because I was a lesbian. I knew Carmen, I had known Carmen. So Carmen called me with egg on her face and apologized: "Well, geez, we're really sorry. You still interested?"

I said, "I don't know. What is this shit?" Now, it's really a funny story. In hindsight, what I realize is like, you know, we were learning. The building was learning. None of the women who were on staff, or the collective, or whatever their status was, none of the women who were responsible and accountable for the actual building and the daily running of the building ... I don't think that they'd really run an agency before. ...

I don't know what they were doing with the other interviewees, but they decided that they liked me and they were offering me the position. I think they were afraid I wasn't going to take it, because we started out with the building fucking up and me yelling at the building.

As a consciously feminist group, the collective placed a high value on having no hierarchy. Informally, however, several women consistently stepped forward to provide visible leadership, including Roma Guy, Carmen Vasquez, and Diane Jones. Another of the original founders, Jean Crosby, was also a constant behind-the-scene voice, especially as the one who handled much of the financial work of maintaining the organization.

Other members of the collective had been there for several years or more: Holly Reed, Deena Clevenson, Leslie Kirk Campbell, Janice Toohey, Graciela Perez Trevisan, Flo Tumolo, Holly Fincke, Deb Riley, Pam Weatherford, Tiana Arruda, Flavia Maucci. There were also women who had been very involved in the first couple of years who continued to be named as members of the paper board of directors, on call for support on specific projects: Tracy Gary, Jean Livingston, Jeanne Adelman Mahoney, and Pam Miller.

This collection of women weren't merely co-workers. Weathering crisis after crisis, they forged very close bonds. The Women's Building "family" was ever-growing, because even as women left the collective, most kept those ties alive, returning to the Building again and again for events and meetings and continuing to give money.

Friendships also formed between women from the tenant organizations. Efforts were made to formalize a tenant's council, but the real ties were those made by women passing on the stairwell, or meeting at a nearby coffee shop or taqueria. Most of the organizations had small staffs, so being around like-minded women and organizations helped combat the isolation. There were other buildings in San Francisco that housed a concentration of nonprofit organizations, but the context there was more like being neighbors. At The Women's Building, it was more like being roommates within a single house. In part, this was because of the physical characteristics of the Building— it wasn't a hall lined with separate doors for each organization. Sometimes, getting access to an office meant passing through another office. But another factor was that everyone was dealing with aspects of women's condition and the effort to gain more rights for women. One group's victory—or setback—was shared by all. The supportive context made it a little easier to deal with issues that by nature were stressful. The benefit that this provided to the movement as a whole is hard to calculate, and indeed was often unacknowledged. But the spirit of community that existed in the Building was real.

Evolution of the Collective

By the late 1980s, the four women who had been such important anchors were ready to move on, or had already done so. Roma Guy was co-directing the Women's Foundation, then housed at The Women's Building and very involved in international solidarity work. Carmen Vasquez was the director at Community United Against

Violence, one of more vocal players in the gay community, and she was beginning to contemplate a move back to New York. Diane Jones had finished her nursing degree and was working full time in the AIDS ward at San Francisco General Hospital, supporting her young daughter. She was also very involved in solidarity work with women in Central America. None of these three had been paid members of The Women's Building collective since the mid-80s.

Jean Crosby, who had been part of the SFWC since its inception, was the bookkeeper for the Building until late into the 1980s. Over the years, this included working with many of the sponsored projects that went on to form independent nonprofits, and slowly she found herself with her own business, consulting as a bookkeeper with a number of them. In 1988 she turned over her bookkeeping responsibilities and drew back from direct involvement in The Women's Building staff collective.

Losing key volunteers was certainly a blow, but all four continued to be active supporters of the Buildings, making themselves available in various ways in the subsequent years.

Since the purchase of the Building, a "paper" board of directors had been maintained to meet legal requirements. Over the years, new women were added to the list as they came into the collective, but names were rarely dropped, even as women became less active. The board rarely met, beyond the required annual meeting to "re-elect" itself and add new names.

Following the 1982 strategic planning, the concept of a Community Advisory Board was revived as a way to keep up relations with the broader community. It met periodically throughout the eighties, providing a useful context for airing issues and processing decisions. In 1986, as part of developing the collective's accountability, it was decided that the Board of Directors would include only active collective members. Six women who had long been on the paper board but were no longer active in the collective were dropped from the list: Tiana Arruda, Jeanne Adelman Mahoney Tracy Gary, Jean Livingston, Pam Miller, and Janice Toohey. Of these, Tiana, Pam, and Janice had all at one time been active members of the Building's collective. The other three had been involved in the purchase and were active supporters in the early years. The board was now comprised of the current paid staff and those volunteers who were putting in hours of work every week to keep the Building operating.

As Roma, Carmen, Diane, and Jean were beginning to step back, the collective called and met with dozens of women to recruit women to take their place. It soon became clear that the commitment level they were asking of new volunteer board members was very high. The days when a volunteer could attend weekly staff meetings and put in ten to twelve hours per week helping to run the Building were in the past. Even the paid collective positions were hard to fill, as the pay continued to be relatively low, and benefits limited.

The process did bring in a few women; Regina Gabrielle was hired as the bookings coordinator in 1987, and Hilary Crosby, a CPA, volunteered critical financial advice. Leni Marin and Rosa (Smokey) Rivera offered political input and community ties, Leni from her position at a Family Violence Prevention program and Smokey as a Mission District businesswoman. Carmen and Diane stayed on the board to provide continuity, still putting in hours of work every week.

Still, the limits of this "working board" became clear, and in 1988 they began yet another transition in the board concept. Now, the idea was to make it a board of volunteers who would direct policy and future planning but not be involved in the daily operation of the Building. To maintain communications with the paid staff collective, two staff members were also appointed as voting members of the Board of Directors; Regina, the bookings coordinator, and Holly Fincke, the fundraiser, joined the board. In 1989 the other members of the board were Carmen, Diane, Hilary Crosby, Leni Marin, Rosa Rivera, Beverly Ovrebo, Patricia Figueroa, and Midgalia Rosado. The rest of the paid staff still worked as a collective, but they were no longer part of the formal leadership of the Building.

As the new board took shape, the limits of the collective staff structure were also showing. The job descriptions that had been developed over the years for the paid staff became more solidified as the number of paid positions increased and as more and more of the daily and weekly work was done by paid staff. So a new position, director of administration, was developed. This position was designed to provide more than just coordination of the work, and it was the first step in establishing an executive director for the organization.

Determining how the board, the executive director, and the staff would work together took some doing. With four of the women who had provided leadership now gone from the daily work, defining the new leadership was an undercurrent in many discussions at the Building. A functional, volunteer board couldn't relate to the staff as a whole, nor could a board just spring into life and function without someone being responsible for working with it.

By now, many organizing projects and most groups providing direct service functioned along the nonprofit model. There was lots of advice and experience to look at in defining the respective roles of staff, executive director, and board members. There were also many stories of organizations caught up in political battles between boards and staffs, making the women wary of that model.

It took some time, but by 1990, Regina Gabrielle of the current staff agreed to step into the new position as administrative director. Regina had been attending events at The Women's Building since it opened, and initially she envied the women who worked there. In 1986 she was hired to work part time as a consultant, keeping a very high-paying part-time position at San Francisco General Hospital. In her position with The Women's Building, she worked on the several lesbian of color conferences and on other programs for young lesbians.

In 1987, Regina accepted a full-time job at The Women's Building as the bookings coordinator. This meant leaving her job with flexible hours at the hospital to take on a lower-paid, full-time position with no real security. Two years later, it was a big step for Regina to take on the new title of Administrative Director, without clear responsibilities. Regina recalls that time:

The building was a collective then (1987), and so I was part of what we called the admin team. Roma would come to that. Her assignment was to come in and basically work with the admin team. Every Monday or Tuesday or whenever it was, we would meet for a couple of hours in a staff meeting. That's where we would take care of administrative details, and we would check in about each other's lives, and also about what was going on with the building, and basically fleshed out the day-to-day happenings. So that was very important, because we had, I remember, a collective of about seven women, some were full time, some were part time, so we didn't see each other all the time and [were] doing very different jobs. [The admin team] had the responsibility to run the women's building...

I think that's where Roma must see my potential, being an administrator. Even then, I didn't know what administration meant. I'm the chair of the admin team, so I'm supposed to come in and run these meetings. That was cool. So I'd create the agenda, make sure everybody was checking in with me, and what's on the agenda, try to make some sense out of chaos. I think that Roma really saw something in me, and I think other people who were around the building saw some potential in me. I guess there was a plan for the building. I was so oblivious.

There was a plan. I think part of the plan was that really the building needed to move to the next step, and we needed to break away from the admin chair. And we needed to find someone to be a director of administration. We need to find a board that's actually going to be a working board, while we define who we were and how we're going to govern. Roma approached me and said, "And how would you like to be The Women's Building's first director of administration? I will work with you and groom you for about a year, get you ready for this." I just remember looking at her and laughing, and I really think that's what changed my life because up until then, I don't think I had a lot of direction in terms of career or profession. So anyway, then I began going to conferences and trainings to learn about management, supervising, bookkeeping, nonprofit accounting, budgeting et cetera, et cetera.

Regina held the position as Administrative Director through its development into an Executive Director. (See Chapter 9 for more on this story.)

Moving toward Financial Security

In spite of all the organizational and personnel turmoil, the Building itself was slowly taking shape. The assets of the SFWC steadily increased through the eighties, from $550,000 at the start of the decade to about $1,000,000 by the end. This was mainly due to increases in the value of the Building and the land it sits on. The mortgage still due in 1989 was $382,000, down from the $425,000 listed on the July 1981 balance sheet.

Despite the steadily growing balance sheet, the figures were far more modest in terms of actual cash income, as Table 2 shows.

Table 2: Women's Building
Annual Income
1982 - 1989

Year	Income
1982	$219,000
1983	$263,000
1984	$270,000
1985	$450,000
1986	$462,000
1987	$340,000
1988	$462,000
1989	$289,000

Through the eighties, annual rental income rose steadily from $70,000 to $100,000, with the increases mostly coming with the increased amount of office space available for rent as various re-modeling projects were completed. Income from one-time events was important, but it was harder to count on than regular month-ly rental income. Square footage rates of far under $1/foot meant that the space was affordable, and the Building was usually at full occupancy.

Throughout the decade, income levels from basic fundraising and rental income was just under $300,000 per year. The big jumps in in-come in 1985, 1986, and 1988 reflect the funds granted, principally by the Mayor's Office of Community Development, to undertake ren-ovation and safety upgrades for the facility. In total, the city granted nearly $350,000, which was used to install sprinklers on the first two floors, to put in wheelchair-accessible bathrooms on the first and third floor, to remodel the lobby to put in a reception and security area as well as a small office on the ground floor, and to soundproof the au-ditorium and the Harriet Tubman Room on the third floor. Slowly, the shape of the Building was changing to become a space more useful to the community it was serving.

In 1988, a marketing survey was undertaken to assess who used the Building, in what manner, and how other organizations in the community might use the Building. Out of this study, a new, more comprehensive renovations plan was developed. Before it got much past envisioning a transformed first and second floor, however, the 1989 earthquake put all renovation work in a new light—and with a new budget and timeline. While actual damage from the earth-quake was limited, the Building was made of unreinforced masonry, and so its vulnerability to future quake damage was very high. The collapse of similar buildings in the Marina District highlighted the danger, and all such buildings were identified by the city as requir-ing a retrofit.

With the grants coming in for various renovation projects, the women were able to pay for building management and bookings, and other fundraising efforts were able to cover other administrative work and some programming. In addition to rent, the core of the annual income came from individual contributions, up to $100,000 per year, and from major special events, like the Walk-a-Thon and the crafts fair.

In terms of grants, the main source of funding for the Women's Building came from various city agencies, in particular the Mayor's Office of Community Development. These grants funded the remodeling of the second-floor dining room. The space was separated into two main sections: The first half became a larger meeting room,[23] and the other half was carved into office space, meeting an ever-growing demand for low-cost office rentals. Other grants were spent in remodeling the entrance and reception area and carving more meeting space out of the third floor. By the time of the 1989 earthquake, the Building was filled to capacity. Income from tenants and rentals became the one steady stream of revenue, ensuring at least a couple of paid staff positions.

Renovation grants, the occasional foundation grant, and rental income provided a basic financial foundation for the organization. Since the low point in paid staff in 1984, when only two women were paid, the percentage of the collective to be paid had gradually increased. After the initial years of a dozen paid members and then the sudden drop to just two women, the paid staff stabilized at five or six people, including a building / renovation manager, bookings coordinator, finance / administrative director, receptionist / information and referral person, and fundraiser. Staffing for various programs was fairly ad hoc; women were hired for specific projects out of various grants, or the tasks were taken on by staff in addition to their regular work or by volunteers. In order to pay even the modest wages of the time, The Women's Building needed additional streams of income.

At the core of ongoing fundraising was support from a base that made annual membership pledges of $25 and up. A few of these donors gave hundreds of dollars per year, and some gave in the four

---

23 This meeting room including the original bar—the only bar that survived all the stages of remodeling that had been done over the years.

figures, but most of the base gave less than $100 each. Remember, this was the eighties, and while $100 didn't stretch the way it had in the early seventies, inflation had slowed by mid-decade, and $100 would pay a few day's salary, or a good portion of the monthly health insurance premiums.

After three years, the Run/Walk-a-Thon sponsored by The Women's Building was discontinued. A similar format had been picked up by another group, Volunteers of America, and for a couple of years, staff and supporters of The Women's Building collected pledges through this event. But none of the subsequent years were as successful as the first in raising either funds or visibility for The Women's Building.

Women's Holiday Crafts Fair

The major annual event that replaced income from the Walk-a-Thons was the annual Celebration of Craftswomen. The project was viewed as a program as well as a fundraiser. A committee of craftswomen was brought together to help solicit exhibitors and to run a juried selection process. Training sessions were held to help the craftswomen learn various skills of the trade: how to best exhibit their wares, how to track sales and inventory, how to keep financial records and deal with taxes, etc.

Throughout the eighties, for two weekends in December, the first three floors of the Building were turned into a women's community indoor market, the Annual Celebration of Craftswomen. Food booths featured local groups and restaurants. Throughout each day, a steady stream of entertainment in the form of dance, music, spoken word, and poetry was presented while visitors ate or just took a break from shopping. The Women's Building made money from the entrance fees and from hourly raffles of goods donated by exhibitors. Fees from the exhibitors and food vendors basically covered the cost of using the facility, including the substantial electrical and lighting that had to be brought in to sustain the dozens of booths and the loss of other rental income over the two weekends.

—————————10TH ANNUAL—————————

WOMEN'S BUILDING
ARTS & CRAFTS FAIR

A DECADE OF CELEBRATING WOMEN'S CRAFTS
Sat. & Sun. • Dec. 10, 11 & 17, 18, 1988 • 10 a.m. to 6 p.m.
The Women's Building • 3543 18th Street, S.F. (at Valencia)

This annual event brought hundreds of women, men, and children to the Building and involved dozens of volunteers in addition to the staff, exhibitors, and entertainers. After the first few years, as it became clear that this was a successful event, a staff person worked nearly year-round on this project. The committee of craftswomen continued to function on a volunteer basis, and those participating were assured of a space at the fair. The popularity of the fair and the relatively low cost booth fees meant there was never a lack of potential exhibitors. Even with two weekends to work with, craftswomen were turned down every year.

By the late 1980s, the event had outgrown The Women's Building. At the same time, the increasing use of the Building's space by offices meant that less room was available for the event. In 1989, the Annual Celebration of Craftswomen was moved to a large building at Fort Mason, in the Marina District. This entailed far more expense it terms of rental fees, but the fair was also able to double in size, and it continued to be a significant annual fundraiser for the Building. In addition to the direct income from the event, ranging between $50,000 and $75,000, the raffle program was a continual new source of names and addresses that could be approached in other fundraising appeals.

Though the October '89 earthquake raised whole new issues about the physical feasibility of the Building, at the end of its first decade of operation, the organization had established a fairly secure sense of purpose and a basic organizational structure and financial base to take it into the next decade. Although few enjoyed unplugging the occasional clogged toilet, collective members no longer questioned the value of owning the Building.

CHAPTER 7

RADICAL ROOTS AND RICH RELATIONS

THROUGHOUT THE EIGHTIES, The Women's Building had special relationships with two organizations: the Alliance Against Women's Oppression and the Women's Foundation. Neither group could be characterized as the offspring of the San Francisco Women's Centers (SFWC), but there was a familial dynamic with each. These groups had their own distinct purposes and organizational structures, but an overlap in individual women involved in the groups created close ties between each and The Women's Building.

Of course, the women at the core of the Building were also involved in many other organizations, but for a variety of reasons, these two organizations were most important to the development of The Women's Building. With other organizations, such as various sponsored projects, the relationship was mostly about what The Women's Building was able to do for them. In the case of these two groups, the relationships were more complicated, and they more directly impacted the growth of The Women's Building itself, making them more like sisters.

The Alliance

Though the Alliance Against Women's Oppression folded up shop in 1989 and had little to do with the SFWC prior to the purchase of the Building, the relationship with this organization was significant throughout the eighties.

The SFWC first came into contact with the Alliance (as they called themselves) in the mid-70s, while doing outreach for the "Violence Against Women" conference. The women of the Alliance were not involved in the conference as an organizing or sponsoring group, but members did attend the conference, beginning political relationships that would endure for years to come.

The group began meeting in the 1960s as a Black women's caucus within the Student Nonviolent Coordinating Committee in New York City. The initial impetus for meeting was to deal with the sexism the women confronted within their organization. They soon found allies among Black women in other organizations and broadened their group to become the Black Women's Alliance. Within a few years, they broadened once again to involve Puerto Rican and other Latina and Asian women, becoming the Third World Women's Alliance. Active for many years in New York, their most visible presence came through their publication Triple Jeopardy. With a political focus that challenged imperialism, racism, and sexism, the organization presented a clearly radical program, even though much of its function was to provide support for the activism of women of color.

In the early seventies, Alliance member Cheryl Perry moved to Oakland and formed a local chapter. In addition to supporting the activism of its members, the new chapter was involved in a variety of political campaigns, perhaps most notably their work in identifying and challenging the high rate of infant mortality within communities of color, especially in Alameda County. They were also active in support of strike actions by workers for Blue Cross, opposing court decisions undermining affirmative action in the Bakke and Weber cases, and offering international solidarity to sisters around the world.

Though the New York chapter folded in the seventies, along with the newspaper Triple Jeopardy, the Bay Area chapter thrived. They also hooked up politically with other radical groups that put the struggle against racism at the core of their political strategy. The U.S.

left of the sixties had begun to evolve into what became known as the "new communist movement," and many members of the Alliance joined forces with members of the Union of Democratic Filipinos (KDP)—a national radical organization based in Filipino communities addressing the domestic issues of immigrants and challenging the dictatorial rule of Ferdinand Marcos in the Philippines—and the Northern California Alliance—a multiracial group of socialists—to form the Line of March. This group was one of the many "pre-party" communist formations that emerged out of the 1960s and functioned through the 1980s. Ultimately, the upheaval within the socialist left, most dramatically symbolized by the collapse of the Berlin Wall in 1989, led to the collapse of most of these organizations, including the Line of March.[24]

Not everyone in the Alliance joined the Line of March, but most did, including the leadership of the organization. A few women left the organization because of the affiliation. There was, however, an effort to maintain a distinction between the groups. The Line of March was a consciously, explicit communist organization. Alliance members, on the other hand, needn't be communist, or even socialist. As a so-called "mass organization," its aim was to maintain itself as an organization with less radical politics. For the Line of March, the role of mass organizations like the Alliance was to expose new people to revolutionary thinking and ultimately expand the ranks of the communist movement.

In the short term, the overlap between the two groups had no immediate impact on the functioning of the Alliance, nor did the Line of March tell it what to do. Though the Northern California Alliance did dissolve as a distinct group, both the Alliance and the KDP carried on as mass organizations, with their own existing programs and their own leadership.

One major change in the Alliance did reflect the needs of the Line of March, and this brings us back to The Women's Building. Members

---

24 For a history of this movement, see Max Elbaum, *Revolution Is in the Air* (London: Verso, 2002).

of the Line of March worked with various coalitions and organizations around issues of racism, workers rights, and international solidarity. The Alliance was seen as their vehicle for working with the women's movement, but its identity as a third world organization limited its ability to relate to progressive and socialist-minded white women.

Up until the late 1970s, the Alliance didn't identify as a feminist organization or see itself as part of the women's movement. They refused to be one of the groups sponsoring the 1976 women and violence conference in part because there was no history between the groups and therefore no reason to trust where the organizing would go. At the time there was also considerable ambivalence within the Alliance about having any relation with the white women's movement, and in particular with lesbians. Most of the Alliance membership was straight, and some were outright homophobic, making it an inhospitable organization for lesbians of color. In the wake of that conference, the Alliance had an internal struggle over the issue of homophobia and lesbian/gay rights, and it came in the end to support gay rights, losing a few members over the issue.

In 1979, at the initiation of leaders who were part of the Line of March, the Third World Women's Alliance went through a lengthy study and debate assessing the current state of politics in the United States and what role their organization should play within it. Since its founding, the organization's radical politics had focused on a triad of targets: racism, sexism, and imperialism.

The challenge to capitalism had meant implicit support for socialism, but not all members identified themselves as socialist. This was an era of national liberation struggles around the world, and this was reflected in the United States by the rise of nationalist ideologies among radical groups. The Alliance was a multiracial formation that excluded only white people and few if any in the group were of a dogmatic nationalist bent. No one wanted to change the basic political foundation of the organization. Rather, the goal was to clarify a strategic priority that focused the organization on the issues of women's liberation.

During the course of this discussion, the Alliance, at the invitation of The Women's Building, rented an office on the Building's second floor. When the discussion on identity within the Third World Women's Alliance came to an end in August 1980, the group identified itself as an anti-capitalist, antiracist, working-class organization of women. Its goal was the pursuit of women's liberation as an integral part of building a people's movement in the United States. With their focus clearly on women's issues and the women's movement, the group opened its membership to white women. The name was changed to the Alliance Against Women's Oppression. Since the Third World Women's Alliance was already referred to as "the Alliance," the new name allowed them to keep this shorthand and make the transition smoother.

A three-month-long weekly study seminar was developed to acquaint potential members with the political perspective of the Alliance. A weekend conference in 1981 brought most of these women together to launch the new Alliance Against Women's Oppression as a national organization, with chapters in New York, Boston, Washington, D.C., Seattle, and the Bay Area.

In the Bay Area, several of the women involved with the newly purchased Women's Building participated in the women's study project. Roma Guy, Carmen Vasquez, Diane Jones, and Jean Crosby, four of the central collective members of the SFWC, were members of the Alliance through the eighties. The Alliance kept its office at The Women's Building for about five years, moving to the third floor after the 1980 fire. It was an all-volunteer organization, so most meetings were held in members' homes; the rented space was used primarily for storage and to provide staging for events held at the Building or elsewhere in the city. It was yielded by the mid-80s to make room for never-ending renovation and growing demand for office rental space.

There was no formal relationship between The Women's Building and the Alliance, or the Line of March. Many of the socialist-left organizations of the time had a reputation, partially true, of trying to bend mass organizations to their own will—taking over the leadership or stacking the membership to get the decisions they wanted. Between the many party-like formations from the new communist movement and numerous splinters from the Trotskyite socialist left, independent left-wing women activists and their organizations (like the SFWC) were regularly courted to join someone's revolutionary group. More than one coalition would fall apart because of sectarian behavior between left-wing groups jockeying to claim parts of the movement as their own. Many radical feminists were justifiably repelled by such antics, if not by the political positions some of the groups took with regard to women's and lesbian/gay rights. By the eighties, most wanted little to do with the organized left. This meant that revolutionary organizations that did want to work with the broader women's movement had to be very careful about how they related to existing organizations.

Although the Line of March and the Alliance were separate organizations, with distinct principles of unity and membership requirements, by 1980 there was a significant overlap in membership, with most Alliance members also members of the Line of March, particularly in the chapters outside the Bay Area. For many in the broader movement, the Alliance Against Women's Oppression was mainly seen as a branch of the Line of March. The intertwined nature of the two organizations was underscored when the Line of March went into its tailspin.[25] Although there was a separate summation and logic to the decision to fold each group, it's hard to see how the Alliance Against Women's Oppression would have continued as an organization once the Line of March folded its tent.

The same cannot be said of the relationship between the Alliance and The Women's Building, which maintained its own identity and

---

25   The Line of March collapsed as a result of an internal leadership crisis in 1988. As part of this internal turmoil, the Alliance Against Women's Oppression went through a year-long summation of its own work and decided to fold the organization as women turned their attention to other projects. Its resources, a few thousand dollars, were donated to the Women of Color Resource Center, a project founded by several long-time members of the Alliance, and to The Women's Building.

base."} Nonetheless, the Building had a very close relationship with the Alliance Against Women's Oppression, and therefore with the Line of March. The Building had relations with other revolutionary organizations, for instance Radical Women and Freedom Socialist Organization, but these were characterized by ties of support for an occasional renter or sponsoring a specific project. A significant number of the women from The Women's Building collectives were at some point members of the Alliance, and a few were to become members of the Line of March.[26]

One of the characteristics of the Line of March was a strong emphasis on theoretical study to inform practical organizing. Most of its members went through a rigorous ten-month seminar to study some of the classic Marxist and Leninist writings and the current dynamics of capitalism and socialism. Several of The Women's Building collective members participated in this "long course" of study, and others participated in a shorter three-month introductory version of the same material. These collective studying habits, and in some cases the materials, were brought back to The Women's Building in its own internal education meetings.

Diane recalls how the relationship between the Building and the Alliance developed after the initial contact in 1976:

> Then [after the transformation from the Third World Women's Alliance] they were prepared to deal with us, and we were by then in a better place also. We had more of a developed understanding of what it was going to take to build multiracial coalitions and to become a multiracial organization. By this time the building was bought and we were in the building. And they became a tenant in the building. And then many of us who were at the core of the building joined the Alliance Against Women's Oppression.
>
> What they contributed was a very high level of theoretical

---

26 Most of these memberships were not open, since by the mid-80s, open affiliation with a communist organization would often undermine an activist's credibility.

and political analysis around the question of women's oppression, and how it intersects with race and class and the international question. And that's the contribution they made that really pro-pelled the building ... because of the tradition they came out of, which was a Marxist tradition, a leftist tradition. ... [T]hey brought to the organization an ability to work with the subjective factor, and people's individual experiences and distrust and whatever. And through rigorous analysis and study and understanding of history and understanding of movements, an ability to transcend your subjective experience, to be more objective. Then to be able to look at [and], on some level, de-personalize these issues, or understand how to take personal responsibility for whatever your behavior was but also understand it within the larger context.

To me, what was most helpful was it took it out of the mor-al realm. Back around the violence conference, the question of sexism, or heterosexism, or racism had a very, very moral and moralistic twist to it. And it became profoundly destructive and upsetting to people when a racial dynamic would occur. But where I think we were more successful, not always but where we were more successful several years later is that when a racial dynamic would occur or something would happen within the or-ganization, people would work together to try to unravel it and understand something. Through an ability to be more objective and more analytical and understanding, that helped people move through an [issue] faster and make certain decisions. For exam-ple, the policewomen's question, [the] controversy around when the policewomen wanted to come and meet at the building.

By the mid-1980s, both Roma and Diane were part of the nation-al leadership of the Alliance, and other Women's Building collective members worked on local projects with the Alliance. But the opera-tion and programming at The Women's Building was not considered to be the work of the Alliance. No formal direction was given to Alliance members who worked with the Building as to what should be happening or how to make it happen. Any ideas from the Line of March about pulling Women's Building activists more centrally into other aspects of their program were held in check by a recognition that to do so would take their attention away from The Women's Building and risk destabilizing what was seen as an important movement resource. Even though the Line of March was itself part of the dogmatic left of the eighties, it did retain some sense of boundaries and respect for "mass organizations."

The Women's Foundation

The other organization that The Women's Building had a special relationship with was the Women's Foundation, an organization quite different from the Alliance. The Women's Foundation grew from a progressive political impulse, and its goal was to raise money for projects working to improve the conditions of women and girls within society. Its base was middle and upper-class women with money.

From the initial inception of the SFWC back in the early 1970s, finding ways to get money for women's rights organizing had been part of the organization's vision. This was the impulse behind the Bay Area Feminist Federal Credit Union—to combine the communities' money in order to assist individual women. But the credit union was never stable enough to lend money to movement efforts. Over the years, the SFWC sometimes did direct fundraising for specific projects like the Women's Building Project, but more often its work was less direct. For example, workshops were held about different ways to raise money, from direct mail appeals to personal requests. A day-long program in 1976, "Women Producing Women," was held to teach women the basics of event organizing. The SFWC helped women write grants, funneling monies received through the SFWC's nonprofit status for tax purposes.

Funding Feminists Coalition was the first effort by the SFWC to build an organization that would be dedicated to getting money for women's movement organizing. Beginning in 1974, the SFWC pulled together about a dozen women's groups and advocates that would work together to push more generally on the foundation world to give money to women's issues. Funding Feminists identified two purposes: (1) political action to raise awareness of the issue and pressing for funding on women's issues and (2) providing technical assistance to groups looking for foundation support.

The group renamed itself the Project Directors Group, conducted a review of the current state of funding for women's projects, and held a few educational programs to address the issue. One important contact made was with the Bay Area Research Council and its director, Ruth McGuire. This group had formed in 1972 with the purpose of researching foundation funds available to women and pressing for increased funding. But without a clear plan or staffing, the Project Directors Group soon became one of many volunteer efforts that existed in name only.

After The Women's Building was purchased, the SFWC continued to assist sponsored projects with administrative services, but its ability to raise money for them was limited. As the women were settling into the Building, several who were very involved in the purchase decided it was time to form their own foundation that was dedicated to funding women's issues. Funding Feminists was revived and received a $1,000 grant from the Ms. Foundation to get the process started. Roma Guy, Marya Grambs, and Tracy Gary approached Ruth McGuire about joining forces to launch a new foundation. By this time, the Bay Area Research Council was nearly defunct, and Ruth put all its resources into the new project. Together, the group pulled together an initial endowment and established the Women's Foundation. By 1981, they had gotten their own charitable foundation status with the state and federal tax agencies.

Roma, Marya, and Tracy had all been instrumental in raising the funds to purchase The Women's Building. Though Roma continued to be active with the Building after the purchase, both Marya and Tracy were soon burned out. Partly this is because they undertook so much work to raise the $160,000 it took to close the deal. But it was also because of the undercurrents of class dynamics. Their more privileged class backgrounds had given them access to the kind of money that was needed for the down payment. But because the goal was to have women of color at the core of the Building project, most of the collective came from more working-class backgrounds, and many were suspicious of anyone with wealth, including women. Tracy and Marya kept their names on the paper board and gave verbal and monetary support to the Building, but they were not actively involved with the Building after its first year.

To them, a Women's Foundation was different because it did not tie its fate to any one organization. Rather, its role was specifically to raise money for the broader women's movement. The Women's Building was just one of the organizations that could, and did, apply for grants from the foundation.

Some of the initial donors of the new foundation were also donors to the Women's Building Project. Many others, however, were women who weren't interested in giving to only one project, or for whom the politics of the SFWC were too radical. Nonetheless, the fact is that the two organizations both based in San Francisco and with overlap in core volunteers, were trying to raise substantial funds for a major women's project, and drawing from some of the same base. Though there wasn't open conflict between the two groups, there was some concern that the success of the Women's Foundation would undermine the potential funding base of The Women's Building. Carmen Vasquez described the conflict in an interview with Frances Doughty:

> This is maybe a controversial thing to say, but I'm going to say it anyway. I think that ... the creation of the Women's Foundation pretty much at the same time as the development of The Women's Building was a mistake. I think it should have never happened. Or that it should have happened later. But I think that the space for funding something of the magnitude of a Woman's Foundation and a Women's Building was just not there in the Bay Area. Too hard to do. Now the fundraisers will say, "No, they're different

things and people give in different ways and da da da." But I say, haha, that it's too much competition. And again it's almost like the reverse of Women's Centers and The Women's Building.

FRANCES: The Women's Foundation is the posher one.

CARMEN: Right. And the Building is sort of the little stepchild and the poorer thing [for] those activists. And I think that it's not just the donors, not just the pool of donors but the energies of some of the best fundraising feminists in the Bay Area had to go into making money for the foundation. Maybe they were not going to be willing to raise money for the Building any more. I don't know if that's true, but I think it was a mistake, in retrospect.

FRANCES: So you think that some of the money that went to the foundation would in fact have come to the building? Or do you think it's more the diversion of energy and vision of the people who were involved in trying to make the foundation happen, or some of them?

CARMEN: Some of both. I mean, I think that probably more of the latter, ... the diversion of energy of people who would have been central to a development campaign for the building. Because really what it meant, when Roma went off to do the Women's Foundation, and Marya, the building didn't have fundraising. ... We brought people in who had very little experience as fundraisers, and we trained them. Roma and Marya and whoever else trained them. And as soon as they got trained they'd go off. Of course, because if you can raise $100,000 a year or more, why should you be working someplace for $12,000 a year or less? So, you know, in retrospect I feel that it should have been a project put off for three or four more years until there was a more solid basis for the building. There are folks who would never give to The Women's Building that would write a check or do whatever these people do—a bequest—to the foundation. But would never do it for the building. But despite that, I think that there are enough other kinds of folks who are progressive who would give money who would have done more in terms of supporting the building if they hadn't been diverted into something else.

These are comments made ten years after the fact. At the time, such concerns were rarely aired publicly. In the public eye, the two groups were seen as closely allied organizations. Some people didn't even know that they were separate groups. This perception was fed by the fact that the Women's Foundation made its home in The Women's Building until the 1990s.

Beyond the potential competition for donors, both groups benefited from their close relationship. In general, there were good relations between the women involved on both staffs. The friendships they built helped to alleviate some of the isolation and frustration of the daily work of the respective groups. Roma, who continued to be active with The Women's Building collective, was able to split her time between the two organizations. Her central and public role in both organizations contributed to the tendency to merge the two groups in people's minds, but it also helped smooth out relations between the two groups. It also made for an easier transition of Roma's workload as she became more active with the work of the Women's Foundation.

While SFWC was still functioning as a collective, the Women's Foundation started right out with the more traditional organizational form of a charitable nonprofit agency. A staff was hired and a board of directors appointed. The organization was also launched with a significant amount of capital already in hand. The one nod to the more collective origins of the project was the existence of a co-directorship rather than a single executive director. These positions were initially shared by Marya and Roma. In the 1990s, the Women's Foundation dropped this shared position and established a traditional executive director position.

The Women's Building did receive small grants from the Women's

Foundation for a variety of projects over the years, but no one could accuse the Women's Foundation of favoritism toward the Building. There was no guarantee that a proposal from The Women's Building would be approved. Nor did these grants ever add up to a significant part of building's annual budgets.

Probably the biggest financial benefit to the Women's Building of having the Women's Foundation as a tenant was their role in undertaking a major remodeling of the fourth floor. Vida Gallery had occupied about half of the fourth floor until it closed in 1984, and it had been vacant ever since. In fact, the remodeling work uncovered walled-off areas that no one had even been aware of. Separate offices, with windows looking out over the Mission District and with downtown in the background, were put in along both outer walls of the Building. Larger meeting rooms, a common kitchen area for use by various staffs, and storage areas were carved out in the space between. The Women's Foundation occupied most of the offices, with a few of the smaller rooms rented to other women's organizations. The rent at that time was sixty-five cents per square foot.

Meanwhile, The Women's Building staff moved its offices around, depending on the current configuration of office space and other tenants. Quite often, that meant less than ideal workspace—desks were fit in haphazardly, sometimes with cubicle partitions and only rarely with an office door that could be closed. For many years, the Building's administrative offices were on the third floor, in a large space next to the Harriet Tubman Room and sharing its very high ceilings. With only portable cubicle walls separating women, the noise level in the room was at times oppressive. The contrast to the freshly remodeled space used by the Women's Foundation no doubt fed some of the resentment that built up toward the foundation. When the foundation moved its offices downtown in 1994, to be closer to other foundations and in a setting presumably more comfortable for visiting potential donors, The Women's Building moved its administration offices into this preferred space upstairs.

With the move, the distinction between the two groups became clearer, and the parting was on amicable terms. The Women's Foundation is still going strong, continuing to raise money and provide technical support for projects aimed at improving conditions for women and girls across the U.S. and the globe, including occasional programs of The Women's Building.

CHAPTER 8

ORGANIZING IN THE 1980'S

POLITICS IN THE 1980s looked very different from the militancy and mass mobilizations that had characterized the sixties and the first half of the seventies. There were some significant national marches in the eighties: over a million people took to the streets in New York City in 1982 to demonstrate for peace, and in 1987, nearly a million people marched in Washington, D.C., for lesbian and gay rights. As one of the few remaining liberal hot spots, the Bay Area was the location of occasional demonstrations, usually focused on international solidarity and peace issues, or AIDS policies. But most were small by sixties standards, numbering at the most in the thousands, and protests were often met by intimidating mounted police. More than one activist was injured by police batons emboldened by the country's rightward swing.

In national politics, the right wing of the Republican Party controlled the executive branch and through appointments was beginning to reshape the judiciary. Democrats were scurrying to the center in an attempt to win back the white base that was abandoning it. Enacting progressive policy at the national level was an uphill and long-term battle. Blocking reactionary and repressive legislation and policies was the main thrust of most national progressive campaigns.

Unable to have much positive impact on the "big picture," many activists looked for ways to take on some piece of that picture. Many turned to local politics as the arena where they would be most likely to have an impact. Others took up a single issue; there were dozens of possibilities on both the domestic and the international front.

The result of these factors was the growth of a very fragmented movement. While the Vietnam War had provided a common thread for organizing in the sixties and seventies, in the eighties there was no such clear common cause. Lip service was often given to related issues, but most organizing was more narrowly focused, and the mobilization of people, whether to infrequent street action or to the voting booth or letter writing campaigns, was focused on a narrow community on behalf of a specific issue. One response to the fragmentation was to embrace the concept of "identity politics." Throughout the eighties, and well into the nineties, the foundation of common political action often had more to do with shared conditions of being such as racial background or religious belief than with having a well-defined political perspective. The struggle around the issue with the police women was just one of many that pitted identity against broader political ideals.

Conferences

One thing that did bring activists together was attending conferences. Organizing and attending conferences was an important means of keeping the movement alive, even if in a fragmented form. With so few palpable results from organizing efforts, organizing a conference itself often became the goal, rather than any actions that might result from the conference. Conference organizing focused on providing attendees with education on the issues at hand and with the opportunity to network with like-minded people.

The women's movement had numerous national conferences every year. Some were the annual meetings of organizations like the National Organization for Women (NOW) and the National Women's Studies Association. Others convened around specific issues, like reproductive rights or misogynist violence. I attended four conferences of the Reproductive Rights National Network in the early 1980s, including one held at the recently purchased Women's Building in 1981. My memories of all the caucusing that went on are more vivid than any of the actual organizing efforts that were discussed and adopted. While some of the educational aspects of the conferences focused on the nuts and bolts of organizing and on details about reproductive health care, a lot of what we learned came more informally and spontaneously through the conflicts and resolutions addressed through caucuses and the plenary meetings of the entire conference. By definition, the caucuses were usually identity based: women of color (sometimes as a multiracial group and other times in ethnic-specific groups, including African American, Latina, Asian, and Pacific Islander women), lesbians, Jewish women, and disabled women. Sometimes caucusing was scheduled into the conference, but often it would occur during the breaks, in lieu of workshops and during mealtimes. Some of the most controversial and divisive topics of the conferences emerged from discussions that began within the caucuses and were then brought back before the full conference.

The San Francisco Women's Centers (SFWC) continued its tradition of promoting the growth of the movement by supporting numerous conferences throughout the 1980s. Some of these conferences were held at The Women's Building, but larger gatherings needed public school or college settings for the numerous workshops. For some conferences the SFWC was a sponsor, lending its name and limited logistical support; for others, collective members threw themselves into the organizing effort. Members of the collective struggled to hold onto their understanding of operating a building as a political action, and supporting conferences was one of the main ways that this took a clear and concrete form. For days after a conference gathered at the Building, the woman-energy continued to resonate throughout the Building, making all the effort seem worthwhile for those who worked there.

Of course, convening conferences at The Women's Building presented many challenges. In the eighties, remodeling was a haphazard and nearly ongoing feature of occupancy. Much of the facility continued to be run down, with dim lighting, often poor acoustics, and extremely uncomfortable chairs. Heavy wooden chairs were kept under the stage in the auditorium, and pulling them out and putting them away required at least two women, and usually half a dozen or more were involved. Lighter weight wooden chairs, often a bit rickety, and folding metal chairs made up the rest of the seating, aside from the benches and thrones in the Harriet Tubman Room on the third floor. Tables were also heavy and well worn; bright African cloth was regularly used to cover the stains. Most of the time the elevator worked, which was fortunate for those moving furniture, but most conference participants went up and down the spiral stairway. But for all that was lacking in logistical resources, the energy of women gathered together in their own building was usually high enough to make all such problems seem trivial.

Bay Area Lesbian of Color Conferences

Probably the most significant conferences The Women's Building was involved in were a series of conferences focused on lesbians. Lesbians had always played a central role in the Building. A significant percentage of the Building staff were lesbians, including a number of lesbians of color.

However, in the Building's early years, the fact that most of the audience members for events were lesbians was seen as a problem, and efforts were made to make straight women more comfortable. In reaching out to the Mission community, and in efforts to get city funding for various renovations and upgrades of the facility, the collective fought the image of being a "lesbian organization" by stressing its general commitment to women and girls. The involvement of lesbians was never hidden, but neither was it highlighted. With the emergence of the AIDS epidemic, The Women's Building joined in the opposition to ballot initiatives and other policies targeting people with AIDS. This brought the Building more directly into the gay movement, but the specific issues of lesbians weren't a direct focus.

The eighties were a vibrant time in the history of feminists of color, including many lesbians. Kitchen Table Women of Color Press began publishing works by women of color, including *Home Girls: A Black Feminist Anthology* (1983), edited by Barbara Smith and *This Bridge Called My Back: Writings by Radical Women of Color* (1984), edited by Cherrie Moraga and Gloria Anzaldua. Many other progressive presses and journals followed suit.

By the mid-80s, there was a rumble of concern from both staff and supporters about the growing invisibility of lesbians. In 1985 The Women's Building successfully applied to the United Way for money to develop programming for lesbians. This was one of the first substantial grants dedicated to programming for The Women's Building. Up to this point, most grants had been dedicated to upgrading the facilities. This grant helped to subsidize staffing to develop a program for The Women's Building. After discussion, the collective decided that the central aspect of their lesbian programming would be to support lesbians of color. Drawing from the collective and from other friends in the community, a committee was formed to organize a conference for lesbians of color. It was for this project that Regina Gabrielle first came to work at The Women's Building.

The first conference was held in June 1986. Under the title "Coming Out and Surviving," the program covered a wide range of topics, from organizing issues to relationship challenges. White lesbians and straight women were tapped for logistical support, mainly behind the scenes, and they were welcomed to the public party at the conference's end.

The conference was hailed as a fantastic success by all in attendance. Several hundred lesbians participated or worked behind the scenes. Unlike other, more mainstream conferences, here they had the opportunity to meet with other lesbians of color in a context where they were not the minority. For once they could simply offer each other support and did not feel obligated to challenge the ideology of the majority of conference attendees. It was a positive, uplifting experience.

The success of the first conference encouraged the group to continue working, with the aim of producing future conferences. Formalized as the Bay Area Lesbians of Color (BALOC), the group would sponsor two more conferences, in 1987 and 1988. The 1987 conference, titled "Coming Out and Coming Home," resulted in the establishment of Nia, a Black lesbian social organization that continued to hold retreats for the next decade. Several other social networks, including Asian and Pacific Islander Lesbians, Latina Lesbians, and Arab Lesbians, would also form from contacts made at these conferences.

The third conference was titled "Perseverance: Creating Our Place and Gaining Ground." Regina and Carmen Vasquez opened the conference, with keynote speaker Andrea Canaan. An evening cultural program featured poetry by Andrea and by Cherrie Moraga. Over twenty workshops were held on topics like "Politics as a Matter of Survival," "Homophobia and Racism," "Disabilities, Images and Attitude," and "Those Who Carry Manchildren from the Womb." These two conferences were also held at The Women's Building, with staff resources devoted to the organizing work. The Building's lesbian credentials and its base in the gay community were stronger than ever.

Dynamics of Color Conference

In planning for the 1989 conference, some of the women from BALOC approached a group of white lesbians, some affiliated with Lesbian Agenda for Action (LAFA), to produce the "Dynamics of Color," a conference on racism for the entire lesbian community. After several delays, it was held in November of 1989. LAFA had been formed in 1987 as a multiracial lesbian political action group, an alternative to the Democratic Party club system. The Alice B. Toklas Club and the Harvey Milk Club were the two official Democratic Party clubs representing gay men and lesbians, but men dominated the leadership and lesbian issues often were overlooked. To its credit, however, the Harvey Milk Club had been holding its meetings at The Women's Building in a show of support since the early eighties. Some of the work LAFA did was modeled after these clubs, particularly in its approach to electoral politics. However, its umbrella was wide enough to involve women interested in non-electoral organizing. In 1989, an off-year for elections in San Francisco, much of the energy of its members was put into the organizing of the "Dynamics of Color" conference.

LAFA had an office on the third floor of the Building, and many of the organizing meetings for the "Dynamics of Color" conference were held there. The conference itself was held a block up the street at Mission High School. Unlike the lesbian of color conferences, this conference was not a direct project of The Women's Building. The Building did adopt the conference as a sponsored project, providing administrative back-up, but beyond that no staff time was dedicated to the organizing. Jean Crosby, still on staff as the bookkeeper, stepped up to take a major volunteer role in the organizing, becoming one of the three chairs.

After eighteen months of planning, over one thousand lesbians attended the conference, held in November 1989. Nearly a hundred women were actively involved in organizing various aspects of this conference. It was postponed twice because practical logistics were often set aside to deal with racial dynamics that occurred within various subcommittees, or because work was delayed while a balanced racial composition within committees was established. Particular care was taken to make the event fully accessible, for the hearing and sight impaired as well as for women with mobility problems. There was an acknowledgement of the growing problem of environmental illnesses, and efforts were taken to limit scents. The program for the conference, including numerous paid ads collected to help pay for cost of the conference, was a thirty-two-page booklet.

The conference was almost canceled entirely in the wake of the

October 17, 1989, Loma Prieta earthquake. Fortunately, the conference was not being held at The Women's Building, which sustained more damage than Mission High School, where the conference was held. Still, it was an anguishing week or so while all public buildings throughout the city were cleared for use. After several weeks of aftershock tremors and widespread uncertainty, the conference did go ahead. The energy of the gathering was clearly impacted by the earthquake, with more than one woman quite nervous about being inside a large building.

As a conference, "Dynamics of Color" was very successful. Literally dozens of workshops and affinity group meetings kept women running nonstop, most going fairly smoothly despite the larger than expected turnout. With a crowd already edgy because of the earthquake, the dozens of women assigned to monitor dynamics within various settings were kept busy identifying and defusing conflict. The commitment to education prevailed, however, and most left the two-day gathering with a sense of personal growth and belief in the power of women united. Most of the organizers also learned a lot through bringing the conference to fruition, but were fully exhausted by the experience.

The cause of their fatigue was more profound than just the hard work of bringing the conference to a close. When the main organizers reconvened a few weeks later to assess where to go next, it was clear that those at the center of the organizing were seriously burned out and unable and unwilling to take on anything else for at least the near future. BALOC had forgone its 1989 Lesbian of Color conference in lieu of building the "Dynamics of Color" conference, and though the personal ties built endured, as did some of the networks spawned by the conferences,[27] the group itself did not. Some members of LAFA less engaged in the conference organizing carried on with the electoral aspect of its work for a few years, but it too folded, with most of its remaining members affiliating with the Harvey Milk Club.

---

27   One project that did emerge from the conference to carry on for the next fifteen years was Lesbian Visual Artists.

International Women's Day

Internationalism was present from the early days of the SFWC, and the tradition became even stronger once the Building was purchased. The core collective included a number of immigrant women, and some of its white members had been in the Peace Corps in Africa, making internationalism a natural perspective. These politics were woven into all the political work of the Building, including the sponsorship of projects like the Middle East Cultural and Educational Foundation, Venceremos Brigade, and Women for a Nuclear Free Future. Support for these projects was also one of the ways that collective members could concretely see the political benefits of owning a building.

The most explicit and consistent expression of internationalism was through the participation in annual celebrations of International Women's Day, celebrated on March 8 around the world. The date honors women textile workers in the United States who stood up for their rights in 1908, but it is not a widely recognized holiday in the United States. At the time it was primarily celebrated in the socialist world. Even the women's movements in capitalist-based European nations commemorated the date more than the U.S. women's movement did. The fact that the SFWC was even aware of the significance of the date set it to the left of the mainstream U.S. women's movement. The first celebration of International Women's Day at The Women's Building was held on March 8, 1980. The program was a dance and celebration of the first year in the Building.

Celebrating International Women's Day had been a central part of the work of the Third World Women's Alliance. The Alliance carried this tradition on after its transformation, with most of its programs during the 1980s held at The Women's Building. Each year, the Alliance Against Women's Oppression assigned some of its own members and recruited other women to a Committee to Celebrate International Women's Day. Members of the Women's Building collective often participated in this committee, and most attended the events.

No matter how simple or elaborate the event being planned, the work usually wore the organizing committee to a frazzle. With an early March date for the event, initial planning needed to start before the winter holidays, and most of the actual work got done in the first eight weeks of the year. The programs were always well attended and generated a euphoria that kept organizers going in a decade when most of the political news was bad or worse.

Regardless of format, all the activities focused on the key domestic and international issue of that year, offering an assessment of the current status of women. With Ronald Reagan in the White House for most of the eighties, the domestic themes didn't vary much: defense of reproductive rights, defense of lesbians and gay men, and opposition to cuts in social services that hit women and children particularly hard.

Generally, the domestic commentary wasn't controversial, though part of the style of the Alliance Against Women's Oppression, reflecting its ties to the Leninist left, was to pose its argument as a polemic with other allies. A prime example of this was the criticism of the phrase "feminization of poverty." The liberal wing of the women's movement coined this phrase in response to the increasing impact of the cuts in social services that were at the core of Reaganomics. The Alliance pointed out that this analysis basically ignored the fact that poverty had long been racialized in the United States, and while more white women were now impacted, women of color were hit even harder.

A related point of controversy on domestic issues was the 1984 International Women's Day program identifying Jesse Jackson's Rainbow Coalition as the best agenda for women's rights in the coming presidential election. This was also the year that many women activists in the Democratic Party were pressing hard for a woman to fill the second spot on the ticket. A gender gap in voting patterns was for the first time a significant factor, with female support of Reagan at 52 percent versus 63 percent among men. For the first time in its history, NOW made a presidential endorsement, backing Walter Mondale. They made this endorsement very early in the election season, which was seen by many women of color as a rejection of the Jackson campaign. For some women, backing Jackson, who they believed had no chance of winning the nomination, was seen as detracting from their effort to take a seat with the big boys. Many of these women did not acknowledge that a majority of white women were still voting Republican, tacitly supporting policies that hurt poor women and women of color.

For the Alliance Against Women's Oppression and The Women's Building, the color line was very clear. For them, Jackson was the only candidate who articulated and defended the political interests of poor women and women of color, those most impacted by Reagan's policies. Poor women and women of color, therefore, should be the strongest base of support for the Democratic Party, and the candidate should appeal to them. Those who were supporting Mondale were selling out.

Central America

The first several years of International Women's Day events at The Women's Building were very long and packed evening events including music, dance, poetry, speeches, and presentations from the kids who had been in child care for the day while their moms set up for the event. In 1985, a more ambitious plan was conceived—a two-day conference held at nearby Mission High School, with child care and other logistical support from The Women's Building. Titled Somos Hermanas: A West Coast Conference of Women in Central America, the event was meant to build on a campaign launched in 1984 by the Alliance Against Women's Oppression.

The purpose of Somos Hermanas (We Are Sisters) was to convene multiracial groups of women from around the country who would visit with women in Nicaragua and El Salvador and then come home and build support for them and opposition to U.S. policies. The first day of the gathering was a successful educational effort, with workshops addressing conditions of women in Central America, South Africa, and here in the United States. The second day, meant to launch a new group, was less successful.

Somos Hermanas would continue for several more years as a Bay

Area–based project, and delegations were sent to Central America in 1985, 1986, and 1987. Political ties were made with two organizations, the Asociación de Mujeres Nicaraguenses Luisa Amanda Espinoza (AMNLAE) and Asociación de Mujeres de El Salvador (AMES), both affiliated with revolutionary parties in their respective countries.

One of the major international issues of the 1980s was the undeclared U.S. war against revolutionaries in Central America. The victory of the Sandinistas in Nicaragua and the similar challenges by revolutionaries in El Salvador alarmed the Reagan administration. Because the administration was still hampered by the fallout from the U.S. defeat in Vietnam, its strategy was to quietly arm the contras in their effort to overthrow the Sandinistas and to send aid to dictators battling popular revolts and training death squads to unleash terror on the people. The Mission District was directly impacted by the wars in Central America, as refugees headed north often found their new home there. Nor did the intimidation end at the borders, as immigrant organizers were often targeted for harassment.

As a supporter of Central American revolutionary efforts, The Women's Building was also a target. The Building was broken into during the early morning hours of March 11, 1987. Files were rifled, photographs and computers were stolen, and a small amount of money, less than fifty dollars, was taken. Around the same time, other Central American solidarity organizations also had their offices broken into. Of course, there wasn't much of an investigation by the police department but The Women's Building held a press conference to publicize the incident. Several news outlets, including daily and weekly newspapers, reported on the break-ins as political in nature and in the context of similar break-ins at offices of other organizations, both in the Bay Area and nationally.

With its home in the Mission District and many Latinas on its staff or as close supporters, it was only natural that The Women's Building was one of the centers for Central American solidarity work. The participation of Women's Building collective members on trips to Central America helped them develop ties with women around the world.

One very visible reflection of this solidarity is the portrait of Rigoberta Menchú that appears so prominently on the mural now covering The Women's Building.

The UN Decade of Women

The United Nations declared 1975 the "Year of the Woman" and convened an international gathering in Mexico City to assess the state of the women. This gathering launched the Decade of Women, to culminate in 1985 with a worldwide assessment of the current status of women and goals for improving that position. In 1977, the U.S. government convened a conference in Houston to develop an action plan for women in the United States.

The SFWC worked with others throughout California to send a delegation of women from the Bay Area, raising funds to enable women to make video recordings of the gathering. A number of women from the right wing, such as Phyliss Schlafly and Anita Bryant, were planning to attend, and even support of the Equal Rights Amendment (ERA), still a live issue in 1975, was challenged. The progressive coalition that included the SFWC supported the ERA, reproductive rights (including support for abortion on demand and an end to forced sterilizations), gay rights, better access to child care, and equal employment and education opportunities.

The Decade of Women culminated at a conference held in Nairobi, Kenya, in August 1985. The official U.S. delegation consisted of twenty-nine women led by the president's daughter, Maureen Reagan, whose politics were far to the right of those of most in the U.S. women's movement. Pressure from mainstream women's organizations had resulted in an expansion of the initial delegation of twenty, adding some depth and color. But many remained skeptical that the true interests of women in the United States would be represented in Nairobi. In a world still defined by cold war politics, all international gatherings were viewed as an opportunity to put a check on any upstarts from around the world that challenged U.S. hegemony.

Many feared that the priorities that might actually improve the status of women would be lost in the midst of this posturing.

This two-week gathering was certainly fraught with controversy. However, in the end the U.S. delegation did sign onto the final document, "Forward Looking Strategies for the Advancement of Women." This success came only after the delegation voted against the wording of three sections from the document's introduction: (1) placing blame on the developed nations for refusing to redistribute their wealth, (2) a call for economic sanctions against apartheid South Africa, and (3) criticism of Israel for its continuing occupation of the West Bank. In response to this last issue, the official U.S. delegation initially walked out of the convention, declaring that the issue of Zionism was outside the purview of a conference on women's issues. After acrimonious debate, the wording equating Zionism with racism was eliminated from the document. For Maureen Reagan, keeping the word "Zionism" out of the document was a significant victory, making it possible for the delegation to sign the document.[28]

While the official delegates were meeting to approve the official document, a parallel conference composed of members of nongovernmental organizations (NGOs) was also convened. Forum 85, as it was called, involved more that thirteen thousand participants from around the world, including two thousand from the United States. Participation in this part of the Nairobi gathering was self-selected;

---

28 Ten years earlier, in 1975, international forces supporting the Palestinian struggle for self-determination had put forth a resolution equating Zionism with racism, which the UN General Assembly passed as Resolution 3379, determining that Zionism was a form of racism and racial discrimination. The United States, among others, would certainly have vetoed such a resolution within the more powerful UN Security Council, but in the General Assembly, the resolution was approved by a vote of 72 to 35, with 32 abstentions. In nearly every subsequent large gathering sponsored by the UN, this issue was brought to the fore and efforts were made to add the language to official documents. More often than not, these efforts were enough to prevent the United States and other "first world" nations from signing onto final documents. The Nairobi conference was one of the first to work past this controversy and find language acceptable to all. In 1991, the UN would pass a second resolution, number 4686, revoking Resolution 3379.

whoever could get there was welcome. Women from all over the country, both as individuals and representing local and national organizations, made their way to Nairobi. A Peace Tent was erected in the mall at the University of Nairobi, and for two weeks it was the focal point of nonstop dialogue, education, and performance.

Given the expense of traveling to Africa for two weeks, $2,000 at a minimum and often much more, most of the women from the United States were white and had at least some financial security. Most were to the left of the official U.S. delegation, but beyond that reflected a wide range of political perspectives.

The Alliance Against Women's Oppression made an effort to get radical women's voices, and particularly the voices of women of color, to the conference. Money was raised to send a multiracial delegation of women from around the country, with most of the participants from the Bay Area and New York. Roma Guy, who had attended the 1977 conference in Houston, raised her own fare to attend as a representative of The Women's Building, and several other current or past members of the Women's Building collective also attended the conference. While in Nairobi, the model of The Women's Building as a community was shared with women from around the world.

Here at home, the Building was used to build support for the effort, hosting press conferences and programs both before and after the gathering in Nairobi. By the mid-80s, the Building collective had recognized that its primary contribution to the movement was operating the Building. These conference-related events helped to keep this role clear in their minds. The radical policies and perspectives that they stood for helped to alleviate concerns that they were somehow selling out their politics by owning property.

In 1986, the gathering was brought home at the International Women's Day event cosponsored by The Women's Building and the Alliance Against Women's Oppression. A one-day conference titled After Nairobi: Forward Looking Strategies included dozens of workshops and panels looking at many of the issues that had been addressed in Nairobi. The morning sessions were held at the nearby

Instituto Laboral de la Raza. The afternoon and evening parts of the program were held at The Women's Building. The one-day gathering mirrored more than the content of Forum 85; it packed enough activity into a sixteen-hour day to reflect the frenzied pace of nearly nonstop activity that had characterized the two weeks in Nairobi.

International women's issues weren't new to the U.S. women's movement, particularly among the more radical sectors and among women of color and immigrant women. But for the movement as a whole, the year of activities surrounding the Nairobi gathering raised the debate around women's equality to a new level. Any argument that women in the United States were coming close to equality was increasingly undercut by a recognition that around the world, women continued to bear a heavy burden in supporting society while being denied many basic legal and social rights enjoyed by men, and often facing cruel, inhumane attacks just because of their gender (e.g., genital mutilation, bride sacrifice, and unrestrained domestic violence). For a movement that had foundered in a failed attempt to pass the ERA, the year gave women fresh impetus to pursue new avenues in promoting women's equality.

Jewish Feminism, Zionism, and Palestine

The most controversial issues in Nairobi were those arising from the politics of the Middle East. Debate over the questions of Israel, Zionism, and Palestinians wasn't new, and the issue arose in many movements and communities. However, it took on a particular form within the progressive wing of the U.S. women's movement.

In the early 1970s, Jewish feminists issued a challenge: to change sexist aspects of the Jewish religion, including the right of women to bear witness, to initiate divorce proceedings, to be counted as part of the *minyan* (the quorum required for worship to take place), and to move into leadership positions. Over the decade this movement expanded across the country, and through both Reformed and Orthodox strains of Judaism. One clear result of this movement was the decision in 1983 by the Jewish Theological Seminary, one of the premiere educational institutions of Reform Judaism, to open its rabbinical school to women.

Outside the synagogue, Jewish women also gathered within their local communities, in both secular and religious contexts, to further this reform. Many a Seder was held with the wording of the story changed to reflect feminist perspectives. At women's conferences, from women's studies gatherings to conferences of political organizations such as NOW and the Reproductive Rights National Network, Jewish women caucused as a group and brought resolutions back to the full bodies.

In 1982, Bay Area Jewish feminists began planning for a major conference. By this time, many of the gatherings of Jewish women were dominated by concerns over religious issues, often from more conservative Orthodox women. Many feared that more radical perspectives and secular issues were being lost. The goal for this conference, supported by The Women's Building, was an explicitly progressive gathering of Jewish women, and their allies, to address the wide range of issues affecting Jewish women and to discuss how to mobilize Jewish women in support of other progressive issues.

By the time of the conference, Middle East issues had taken the front page, and this impacted the tenor of the conference. In June 1982, Israel invaded southern Lebanon, where the Palestine Liberation Organization (PLO) had its base at the time. The immediate cause of the invasion was an assassination attempt on the Israeli ambassador to the United Kingdom, Shlomo Argov. In many ways, however, this push by Israel was just the next step in the push/pull relations with Israel's Arab neighbors. The original source of the dynamics lay with the 1947 UN partition of the Middle East that had established the Israeli state in the first place. But in more recent history, long-simmering hostility first broke into active war in 1967, when Israel launched its Six Day War against Egypt, Syria, Jordan, and Iraq. At the end of the engagement, Israel expanded its borders to include Gaza, the West Bank, the Golan Heights, and parts of the Sinai Peninsula. Six years later, on Yom Kippur, Egypt and Syria struck back, and initially won victories reclaiming territory in the Golan Heights and Sinai Peninsula. This second round is what led to the U.S.-led Camp David talks, out of which Egypt officially recognized Israel's right to exist, the first Arab nation to do so since the 1947 partition was set in place.

Though Middle East politics remained volatile, by the eighties tension with other Arab countries had lessened, while tension around the issue of Palestinians originally displaced by the 1947 partition moved center stage. The PLO emerged as the principal representative of Palestinians, many living as refugees in Lebanon or Jordan, or living as second-class citizens within the expanded borders of Israel in Gaza and the West Bank. There was growing international support for Palestinians, with an internal debate over strategy: should the demand be a single, secular nation to replace the Jewish state of Israel, or should the goal be to accept Israel as is and carve out a second, Palestinian state? By the end of the eighties, most, including the PLO, were supporting the latter, known as the two-state solution. To this day, what exactly that means and how to set the states up remains a burning question for both Israelis and Palestinians, and for all who want to see peace in the Middle East.

In the United States, the women's movement was also deeply divided over the Israeli-Palestine debate. To some, Zionism was equivalent to racism; to others, opposition to Zionism or Israel was equal to anti-Semitism. Clouded over by the debate was the broader question of how war and militarism were women's issues.

The first Bay Area Jewish Feminist Conference was held Memorial Day weekend, 1982, just a week before Israel went into southern Lebanon. The Women's Building endorsed the conference and some of the planning meetings were held at the Building, but the conference itself was held at nearby Evert Middle School. Over seven hundred Jewish women and two hundred allies attended the three-day conference. Saturday and Monday were limited to Jewish women; the Sunday session was open to allies. There were dozens of workshops, as well as panel presentations to the group as a whole. Predictably, issues around Israel, Zionism, and Palestine were the most contentious. A spirit of harmony ruled, however, and much of the debate was more about educating each other and learning about different perspectives.

The June 1982 invasion of Lebanon gave new spark to support for the PLO, internationally and in the United States, where support of Israel had traditionally been almost a requirement for national politicians. Sympathy for the plight of Palestinians grew even stronger several months later. In September 1982, hundreds of Palestinian refugees in camps at Sabra and Shatila, just outside of Beirut, were massacred, including many women, children, and elderly. The actual attacks were carried out by pro-Israeli Lebanese Christian militias in furtherance of their efforts to topple the current Lebanese government. While Israel denied that its soldiers played a role in the massacres or were even aware of the killings, the Israeli military was responsible for the security of the camps and soldiers were physically surrounding the camps at the time of the attacks.

During the summer of 1982, The Women's Building joined with the Alliance Against Women's Oppression to sponsor a community forum to address the Lebanon invasion. Though careful not to directly oppose the right of Israel to exist, the panelists did challenge the premise of Zionism as the basis of a democratic society. Just the fact of questioning Israel's action was enough to draw fire from some Jewish feminists, who charged The Women's Building with anti-Semitism.

The Middle East was also one of the topics that the collective took on as part of its internal educational work. On more than one occasion, The Women's Building received letters from supporters angry that a platform for Palestinian views was provided at various International Women's Day events or at other events held at building.[29]

Meanwhile, the high from the success of the first Bay Area Jewish

---

29 These same issues were still being raised decades later, at a 2005 International Women's Day program organized by a Mission District youth organization and held at the Building.

Feminist Conference kept some of the organizers together to organize a second conference. The conference was held in the East Bay, and The Women's Building had no significant role in it.

Part one of the conference was convened in September 1983 and was for Jewish women only. It was followed a month later by part two, open to non-Jewish allies. The goals of the gathering were to share cultures, to explore commonalities and differences among Jewish and non-Jewish women, and to promote dialogue about racism and anti-Semitism. The attendance this time around was far less, and though progressive Jewish women continued to organize in various forms, this was the last major public conference of Jewish feminists in the Bay Area.

While conferences are a more passive means of organizing than mass mobilizations, street actions, or other lobbying campaigns, they did have an important role in keeping alive the sense of a movement. For The Women's Building collective, conferences offered a concrete way for the collective to make a contribution to the movement. The euphoria generated by the actual events was great in the short run, but in the months between gatherings, the collective needed steady reminders that the daily mundane work of renovation and building maintenance could have political ramifications. By the choices they made about which conferences to support, and which communities to highlight in the programs, the women of The Women's Building were able to keep alive their radical political perspective.

CHAPTER 9

RE-VISIONING THE ORGANIZATION

IN 1989, TEN years after the purchase of the Building and twenty years since the inception of the San Francisco Women's Centers (SFWC), American society had undergone enormous changes. Though still far from equal, women had made important advances in legal and economic rights. Societal attitudes had shifted with the aging of the baby boomers and the emergence into adulthood of young people, brought up with new attitudes and less tolerant of racism and sexism.

The U.S. economy was continuing to prosper, but the distribution of its wealth was becoming less equitable. The collapse of the socialist economic order gave capitalism free range as the only economic system. Politically, the entire spectrum had shifted to the right. When Bill Clinton was elected in 1992, he represented a centrist Democratic Party with a platform less progressive than that of Nixon-era Republicans. The first Gulf War was clear proof that the United States was still playing the role of international bully in support of big business.

Radical movements continued, but they were very marginalized and lacked any clear alternative program to capitalism. Progressive struggle was no longer about replacing the economic system. The goal now was to try to rein in the worst excesses of greed and to improve the quality of life for all. After all, the collapse of socialism didn't mean the capitalist system was suddenly taking care of the rights of poor women or women of color.

The SFWC still considered itself part of a progressive tradition, even as it went through the transformation from a volunteer collective to a more traditional nonprofit organization with a paid staff and volunteer board. While clear organizational distinctions were being drawn between the board and the staff, they still had shared political perspectives. Part of this perspective was a commitment to collective and cooperative work style, despite the establishment of formal hierarchies of power. The transformation was a rocky process that would take a couple years to fully unfold, but by the start of the 1990s, a distinct board and staff were functioning.

The Loma Prieta earthquake had raised a whole new set of issues about what the future building would look like, providing an immediate challenge to the new organizational structure. Even though the actual short-term damage to the Building was relatively minor, the required retrofit was a significant cost, even if the cheapest (and ugliest) route of bolstering the structure was taken. Ten years earlier, women had the vision to buy the Building and made it happen. Now new visionaries were needed to imagine what new shape it could take in the course of the retrofit and to make the new dream come true.

Evolution to an Executive Director

The first several years under the new, more traditional nonprofit structure was as tumultuous as the first year in the Building. In a traditional structure, the board takes responsibility for broad policy and legal governance and hires the executive director. The executive director is accountable to the board and hires the rest of the staff. The daily work of the organization is undertaken by the staff. In the first couple of years, these lines were often crossed, even to the point where Regina Gabrielle was both executive director and a full member of the board of directors. Regina recalls:

We did a wage survey, because at that time, everybody who was in the collective, regardless of their skill and regardless of their seniority at the building, we were all paid the same wage, like $8.50 an hour, or $6.50 an hour or something ridiculous. We were all paid the same because we were collective. I don't know, we started discussing that maybe we needed to have wage differentials if we are really going to break away from being a collective ... so Holly and I investigated different nonprofits with similar budgets, similar mission and staffing patterns, what people are getting paid. We did ... the management centers wage survey. It was fun. So that was in 1989, [when] we were ready to do this and implement the budget.

Oh, and in the meantime, the building had gotten itself together in terms of recruiting a Board of Directors that was committed to seeing through this period, and really getting the building on track. And being more in line with what a nonprofit should be, without losing the mission.

That was a great first board. Wild. We were wild. So we had two seats that were staff seats, and it was the director, me, and Holly, the fundraiser. And then the rest were volunteers. Carmen was on the board, Carmen Vasquez; Diane Jones was on the board. Hilary Crosby was on the board, she was our treasurer. Smokey Rivera, she was on the board. She was a merchant. She owned a restaurant. Very diverse women. Leni Marin joined the board from the Family Alliance Project. So we had a Filipina woman, a Puerto Rico woman, white women.

I don't want to leave anyone out [Author's note: The other board members were Norma del Rio, Lily Wu, and Judith Klain], but what I'm letting you know is that it was a good mix and everybody had their hearts in the right places. It was dramatic. We did a lot of good work. And it was frustrating, because we were trying to do something that none of us were really seasoned at doing. We were seasoned organizers, we were seasoned activists, but none of us really knew what the fuck we were doing with the board and running an agency. But we gave it our best shot. That was the year that the building made its transition from the collective to administration, and when Holly became development director, I became the director of administration.

Then a couple of years later, my position evolved, in a really bizarre way, to the executive director. I did that for a year with a new board.

Regina was promoted, somewhat reluctantly, into the position of executive director. She was taking classes to learn how to do the job, while getting most of her training on the job. In the meantime, the board membership changed and new members were recruited to be part of a traditional nonprofit board. They were ready to go forward with the new vision of The Women's Building for the twenty-first century, and they set their expectations high.

Regina made significant contributions to the work of The Women's Building during the 1980s and 1990s. It was her work with the Lesbians of Color conference and other lesbian programming that led to the establishment of the Lavender Youth Recreation and Information Center (LYRIC), one of the more significant sponsored projects of the 1990s. She also held the first meetings with the Federal Emergency Management Agency (FEMA) to begin the retrofit process and to keep the Building opened in the meantime.

In the transition to the more traditional nonprofit structure, the executive director was kept as a voting member of the Board of Directors. In addition, the finance director attended board meetings, though not with voting privileges. The goal was to ensure that the voice of the staff continued to be heard in setting the direction of the organization. But the blurring of lines of responsibility made it hard to establish accountability. Regina tried to make sense of what her job was and how to make the best use of the board. But it wasn't easy. Regina resigned abruptly in late August of 1992. "After a year of fighting with them [the board], and just a year of hell, as Roma put it, I left. I left actually quite abruptly and with a lot of anger just broke down. The board when I resigned was a different board."

Regina's resignation came in the wake of an evaluation process from the Board of Directors. In late 1991, she had met with the board to ask for a better definition of her role as executive director and that of the board of directors. Six months later, the evaluation process led to her sudden resignation. In her resignation letter, she noted, "We've all conceded that it was a mistake to create the position of executive director without clearly defining the role and nature of the relationship between the Board of Directors and executive director. This collective failure made it impossible to empower either the executive director or the Board of Directors."[30]

Maturing the Board of Directors

In the wake of Regina's departure, the bylaws were changed to eliminate the voting power of the executive director.[31] But this was just one aspect of the board growing into its own role and responsibility. Though the formal board included numerous women with professional experience, all of them still came to this from a basic progressive or radical perspective. But the group was still a long way from figuring out exactly what its role within The Women's Building should be. Many of its monthly meetings devoted time to trying to figure it out.

When Regina left, Marta Ames was promoted from financial coordinator to become the acting executive director. The executive director was responsible for staff management, financials, bookings, information and referral, and fund raising for general operations, including the crafts fair. The rest of the staff included Shoshana Rosenberg, the renovations manager, Deborah Miller, the bookings coordinator, Teresa Mejia, information and referral coordinator, Kim Lau, program coordinator, Alicia Sisca, building coordinator, Suzanne Peck membership coordinator, and Deborah Castro, the crafts fair coordinator. Shelly Stortz worked on a

30 Regina Gabrielle's resignation letter. GLBTHS, WBA, collection 3, series 1, subseries 2, box 2, file 19.
31 The Board of Directors at the time consisted of Norma del Rio, Sally Hershey, Diane Jones, Jeanette Lazam, Leticia Pena, Moli Steinert, and Deborah Whitman.

consulting basis to handle the Building's accounting. Roma Guy was working to raise the money for the final mortgage payment.

By late 1992, the board was looking to broaden its membership in anticipation of launching the capital campaign for the retrofit project. One of the women they looked to was Cynthia Gissler, a volunteer who had been attracted to the Building because of her appreciation, as a capitalist, of what it took to purchase a building. She was the first self-identified capitalist to join the board.

Cynthia had first volunteered at the Building while Regina was still executive director. She had an undergraduate degree in finance and international business and worked for three years for the Bank of America before going off to get a master's degree in Public Policy with an emphasis on Women's Studies. After returning to San Francisco and working in high-tech, she began looking for somewhere to donate or volunteer her skills. She stumbled upon The Women's Building, was immediately fascinated, and offered her financial expertise.

In early 1993, the Board of Directors completed its first outside search for an executive director. There were two candidates the board particularly liked. One told them during her interview that some of the things they wanted her to do could be done, but that others would require a more mature organization and could not yet be done. The other woman, Josefina Velazquez, agreed that she could do everything the board was suggesting. In January 1993 she was hired. In retrospect, hiring her was a mistake made by a board still coming to grips with what was possible.

This was about the same time Cynthia was invited to join the board, where she would serve throughout the entire renovations process. She remembers how some of those board meetings went:

> The board meetings should have been two-hour sessions. But they became hideously long meetings that would run for hours and hours and hours and involved a lot of issues that really weren't the issues at hand. But in that setting they were allowed to be the issues at hand.

If you take any other organization that has an established pattern, a corporate environment, then there are books, there are patterns, there are systems, and people kind of fall back on that system. If you take an academic environment, there is a huge bureaucratic structure and people follow the system. But you had this brilliant feminist radical organization saying, "We don't want to do all those things and yet we want to have a board, we want to have a staff and executive director."

And so we went through this painful process of trying to figure out governance issues. They believe very much in consensus, and consensus is good at times. Consensus could also result in no one being personally responsible. ...

Another thing that would happen was issues were brought to the board that never should have been brought to the board. For example, the Women's Foundation went through some incredibly significant evolutions. It was incredibly painful for many people who were board members and staff there. At one point somebody tried to bring in the board of The Women's Building, like the board was supposed to step in and play a heavy and somehow influence the Women's Foundation. And though I'm sure we all had our own personal opinions we had no jurisdiction to influence the Women's Foundation. They were simply a tenant of the building. Now politically maybe it would have made sense for staff members to come in to individual board members who had weight with individual foundation members, behind-the-scenes. [But] it was actually put on the agenda.

The crafts show was another example. ... [We had to work] to be clear about governance, because sometimes the board had a tendency to micromanage the staff and that's a really bad thing. So we had to say, "This is our purview, this is what we need to do." It took the entire nine years I was on the board to get to that place.

Another holdover practice from the collective days that lengthened the meetings and would come back to haunt the organization later was the keeping of the minutes for the board meetings. In the collective days, the role of the minutes had been to provide a complete record of what occurred at meetings. They served as the memory for the collective, with no thought of legal ramifications. As the board began to take its legal role more seriously, reviewing and approving the minutes of the previous meeting was no longer a pro forma event. Time was devoted at every meeting to reading the minutes, and often offering and debating changes before they could be approved.[32]

A Failure of Leadership

As difficult as some of the early challenges in establishing an executive director position had been, they were just a preview of the fireworks that were to come. Josefina's transition into leadership of the Building was tumultuous and would be over by February 1994.

Signs of trouble emerged within weeks. Norma del Rio, a board member for a number of years, had recruited Cynthia to the board. Josefina was opposed to Cynthia's participation for unknown reasons. In the ensuing argument, the responsibility of the board in selecting its members was affirmed, and Cynthia remained a member of the board. However, the nastiness of the argument led Norma to tender her resignation from the board.

Cynthia, unaware of the fight between Norma and Josefina, served on the board as the chair of the Finance Committee. But Josefina's animosity toward her continued to be at play. Cynthia worked closely with Marta Ames in preparing financial reports, and she would press Josefina to provide a budget. But for some reason, possibly having to do with her initial animosity, Josefina was unwilling to share her budget with Cynthia. The first time Cynthia saw it was at a board meeting about a month before the start of the fiscal

---

32 These minutes would become grist for the mill for the lawyers who in 1997 challenged the eviction of the Dovre Club. Board members were caught up in hours of depositions answering questions about what went on at meetings.

year. It was presented as the end result, with the expectation that it would be rubber-stamped.

As the first board member to come with traditional business and finance background, Cynthia was pushing for more professional standards, particularly when it came to managing money. She took her fiscal responsibilities to heart and was unwilling to approve a budget she didn't understand. She was asking some very basic questions about the changes in figures from the previous years. These were the questions that should have been asked in the preparation of the budget, but Josefina was either unable or unwilling to share the rationale behind her budget figures. Instead she reacted as if the questions were hostile and rallied the board to approve the budget.

Cynthia remembers that meeting: "Then at some point they forced a vote to pass the budget, and I'm shocked. And I said, 'I haven't had my questions answered. It's not okay to pass this, this is not an okay process. I need to have these questions answered. And Leticia forced the vote and it passed."

The public confrontation at the board meeting was followed up by a couple more private mediation sessions in which efforts continued to chastise Cynthia for challenging Josefina's authority. Through an emotionally trying experience, Cynthia stood up to the race baiting and guilt tripping, holding firm in her belief that she was standing up for the interests of the organization as a whole. She questioned the charge of racism, but she believed that even if she were racist, her role at The Women's Building was to help with finance, and she knew her questions were appropriate. Instead of quitting the board, she got tough and dug her heels in. She knew the problem was not with her but rather with Josefina and with the way the board was conducting itself and failing to manage the executive director.

Cynthia talked with Norma and learned of the earlier conflict with Josefina. In wake of the first "mediation", Marta resigned as the finance coordinator. Her departure from the staff was another harbinger of things to come.

The difficulties with Josefina went beyond the conflict at the board level. The staff also found her unresponsive to requests for help or direction. Half the time, no one even knew where she was, let alone what she was doing. For a staff that was still learning to work under an executive director structure, her absence as a leader was problematic.

Under the new structure, Josefina was accountable to the board and not to the staff. But it was the staff that was there day to day in dealing with her absences and lack of follow-through on certain campaigns and work. For example, the 1992-93 annual report for the organization was delayed for months; it wasn't published until 1994. This was a critical time in terms of launching the capital campaign for the retrofit project.

Josefina also had poor relationships with many of the women that had been previously active, whether as staff, board members, or volunteers. She seemed to believe that she had been hired with a mandate to remake The Women's Building as a Latina center, and that this effort was hindered by the involvement of the former base of the community. Somehow, in her view, the Latina women, mostly lesbian, who had been around The Women's Building before she arrived didn't count. At the same time, getting the capital campaign off the ground involved reaching out to this former base. A reunion of founders in March 1993 brought hundreds of women back into the active circle of The Women's Building. White lesbians, some of them with disposable income, were certainly part of the circle, and alienating them could sabotage the development of the capital campaign.

Another part of the problem was that Josefina never completely left her other job with PeaceNet, the first progressive Internet service provider. On their behalf, she was still doing consulting work while working full time as the Building's Executive Director. Given the pay scale The Women's Building could afford, it's not surprising that she might feel she needed the money. However, the pay was clear when she was hired and she never raised the issue as a concern, nor did she make it public knowledge that she continued her consulting work.

It didn't take long for frustration to begin to boil up among the staff.

At least partly in response, a plan was made hold a couple of organiza-
tion-wide educational sessions to try to rebuild a sense of unity.

Bringing the Problem to Light

The first session was held in June of 1993, on the topic of race
and class. Josefina was out of the country, on a trip to the Middle East
for PeaceNet, and was not in attendance at the session. An outside
facilitator was brought in, and staff, board members, and volunteers
were all invited. About thirty people were present for a session held
in the Audrey Lorde Room. One of the ground rules for the session
was that there would be no repercussions from anything said in the
course of the evening.

At one point, Elisa Odabasion, recently hired by Josefina to handle the operations financial systems, suggested that the difference
between the pay scales within the staff might reflect racism, as the
white women on staff generally made more money than the women
of color on staff. Salaries were in fact based on the nature of the staff
positions and not on skin color, but the discrepancy still reflected a
common racial dynamic in U.S. society.

A report of Elisa's comment got back to Josefina, apparently from
a board member. Two days later, Josefina fired Kathy. This was done
over the phone because she was still out of the country and had left
no one in charge during her absence. Although she gave other reasons for her decision, many of the women involved in the evening
gathering felt that Elisa's comment at the educational session was the
cause of her termination.

Even though Elisa hadn't been on staff at the Building for long,
everyone on staff was upset on her behalf. And the fact that she'd
formerly had a good relationship with Josefina made them all somewhat nervous about their own status. Some were so upset that they
walked off the job. After a week or so of brouhaha and back and forth
between staff, board, and community members, most staff members
returned to the job. Elisa's termination, however, was final.

Josefina seemed particularly paranoid that her leadership and authority would be challenged by volunteers, who to her represented the old guard. Volunteers were not just the old guard, but an incompetent old guard whose lack of professionalism was a shackle to the growth of The Women's Building.

There wasn't any opposition to strengthening ties to the Latino community by anyone at The Women's Building; in fact it had been the goal to do so since the Building was purchased. Nor was there opposition to broadening the Board of Directors. At issue was whether building a new base would mean giving up the old base. By 1992, the only old guard collective members still centrally active with The Women's Building were Shoshana, heading up the renovations project, Diane Jones, a member of the Renovations Committee, and Roma, who had been drafted to lead the campaign to pay off the mortgage to the Sons of Norway. There was no formal revolt by founders or any attempt to take back control of the organization. On the other hand, no one wanted to see it fail. The retrofit, with its overwhelming $6 million price tag, was looming ever large. No one was against improving the level of professionalism to be able to undertake such a huge project. But disparaging the Building's history didn't go over very well.

The Building seemed to survive the incident over Elisa's dismissal, but the pressures and conflicts continued to boil under the surface. As the year passed, financial issues came back to the forefront as the organization got deeper and deeper in debt. Josefina was using the funds raised to pay off the original mortgage to pay for basic operating expenses.

In fall of 1993, things came to a head once again as relations within the staff reached the breaking point. They brought their concerns directly to board members, putting the board in the position of trying to mediate or to figure out what was really going on. But the board was also in trouble, as several more members had resigned and no new recruits were in the offing. They were also still working to stay within the parameters of their responsibility, which did not include having direct responsibility for the staff. Some of the staff began exploring the option of unionizing, but they soon realized that the small staff and budget of the organization made it unlikely. Rather than continue to work in what was seen as an inhospitable worksite, a number of staff members quit, this time for good.

This raised the level of concern among founding members and other long-time supporters. True or not, many felt that this crisis could force the Building to close because of lack of staff. This in turn would undermine the ability to raise funds for the retrofit. Community members drafted and circulated a letter that challenged the board of The Women's Building to find a resolution. Below are excerpts of that letter, date November 8, 1993:

Dear sisters of the SF WB Board of Directors,

We are writing to you out of deep concern for The Women's Building. Our herstories with The Women's Building are varied, but for all of the signatories, it has been a treasured experience that we still draw from. And we know there are many women of all colors, nationalities, sexualities, and classes who also have an important lifeline with the building. Though some of us are not currently active in our support of the building, all of us have an unyielding commitment to her future.

We want to be absolutely clear that we acknowledge that you, the current Board of Directors, are now the leadership of The Women's Building. We are offering advice and input both as "veterans" and as members of the communities that The Women's Building serves. It's not a step we take lightly, but frankly what we are hearing about events at The Women's Building have seriously alarmed us. To not raise our concerns would be to abdicate our commitment to The Women's Building.

We truly hope that this letter is just the first step of a frank discussion, so we will raise several of the general issues that concern us.

We have heard that the "problems" at The Women's Building are because [of] the old guard of white lesbians, who have been amateurs all these years and/or now won't step back and let women of color take the building to a new level of professionalism. This characterization has several serious distortions in it.

Throughout its history, The Women's Building has struggled over the issue of sustaining a multiracial character, which has meant struggling to understand racism and oppose it in its many manifestations. It's not a done deal yet, and given the world we live in, is unlikely to ever be. And while every crisis has its racist aspects, it's too simple to blame all the problems on racism.

Furthermore, any implication that only white women have had power at The Women's Building flies in the face of reality. We are among the women who have had "power" (though usually [it] felt more like responsibility), and among us are women of color. Please do not deny our experiences and our contributions. The reunion this past March was a graphic display of the multiracial and multicultural experience represented by The Women's Building. We would hope that taking The Women's Building to a new level of development will build upon this historical base, not deny it.

In fact, there is no organized opposition to the transition to a new order. Certainly there is inertia, especially among the broader community of thousands that think of The Women's Building as home but don't have an active relationship to it. Maybe there is controversy over the direction of the restructuring, or the refining of the mission and objectives, but if so not a word of the content of this difference has reached any of us.

Our second area of concern is with the way relations with the staff and volunteers have been handled. It appears that the effort to upgrade the professional level of The Women's Building is being done at the cost of any democratic input by the workers and volunteers. Division of labor and clear lines of accountability can be established without cutting off the voices of the many that help implement policies. For a grass-roots organization, cutting off meaningful participation is slow strangulation. We question the viability of The Women's Building without such a base, and we hope the board is not moving consciously to a structure that eschews its grassroots beginnings. Democracy is never easy in the short run, but it has been key to keeping the building going over the long haul. We believe that this will be true in the future as well.[33]

The letter was signed by Rosa Rivera, Maria Cora, Marta Ames, Holly Fincke, Jeanette Lazam, Patty Chang, Robin Gilbrecht, Sushawn Robb, Diane Jones, Leni Marin, Mickey Rosado, and Norma del Rio.

In addition to those who signed the letter, it was also circulated among another few dozen or so long-term volunteers or former collective members of The Women's Building, including Carmen Vasquez, Jean Crosby, Deborah Castro, Sharon Hewitt, Lily Wu, Carla Rosales, Happy Hyder, Marya Grambs, Wilhelmina Espinoza, Shelly Stortz, Roma Guy, Cecilia Rodriguez, Pam Weatherford, Hilary Crosby, Monica Amoroso, Anne Vanderslice, Molly Steinert, and Virginia Harris. A copy was also sent to Josefina. Though many felt that it was her actions that precipitated the crisis, she was not singled out in the letter.

In response to the community letter, a community meeting of about thirty women was convened at the Building. No action resulted directly from that meeting, but in subsequent private sessions, the board terminated the contract with Josefina.

Cynthia, now the Building's treasurer, recalls the decision:

We fired Josefina. It all happened within a short period of time, because the writing was on the wall, and then it was a long process. I mean, we fired her, and then we had to come up with some agreement and so on and so forth. We fired her; we'd gotten

---

33 Community letter. November 8, 1993. GLBTHS, WBA, collection 3, series 1, box 1, file 14.

rid of this person who wasn't working and was, in my opinion, destructive to the organization. But now we actually had to build a stable staff. The staff was very emotional. They pulled together in the heat of this painful disagreement with Josefina and in essence with the board.

Shoshana Rosenberg, who was then director of the renovation project, was appointed executive director. The staff was rebuilt with a renewed sense of stability. Though the traditional structure of an executive director and a staff was maintained, Shoshana set up an operations team with two other staff members to provide a collective leadership. This was essential in coordinating the general operation of the Building with the retrofit project and helped calm worries that the staff would have no input.

Gradually more board members were recruited. For most of the rest of the decade, the board consisted of eight to ten women. Although Cynthia was the first "capitalist," many of the women recruited over the next ten years came with business and finance backgrounds. They brought skills and insights that were valuable to growing the board and the organization. Generally, politics and society were less radical than they had been in previous decades, but even with the voices of business women, The Women's Building held onto its progressive vision and its internationalist perspective.

CHAPTER 10

RE-VISIONING THE BUILDING

BY 1995, THE staff and board had reached a new level of stability, but they still faced a challenging future. It was six years since the Loma Prieta earthquake and the countdown for the required seismic retrofit was ticking away. The six million dollar price tag was daunting, but there was also growing excitement about what the remodeling would bring. As much as everyone loved the idea of the Building, its physical limitations were becoming clearer and more problematic for staff, tenants and occasional renters. Many sessions had been held to brainstorm about the shape of a new building and the architectural plans were turning those ideas into reality.

Preparing for the Capital Campaign

The first effort to go outside the organization to hire leadership may have ended in disaster, but the organization had enough depth of support to survive. Deciding to forgo another external search, the board appointed Shoshana Rosenberg as Executive Director. Given the challenges the Building was facing, it was an excellent choice. With a background in the women's movement, experience with The Women's Building, and expertise as an electrician familiar with building trades, Shoshana was able to bridge politics with the nuts and bolts of remodeling a building. She formed a leadership team with two other staff members, keeping alive the collective spirit of the organization.

Despite all the stress involved with changing the staff structure, the work did get under way on the capital campaigns, one for the retrofit and the other to finish off the balloon payment on the original mortgage. The mortgage had originally been due in 1990, but with over $300,000 still due at that time, it had been renegotiated to come due in 1993. At that time, $125,000 was still due. It was some of the funds raised for this campaign that were misspent under Josefina Velazquez's tenure. The experience underscored the importance of separating the capital fund from the operating accounts.

The campaign to pay off the mortgage was named "A Room of Our Own." Roma Guy had come back to the Building to lead this campaign, drawing in the support of women who would also be critical to the retrofit campaign. She agreed to do this only if a History Committee was established to set up the archives of The Women's Building, which would be integrated with the Gay, Lesbian, Bisexual, Transgender Historical Society archives. This book could not have been written without these materials.

Meanwhile, the board and staff began organizing the groundwork for an even bigger capital campaign. The cost of the retrofit was estimated at close to $6 million. With FEMA matching funds, that meant the women needed to raise $3 million. It also meant they needed to deal with the time-consuming minutiae of applying to FEMA to establish eligibility for matching funds. Fortunately, they had the financial skills of Cynthia Gissler and Shellie Stortz. They set up the financial systems that made the FEMA report possible and kept it separate from the general operating fund. Cynthia also led the process of getting the Building a low interest line of credit—basically a loan—that would enable them to begin construction by 1998. They did very well at keeping a clear line between the operations of The Women's Building and the funding for the retrofit.

A number of public events were sponsored during the first years of the 1990s to increase the visibility of The Women's Building and begin raising money. These events included the 1993 reunion of women's building "founders," a reading by Susan Griffin from her new book *A Chorus of Stones: The Private Life of War,* the premier of *Dialogues with Madwomen,* a documentary movie by Allie Light and Irving Saraf and Ronnie Gilbert's production of her play *Mother Jones, the Most Dangerous Woman in America.* The Building also had occasional evening fund-raising events honoring different women.

The outside of the building was also transformed. In the early 1980s, a mural had been painted on the outside of the Building. In the nineties, a new mural was planned that would involve hundreds of women. A multiracial collective of seven women were the principal artists of the mural: Yvonne Littleton, Susan Kelk Cervantes, Miranda Bergman, Juana Alicia, Meera Desai, Irene Perez, and Edyth Boone. However, the project was set up in such a way that any community member could come by and lend a hand with the painting. A large street party was held in 1994 to celebrate its completion. Titled *Maestrapeace,* the mural was preserved through the retrofit project, and in 2009 it was extended into the inside of the Building. After years as a sponsored project, the muralists formed their own permanent organization, Maestrapeace Mural Project. They continue to be active as muralists and as teachers, with their works appearing on walls throughout the Bay Area.

Reinforcing the Dream – Raising Capital

Shoshana's term as executive director, though less tumultuous than her predecessors', had its own ups and downs. She had been around the San Francisco Women's Centers (SFWC) since the 1970s, as part of the organizing for the 1976 conference on violence against women. At that time, she was the director of the Women's Center at San Francisco State University. She then went into the trades, becoming an electrician. She donated her company's resources to The Women's Building to provide electricity for the crafts fair in the years it was held at the Building. In this capacity, she came to have

an intimate knowledge of the Building's capacities and structure, making her an ideal choice for leading the organization through the retrofit. She came back on staff in 1991 to coordinate the renovation project.

The first stage of this project was developing a Master Renovation Plan. Over the years, considerable remodeling had been done within the Building, but none of it had been part of a long-term plan. This time it would be different. Extensive surveying and outreach to organizations currently or potentially renting at The Women's Building was conducted to decide how best to remodel the Building to meet the needs of its community. A feasibility study was done by a women-owned architectural firm, Levy Design Partners, which was contracted to see the process through. Some early funds were brought in, in particular to upgrade the Audre Lorde Room on the second floor.

The renovation process itself was complicated, and adding it to the daily operations of the Building made the position of executive director very taxing. For two years, Shoshana juggled all the balls and kept things moving along. Her lack of patience and sometimes gruff way of relating to staff, board, and volunteers made for some difficult meetings and ruffled feathers along the way, but this was also understandable in the circumstances.

She guided the organization's members and volunteers, with the assistance of consultants, through the strategic planning process of envisioning what The Women's Building would look like. Slowly the staff was stabilized and the board became clearer on its role. The groundwork for the capital campaign was under way, with Mary Schmidt hired to direct it

Then, at the end of 1995, Shoshana resigned as executive director for personal reasons. She was looking forward to having a child with her partner. At the same time, there's no question that she was pretty burned out by working with The Women's Building and its cacophony of personal dynamics. Once again, the board was searching for a new executive director.

In 1995, the board again went outside the organization to look for new leadership. They hired Esperanza Macias, a Latina lesbian who had been around San Francisco politics for some time and worked for a Mission District nonprofit, Dolores Street Services. She seemed an ideal fit for The Women's Building. By this time, the designing phase of the retrofit process was nearing an end and it was time to begin putting the contract out for bids. On the money side, however, the process was off to a slower start. It was one thing to put the project out to bid, but for the work to actually begin, most of the money had to be secured.

When Josefina was hired, the expectation was that she would direct the capital campaign, but this proved to be impossible. Even without all of the management drama, it was too much to expect one person to both operate the Building and direct a capital campaign drive. The first step had been hiring Mary Schmidt in 1994. Slowly, the work of the capital campaign started to take shape.

The campaign, named "Reinforce the Dream," was propelled by a leadership committee that by 1997 would include Marta Drury and Ayse Kenmore as the honorary chairs, and members Libby Denebeim, Sofiah Dickerson, Susan Hirsh Simmons, Alina Laguna, Jeanette Lazam, Meghan McVety, Beth Rosales, Vikki Barron, Myra Diaz, Claire Lachance, Christine Olague, Lele Santilli, Deb Montesinos, Mary Schmidt, Lois Shapiro, Andrea Shorter, and Tricia Stapleton.

Fifteen politicians, including Mayor Willie Brown, assembly member Carole Migden, and all the San Francisco supervisors, signed on as campaign ambassadors. Another dozen supporters made up a campaign advisory committee. Everyone on the Board of Directors committed to personally making a significant donation and asking for other donations.

In 1996 Mary left for another job, and two new fundraisers were hired, Rachel Timoner and Gemma del Barrio Cubero. Grant proposals to both public and private foundations were in the pipeline, and individual donations from the broader community were beginning to come in. As of May 1997, $3.8 million had been collected or pledged, as shown in Table 3.

Table 3: Capital Campaign Donations to
The Women's Building Retrofit

SOURCE	AMOUNT
FEMA	$2,650,000
Mayor's Office of Community Development	$583,000
Irvine Foundation	$100,000
Herbst Foundation	$ 75,000
Ayse Kenmore	$ 51,000
San Francisco Foundation	$ 50,000
Phyliss Fried	$ 50,000
Hellman Family Fund	$ 50,000
James Hormel	$ 50,000
Miriam and Peter Haas	$ 40,000
Marta Drury	$ 25,000
Anonymous	$ 25,000
Seven Spring	$ 20,000
San Francisco Arts Commission	$ 13,500
Stalsaft Foundation	$ 10,000
The Women's Building Board	$ 15,000
Reinforce the Dream Leadership Team	$ 9,500
Women's Foundation	$ 8,000
The Women's Building Staff	$ 8,000
TOTAL	$3,833,000

The goal was an additional $1 million from individuals, $600,000 from foundations, and $200,000 from corporations. By 1999, 31 institutions and 129 individuals would donate a combined amount of over $5 million.

With the backing of support letters from dozens of organizations and noted political leaders, the Building was able to negotiate a low-interest $1 million line of credit to cover expenses while the fundraising continued. By the end of the retrofit, the Building would owe about $500,000 on that line of credit. So even though the Building had paid off the initial mortgage, thirty years after the purchase they still owed about the same amount. On the other hand, the value of the Building had increased tenfold.

The retrofit plan was to begin construction in the basement and on the first two floors, with all existing tenants moving to the top two floors. One-time rentals would drop to almost nothing, with the auditorium and the Audre Lorde Room unavailable and the third-floor filled with permanent tenants. San Francisco Women Against

Rape actually moved out of the Building for the duration of the retrofit, concerned about the effect of the construction on the setting for its clients. Most tenants, however, stayed throughout the retrofit construction. The notable exception of course was the Dovre Club. Beyond the money, the bar was the last major obstacle to the renovation.

Dovre Club, Part II

Relations between the Building and the Dovre Club had been in an uneasy truce since the early 1980s. When the club's ten-year lease expired in early 1989, a month-to-month agreement maintained the same rent. Paddy Nolan was aging and had recently been diagnosed with cancer, so neither party had an interest in being tied down by a long lease. However, there was no discussion about changing the relationship. But with the October 1989 earthquake prompting major construction plans, conditions changed. Major retrofit and construction work was bound to affect the physical space of the bar. As the Master Renovation Plan was developed, no voice on behalf of the bar was sought, nor was it heard from.

In the early years of the Building, the collective had been able to come to a compromise that left the bar in place while the organization grew into the rest of the Building. Now, twenty years later, no such compromise was considered in planning the renovation. The staff and volunteer board were all new people, and none had been involved in the original discussions with Nolan.

Not surprisingly, the women never considered maintaining the bar for the long term. Rather, over the years a strong consensus had developed that the Building needed to house a child development center, which would have to be on the ground floor to meet code requirements. In the Master Plan, this child care center would take up the southeast corner of the Building, adjacent to new accessible bathrooms required by law in remodeled buildings. This configuration would cut seriously into the space currently occupied by the

Dovre Club. And there was a silent assumption that the bar would (finally) be evicted, but no one wanted to rush into the battle.

It wasn't until 1996, as actual construction was beginning to loom, that the board began considering what would go into the corner where the bar currently operated. Under the new design, this space would open up into the Building as well as out onto the street. The street entrance could not be made wheelchair accessible without changing the Building's facade, and such a change was prohibited because of the Building's landmark status. So an indoor entrance was necessary. Even were it not, the aim was to bring this space back into the rest of the Building. At that time, the vision of many was that it would be a coffee bar or other small commercial enterprise, possibly run by a youth training program. It would able to generate some income for the Building and provide an informal meeting area, an extension of the lobby.

Starting the Eviction

As fate would have it, Paddy Nolan passed away in November 1996, after a six-year battle with cancer. The board had begun to work out the timing of the eviction during the summer but did not wish to disturb Nolan in the final stages of his life. On the other hand, construction was scheduled to begin the following spring, beginning in the basement and ground floor, effectively occupying the Dovre Club's space.

In December, Esperanza Macias informally notified the Dovre Club manager Brian McEllhatton that construction would begin in April. Formal notice of eviction would be given March 1. With the likes of columnist Warren Hinckle and powerful political consultant Jack Davis as former patrons, the bar was able to generate media coverage about its threatened eviction. Over the next twelve months, this episode was to generate more ink and air time for The Women's Building than any other event in the rest of its entire existence. Much of it portrayed two equally legitimate community centers in a clash, with many calls for compromise.

There was also a lot of concern about alcohol; many identified this as *the* issue. The presence of a higher than average number of bars in the Mission District was already a community issue. A community organizing campaign had demanded and won a moratorium on new bars in the area. These restrictions were one of the obstacles to the solution of relocating the Dovre Club, though with its political clout it was not an insurmountable problem. Esperanza, only recently hired by The Women's Building, had been involved in this effort as an individual and in her work with other nonprofit organizations.

The Women's Building's vision of a community center didn't include a bar, Irish or otherwise, but for the Building it was more about being *for* something else than being against alcohol or drinking establishments. Over the next year, the major media strategy was to try to publicize what The Women's Building was for and what its programs were, and to explain and defend the retrofit plan.

In hindsight, the SFWC made some mistakes, first and foremost in assessing the opposition and therefore their tactics for overcoming it. It was essentially a commercial eviction, and the expectation was that after few months of foot dragging, it would be done and renovation could begin in the summer of 1997, in time to meet city deadlines. The women knew, of course, about the influence of the bar itself, principally through its powerful patrons. Even with Nolan ill and then gone, Davis and Hinckle remained, even though neither were current regulars at the bar. The women underestimated the personal attachment each had to what had been essentially their home away from home during the heydays of their lives. Their opposition was probably inevitable, but the board may have been able to neutralize it better by openly acknowledging their stake and making it part of the renovation planning process. After all, there was other input that was never implemented. For example, the proposals to include a garden café on the rooftop and a darkroom in the basement.

Taking a more conciliatory approach would have undercut an opposition the organization did not foresee: progressives coming to the aid of a beleaguered bar with a history of community support, facing eviction in a city in the throes of crisis over development. For some time, tenant organizations and other progressive groups had been battling the dot.com boom that was changing the face of San Francisco and was just beginning to creep into the Mission. The Dovre Club supporters tapped into this movement, along with the liberal tendency to support the underdog, to give a mass base to their claim that the bar was a community center in its own right. Within days of the first news articles, campaign signs opposing the Dovre eviction appeared on poles throughout the city and in apartment windows in the Mission and Castro districts. Soon, similar signs in support of The Women's Building were put up in response. Petitions were gathered, and the Dovre Club was busier than it had been in years.

In fact, in recent years, the Dovre Club had become a quiet neighborhood bar that probably would have been out of business had it been paying market rents instead of the less than $1/square foot rates that the Building set to keep rates low for its nonprofit tenants. While many community organizations and small businesses were being displaced (read "evicted") through massive rent hikes, mostly unnoticed by the media, The Women's Building never even considered this approach. So here were political forces, tied to the Brown machine that was pushing the dot.com boom, protesting an eviction that would expand community services, yet conveniently silent on evictions pursued in the interests of almighty profit. The real irony of the situation is that progressive voices such as the *Bay Guardian* were supporting the Dovre Club. It worked out quite well for the powers that be to have the eviction issue focus the clash between The Women's Building and the Dovre Club, leaving other commercial eviction stories untold.

As the situation polarized, the Building convened a community meeting on January 30, 1997, partly in response to the call for such a meeting in the *Bay Guardian* but also in accordance with its own traditions. In fact, similar community meetings had already been held in developing the design that now precluded the bar, though none of these meetings were covered by the media, and none were so well attended. Over three hundred people convened, and for three hours, speakers lined both sides of the auditorium to weigh in, most articulately and respectfully as well as passionately.

Some of the support for both viewpoints was clearly orchestrated, but much of the turnout and many of the comments were spontaneous expressions of sentiment. Many called for a compromise. The imperative of the retrofit was explained and the parameters of the new building layout were described. The meeting adjourned on a congenial note, and many from both sides of the debate retired to the Dovre Club for a pint. The meeting helped clear the air and diffused some of the concern, but the clock was still running for the retrofit project to begin. Offers to consider new proposals were made by the board, but none were ever offered up by the new owner, John Cassidy (Nolan's nephew and the executor of his estate) or Brian, the manager of the bar.

Legal proceedings

On March 1, the written eviction notice was delivered, but April

1 came and went with no sign of the Dovre Club preparing to move. Nor did the club come back to the board with any other proposal. With the assistance of a pro bono lawyer, Joe Bravo, The Women's Building took legal action, and court proceedings were begun in April. An initial court date was set for June, but a series of procedural delays by Terry Goggin, the lawyer hired by Jack Davis, delayed the trial until mid-July.

In the meantime, staff and board members found their time taken up in attending depositions held by Goggin, who based his questions on the copious notes from board meetings. These depositions focused on the legitimacy of The Women's Building as a nonprofit and its process in deciding to evict the Dovre Club. Ultimately irrelevant to the legal action, this nonetheless tied up time effectively, as well as wearing down the women's sense of legitimacy.

Presumably, these depositions were to lay the groundwork for the defense, which held that the eviction process violated city law and was therefore invalid. There was also a veiled implication that the SFWC itself was not a legitimate nonprofit because of its failure to follow the law. The other argument the defense was making was that an oral agreement had granted Dovre Club a lease in perpetuity. The trial came to an abrupt end when the defendants claimed that the eviction order had been improperly served, having been addressed to John Cassidy, rather than to the estate of Paddy Nolan. Even though Cassidy was the executor of the estate, the judge seized on the technicality to drop the case, sending The Women's Building back to the start of the eviction process.

Though distracted by the depositions, the Building had continued to organize community support in the months after the community meeting. Statements of support were gathered from tenants, community organizations, service agencies, and prominent individuals. A call-in campaign to the Mayor's Office, launched by the National Organization for Women, overwhelmed his phone lines. In June and July vigils were held outside the Building and the courthouse. Among the supporters of record were supervisors Tom Ammiano, Leslie Katz, and Susan Leal, Assemblywoman Carole Migden, Jesse Jackson of the Rainbow Coalition, Dolores Huerta of the United Farm Workers, and authors Alice Walker, Isabel Allende, and Jewelle Gomez. More than fifty community organizations registered their support.

Most of this support was aimed at supporting the right of the Building to replace the Dovre Club with other services, but there was also a need to defend the Building's right to keep its doors open. With the Dovre Club still in residence, the process of beginning the retrofit construction was delayed. It had already been seven years since the Loma Prieta earthquake, and the city-imposed deadline for the retrofit of unreinforced masonry buildings was closing in.

In July 1997, the Department of Building Inspections sent its Women's Building file to the City Attorney's Office for action. From their point of view, the Building had reached the end of its planning deadline and it was time for actual construction to begin. The effort to obtain permits had begun on a timely basis, but the San Francisco Landmarks Advisory Board had been slow to approve the plans. The deadline to complete the retrofit was November 1997, a deadline that clearly would not be met. By September, The Women's Building received notice from the City Attorney's Office describing what would happen if retrofit construction didn't begin. This included a fine of $500 for each day after the deadline. The only way to avoid the penalty would be to close the doors to the public—including the door to the Dovre Club.

While community forces rallied around the two sides of the conflict and the city bureaucracy and legal fronts moved along in their own fashion, behind the scenes Mayor Willie Brown stepped in to try to force a negotiated settlement. On the one side, he owed favors to both Davis and Hinckle. On the other, support from women was critical to his political future. It was 1997, and the traditional Democratic machine hold on San Francisco politics was just beginning to break down. District elections for supervisors had been approved by voter and were to be in put in place by 1998, leading to a more independent board. Just one year later, Supervisor Ammiano would push Brown into a run-off campaign as a write-in candidate. Davis' role as a political consultant to the 1996 baseball stadium referendum, which had squeaked out a victory in its third time before the public, came under scrutiny in mid-1997. The last thing Brown needed was another controversy keeping Davis in the public eye. So he reached out to founder Roma Guy, presently serving on the city's Health Commission, to try to broker a deal before the issue came back to trial.

True to the form of back-room politics, most of those involved in the negotiations had no actual authority over the disposition of the case. Roma was invited to the meeting, along with Esperanza, as the executive director of The Women's Building, but no other staff or board members were present. John Cassidy, the owner of the bar, was not present, and the Dovre Club interests were presented by Davis. The mayor's main goal for the meeting was to get people into the same room and talking, but he also made it clear that he hoped the two groups could reach a negotiated settlement. The Women's Building goal in the meeting was to clarify the limitations imposed by construction and the new design, and to emphasize the offer to assist in the relocation of the bar.

For the bar's part, Davis made explicit threats to delay permits for the construction project, something that was already happening, even though not directly at his instigation. This was a reiteration of threats already made through the media. Though Brown made no threats of his own, The Women's Building had a proposal for a grant of over $100,000 pending with the Mayor's Office of Community Development, which they were counting on to reach the final goal. Though the Dovre Club presence was a significant delaying factor in signing a contract to begin construction, the Building was also still struggling hard to get the financing in place, and the grant was a significant part of that effort.

Negotiations stalled almost as soon as they began. By the second trial date in early October 1997, The Women's Building had hired a new pair of lawyers, Susan Luten and Martha Caron, to take over from

Joe Bravo.[34] The Dovre Club's position now focused on a supposed superseding oral agreement of permanent tenancy. To support this, they had to dispute the validity of the written lease. This was done by alleging that Paddy Nolan's signature on the lease was a forgery.

In the delay since the July trial, a search of The Women's Building files had uncovered a signed lease between Nolan and the Sons of Norway from 1978, so the Building's lawyers went into the trial fairly confident that they would prevail on the legal issues. But the case did entail paying for expensive handwriting expertise and testimony. But once again the process was derailed.

Several days into the trial, the Judge ordered a mistrial because Martha had asked a witness, Warren Hinckle, if he had been drinking during the lunch recess. He ruled that the question could cause bias against a witness critical to the defense. A date for yet a third trial was set for mid-November. With yet another legal delay, the Building was able get a six-month extension before daily fines would begin.

Effects on the Women of the Building

By now, it had been nearly a year since The Women's Building had begun the eviction process. The staff was seriously overworked, trying to maintain daily operation of the Building and prepare for a major construction project, all the while running a community-based defense campaign. The capital campaign was also moving along, with the media attention a mixed blessing—political support was high and some donations were surely spurred by the battle with the Dovre Club. But for the operations of the Building, the expenses caused by the battle were high: staff time, legal fees, increased security costs. Nor was the publicity good for the process under way to secure the $1 million line of credit from a bank.

Harder to measure was the effect on the unity of the staff and

---

34 What began as an apparently straightforward commercial eviction had become a complicated political skirmish requiring far more time than Joe had expected to give on a pro bono basis.

board. On the one hand, there was a shared progressive unity about the mission of The Women's Building and the end goal. There was less unity about how to get there.

The October staff/board retreat, which had been scheduled with the hope that the eviction would be behind them by then, was dominated by the pending trial. At issue was whether, when, and how to negotiate a settlement versus relying on the outcome of the trial. After the months of legal delays, no one expected a quick result from the courts. The offer in the first round of negotiations to assist with relocation of the bar had gone nowhere. To come back to the table, they needed to offer something new. For the first time, the board gave serious thought to the possibility of the Dovre Club returning in some form after the retrofit. There was always the hope that the new configuration of the Building wouldn't work for the bar, making a new location more acceptable. But they also knew they had to be sincere in efforts to find a compromise.

This position was quite controversial within the board, and was generally opposed by the staff. Emotions ran very high as the debate continued in the days after the retreat. The staff had been consumed by this battle for months, and any solution that left the Dovre Club in place was considered a defeat. But from the board's perspective, winning this battle was meaningless if the delays and subsequent political fallout bankrupted the SFWC and put the whole Building out of business.

This was one of the first serious divisions between staff and the board over political direction. In part, this reflects the inherent difference in responsibilities between a board and a staff. Ultimately, the board is responsible for the fiduciary health of the organization. The staff may have an interest in this, but it is not their immediate concern. But it also reflected the generational differences generally found between the two groups. Most of the board members were of a generation that had fought hard for basic feminist demands. They knew from experience that being morally in the right didn't guarantee victory. In their experiences, battles had been lost and sometimes compromise had been necessary in order to be around for the next battle. Cynthia Gissler, younger than the rest of the board, was the only one on the board who was holding out for the court process to resolve the issue.

Much of the staff was even younger, politicized in the nineties by the cooperative radicalism of the queer movement and anti-war/ youth voice sparked by the Gulf War. For them, compromise was the same as losing. Though they were able to argue their position at the board/staff retreat, ultimately the decision lay with the board. Esperanza was in the unenviable position of upholding a decision unpopular with the staff. As things turned out, none of the various compromise offers ever had to be made.

Resolution at Last

As the third trial began, with jury selection completed, there was a sudden turn in the direction of the case. As it turned out, there was a breakdown within the Dovre Club forces. John Cassidy, the owner, apparently came to the conclusion that the move would have to happen. The acting attorney in the case had been Terry Goggin, hired by Jack Davis. Neither Jack nor his buddy Warren Hinckle wanted to hear about moving the bar. Cassidy went around them and hired his own lawyer to pursue negotiations to avoid the trial. Cassidy's initial proposal was for a move-out date of March 31, 1998, allowing a final St. Patrick's Day celebration and time to stage the move. This was okay with the board, as it would likely take that long to get the construction under way. Other issues in the proposal concerned legal costs, back and future rents, and public acknowledgement of Paddy Nolan. For several days, counter-offers went back and forth, principally concerning issues other than the date.

With the agreement very close, Cassidy suddenly changed the date. Word of the negotiations had gotten out and it wasn't sitting well with Dovre Club supporters. Cassidy began to feel personally threatened. In the week of Thanksgiving, he proposed that the bar be closed immediately, with the premises returned to the SFWC on December 1, 1997, just days away. Other details of the settlement remained as they had been worked out. In evidence of his fear of re-action to the settlement, Cassidy's lawyer asked for and was granted an order to keep the settlement sealed until December 1. The jury would be sent home as if the trial had been delayed. When it recon-vened on December 1, the settlement would be announced and the jury released from service.

The gag order prevented public celebration, but relief and ela-tion prevailed at many Thanksgiving dinners that year. The settlement included enough money to pay the lawyers, with court costs paid by the bar. Rent for the past year was paid, and the bar was to be gone sooner than anyone had dared hope. And as a settlement short of a trial verdict, there were hopes that the political fallout would be lim-ited. On the morning of Monday, December 1, the Dovre Club door was padlocked, and in court the settlement was announced and the jury sent home.

Cassidy was right to be concerned about the reaction of the bar's supporters. When Brian, the manager, found the padlock, he called a locksmith to remove it so he could get into the bar and open for business as usual. The Building staff called the police, but they re-fused to become involved in an eviction process, referring the case to the county sheriff. In the meantime, Brian filed a last-minute appeal, claiming that the bar had been sold to him the previous June and that any settlement without his approval was void. A hearing date was set for later that week. Rather than escalate an already tense situation, the call to the sheriff's office was put off until after the hearing. At the hearing, the judge agreed with The Women's Building position that Brian had already had months to assert his stake. That he had never done so belied his claim and his appeal was dismissed. In the mean-time, the bar had been open for business.

While the Building went to the county to have the eviction served, the party at the bar started going around the clock. Brian and some of his supporters prepared the bar for a blockade, blocking off the outdoor entrance through the basement and gathering material for blocking the front door. At the same time, other patrons were walking off with souvenirs from the bar; it's rumored that someone even tried to take the pool table. Tensions on the street were high, and The Women's Building felt compelled to hire a security guard for the lobby in order to assure its tenants and other visitors of their safety. The night before the eviction was to be carried out, a vigil of Women's Building supporters gathered on the sidewalk. Though the vigil was not convened by the Building staff or board, several attended to urge calm. As the vigil ended, many a past patron of the Dovre Club stopped in for one last drink. At 6 a.m. the next morning, the eviction order was peacefully executed, a quiet and anticlimactic end to a year-long battle.

For its part, the Dovre Club was able to relocate by March to a new location at 26th and Valencia, eight blocks south, where it operates to this day. For The Women's Building, the sudden resolution took all by surprise, and even with the Dovre club gone, it was several months before contracts were signed and actual construction was under way. City threats to close the doors were put on hold as long as construction continued.

Financial Crisis

With the Dovre Club gone, the retrofit process itself could begin. By April 1998, the tenants had been moved around and construction was under way. But a new drama soon presented itself. Most of 1997 had been focused on the Dovre Club battle, but there was also a growing concern about how to raise operating funds for the Building in the midst of such a major capital campaign, combined with an expected decline in rental income. Throughout 1997 the board had been pressing Esperanza for the 1998-99 budget and had been repeatedly assured that things were in hand.

Esperanza had been hired with the recognition that her weakness was in finance. However, that was the strength among the Board members, and the hope was that they would be able to work with her closely on budgeting. Unfortunately, whether it was because there was so much focus on the Dovre Club or just because of personality differences, such a collective was never developed. Esperanza relied on her finance staff person, Raquel Jimenez, who was a bookkeeper and had no experience as a financial planner.

The operations collective that Shoshana had worked with was nominally in place with Esperanza, but it was not a structure with which she was comfortable. She never made full use of the support it could have offered. Like Josefina, Esperanza also seemed paranoid about other staff undercutting her or trying to take her job. Perhaps this is a dynamic that comes with bringing in someone from the outside to take over the leadership of an organization, especially when that someone is not very experienced.[35]

By March 1998, declining income because of reduced rents and fewer donations was leading to a large deficit. The first budget that Esperanza brought to the board that spring wasn't balanced. This was clearly unacceptable, and she was asked to revise it. She came back with a budget that essentially laid off all of the operations staff except herself and the bookkeeper. Staff dedicated to the retrofit was not affected because their funding came out of the capital campaign budget.

Esperanza had been the Executive Director for almost two years, and she played a critically important role in the battle to evict the Dovre Club and in developing plans for the child care center that would move into the Building in 2000. It was also on her watch that the retrofit bids were accepted and the actual construction work was under way. But no one on the board was comfortable with decimating the staff, and they looked for another option. As with any organization, personnel costs were the largest part of the operating budget, so they had to look at personnel cuts to save the $90,000 that was needed to balance the budget for the coming year. The solution that they

---

35 And with the pay The Women's Building could offer, they weren't likely to attract highly experienced candidates.

arrived at was to lay off Esperanza and Raquel, the two highest paid staff, and to temporarily cut back hours for some of the other staff.

It was at this point that the personnel manual came back to haunt the Building. This manual had been put together in the wake of Josefina's tenure as executive director. It focused on defining the rights of employees without clearly defining accountability. During Raquel's year of employment she had racked up hundreds of hours of comp time. More than one staff member questioned when she had time to do all that work or wondered where the product to show for it was. The personnel manual defined limits on comp time, but granted the executive director the authority to override these limits. So the Building had no choice but to pay out a claim of over $15,000 that Raquel filed with the National Labor Relations Board. Fortunately, none of this affected the retrofit campaign, as all of its finances were handled separately from operations in the bookkeeping done by longtime consultant Shellie Stortz.

Teresa Mejia, who had been at the Building since 1992 in a variety of functions, was appointed acting executive director, though her hours were temporarily reduced. Board members stepped in as volunteers to handle the bookkeeping and to work with Shelley. Some fundraising for operations was taken on by the board, and in time the cash flow crunch was eased and staff hours were increased again. Over the next year, Teresa worked very closely with Claire Lachance, the current chair of the board of directors, and with Nancy Corrigan, the board treasurer. She was able to overcome the fear of math and budgets that affects many women. She re-established the operations collective within the staff to provide day-to-day support. In 1999, Teresa was appointed as the permanent Executive Director, a position she still holds today.

A New Building is Born

The renovation project went as smoothly as could have been expected. The Building itself held a few surprises that changed the course of the renovation. Luckily, 1998 turned out to be a wet winter, so the underground creek that flows under the Building was showing itself. This meant that the footings being driven into the foundation had to go deeper than original plans had called for. This slowed the project down, but it also meant the retrofit was stronger and that future expensive repair work would not be necessary. Another surprise was the state of the back interior wall of the Building. The brick character of the Building was well known; it's because of the use of unreinforced brick masonry that the Building was at such risk in an earthquake. What wasn't known was that the brick of the entire back wall was still in excellent shape, having been covered by plaster board for decades. A design decision was made to retain the brick, uncovered, on all four floors of the Building.

By the end of the retrofit project in late 2000, the outside of the Building was largely unchanged. Special attention had been paid to ensure there was no damage to the mural. The inside, however, looked far different than the dark and drab building purchased in 1979. The grand spiral staircase up to the fourth floor was kept, as was the elevator (minus the original brass, stolen by the first company to repair it in the 1980s.) The lobby now extends all the way around the elevator, with a small reception office to greet people as they first enter the Building. New mailboxes and information racks are readily available to tenants and visitors. On the mezzanine floor, the Audrey Lord Room, which had been remodeled earlier in the nineties, still looks the same, but the rest of that floor was turned into workshop rooms and office rentals.

A child care center was put into the southeast corner of the first floor, part of which once housed the Dovre Club. The rest of the old bar space, accessed from the lobby, was to become the information and referral office. With the final wall of the auditorium closed off, the old stage was removed to increase the total space. Some of the old wooden chairs that used to be stored under the stage were auctioned off to raise funds for the operation of the Building and to purchase new, lighter folding chairs. The back brick wall was kept in place, as was the balcony seating. New acoustic ceilings and lighting finally made it a more useful program space.

The third and fourth floors are now reserved for permanent tenants, including The Women's Building's own offices. Other tenants have included Bay Area Teen Voices, BRAVE/Defending Ourselves, Children of Lesbians and Gays Everywhere (COLAGE), Cooperative Restraining Order Clinic, GirlSource, Mission Neighborhood Centers Head Start Program, Mujeres Unidas y Activas, S.F. NOW, Purple Moon Dance Project, The Riley Center, San Francisco Women Against Rape, Neighbor to Neighbor, and ICON/DykeSpeak. ` The spirit of the old Harriet Tubman Room, which had taken up the middle of the third and fourth floors in the old configuration, was maintained by leaving an open common area on the third floor that is open up to the top of the Building. Two of the old throne chairs are still kept in this common area. Offices are laid out around the outer walls of the Building on both floors.

With the retrofit completed, the newly refurbished building was ready once more to be fully filled with the voices of women and girls, ready for the new century. Not that those voices had been silenced during the retrofit project. For much of the nineties, the main focus of The Women's Building had been its own survival. The threats came both from the inside, in the form of various personnel crises, and from the outside, with the challenge from the Dovre Club and its allies. Through it all, the women kept their eyes on the goal: keeping open a building that played an important role in supporting the progressive movement and promoting women's participation. The board and the staff were individually active in political organizing, and there was some frustration that The Women's Building as an organization had limited resources to support these efforts.

Yet the nineties were a very different political era that the years of the Reagan and Bush presidencies. Politically, it wasn't a bad time to let political activism take a back seat. Clinton was elected in 1992, slowing the rightward political direction in the country. Of course, by this time, the liberal Democratic Party was now led by more centrist forces, and rights won two decades before were still in danger. But for much of the decade, economic prosperity, led by the tech revolution launched by the explosive growth of the Internet, helped limit the impact of new conservative policies and programs.

And on the plus side, prosperity provided a good climate for a capital campaign. The Women's Building was able to tap into some of the new wealth to raise the capital for the retrofit. As important as the large number of small donors were, raising $3 million dollars necessitated some larger donations.

This is not to say that The Women's Building took no political stands through the 1990s. In the wake of the first Gulf War, the women of the Building added their voice to opposition to the war. As the impact of Clinton's welfare reform began to unfold, the Building actively supported the developing movement in support of welfare rights. They also threw their support behind efforts to reform U.S. immigration policy and to defend the rights of immigrant workers, still found toiling in sweatshop conditions right in San Francisco.

With the completion of the retrofit, the staff and board of The Women's Building were eager to move to a new level of activism. George Bush had become president, and even though over half the electorate had voted for the Democratic candidate, the power now rested with more conservative voices. A similar conservative political shift was under way in the State of California as well. The need for a place for women to gather and organize was more important than ever.

CHAPTER **11**

EPILOGUE

*To provide women and girls with the tools and resources to re-
alize our full potential, participate as equal partners in the creation
and governance of life, and to improve the world in which we live.*
Mission statement of The Women's Building, 2010

As I complete this book, it has been forty years since the inception of the San Francisco Women's Centers, and over thirty since the
purchase of the Building. I've heard people wonder if women still
need their own building, and unfortunately the answer is a resound-
ing "YES!"

Certainly there have been many changes in society and in the
role of women in society since 1969. In some ways, women and
girls have come a long way toward being fully accepted as equals in
U.S. society. Access to education and careers has expanded consider-
ably; women now make up the majority of those who recently earned
college degrees, including doctoral degrees. More women are being
elected to political office at all levels. A majority of the active work-
force is now female.[36] Even in sectors of society long held to be male

---

36 This is in part the result of the current recession and the collapse of
    manufacturing in the country. But this also indicates the long-term changes in
    the U.S. economy since the 1950s, when a single income was usually enough
    to support a family. Now, the two-income family is the norm, and lower-
    income families often need more than two jobs.

bastions, women have made inroads. Women now hold many more positions within the military branches, and in the world of sports, women are beginning to be taken seriously as athletes, as evidenced by the increasing attention paid to women's basketball.

That said there is a long way to go. Though women fill more leadership roles, they continue to function in a world where patriarchal assumptions still guide economic, political, social, and cultural interactions. There are real differences in how women and men communicate and in what their core values are. I would hazard a guess that the increasing emphasis on collaboration and cooperation reflects the increasing number of women who are setting strategy for organizations. But more broadly in U.S. society, a style of competiveness and polarizing issues still prevails.

In many parts of the world, and even in some sectors within the United States, women are still viewed as subordinate to men. On average, U.S. women still earn 77 percent of what men earn. Forty percent of female-headed households live below the poverty line. Racism continues to define the U.S. class structure, and Black, Latino, Asian, and Native American women are among the hardest working and least paid in the country. But the discrimination percolates up as well. Some higher paid careers still limit women's access; just look at the gender composition in the upper echelons of business. Women often work fewer hours or have breaks in service because they continue to have principal responsibility for maintaining the home and for raising children. And in a pattern that extends back centuries, the value of jobs declines as they begin to be filled by women in place of men. So just as women have begun to fill the majority of managerial positions, the salaries for this work have stagnated or even declined.

Nor is women's subordinate status only an economic issue. One in four women is still likely to be sexually assaulted. The whole range of reproductive health care is harder to access as community clinics close or cut back services. The sexual objectification of women is still a common theme in popular culture and the advertising world. Clearly, struggle for women's rights is not over. The Women's Building came to be in order to provide a place for the movement to call its own while it waged the good fight. That's a need that still needs to be met.

In September 2000, an Open House was held to formally unveil the new building and thank all of those who had made it possible. Every office space was quickly filled and the Building was once again vibrant with the voices of women, girls, boys, and men—all engaged in projects to make the world a better place. The tenants of the Building at the time were Bay Area Teen Voices, BRAVE/Defending Ourselves, Children of Lesbians and Gays Everywhere (COLAGE), Cooperative Restraining Order Clinic, GirlSource, Mission Neighborhood Centers Head Start Program, Mujeres Unidas y Activas, S.F. NOW, Purple Moon Dance Project, The Riley Center, San Francisco Women Against Rape, Neighbor to Neighbor, and ICON/DykeSpeak. Entertainment at the event featured The Wild Mango, Out on a Clef, the Women's Philharmonic, Shalonda Smith, Goapele, Christina Trujillo, Los Cenzontles, and Handmaiden America.

The following year, plans were made for a new September event, Honoring Women of Courage, to launch a new fundraising drive and bring people to the new building. The date for the event was set for Wednesday, September 12. Needless to say, the event was cancelled in the wake of the attacks on the Twin Towers and the Pentagon. The country was plunged into a wartime mentality that framed the debate for years to come.

The Women's Building quickly and publically staked its position as part of a new emerging antiwar movement. The hate-mongering in the country fueled attacks on local businesses. Graffiti attacking Arabs, women, and immigrants appeared on the walls and windows of local merchants throughout the Mission District. The Women's Building mural, with its images of women of color, was among the targets. In response, the Building organized a press conference, challenging reactionary voices that used fear to promote their politics. Funds were raised to help pay for damages. The quick and spirited response was proof that, despite all the vast changes of the past thirty years, the heart of the Building remained. Its basic mission has remained the same: to serve women and girls and families, particularly those in the Mission District but certainly not limited to that population. The goal is to empower women and girls to realize their full potential, and to build a more equitable world for us to do that in.

A more detailed accounting of the first decade of the new century will have to be in the next book. This brief listing of the activities of the past ten years is a testament to the Building's continuing role in supporting social justice efforts and promoting the rights of women:

- The Building continues to offer low-cost rental space to scores of community organizations. It offers new organizing projects a home during the stage of growth that comes between meetings in coffee shops and the full-size, multi-room office space. Women's Building staff are always looking for new ways to be more supportive of the work of their tenants.

- The information and referral program has expanded into a full community resource room, located where the Dovre Club once was. In addition to the traditional housing and jobs listings, free computer and Internet access is available, and workshops and counseling sessions are offered on topics like tax preparation, managing household budgets, and job hunting skills.

- Throughout the first decade of the century, International Women's Day continued to be honored at the Building, with events organized by a cooperative of several Mission District youth organizations. Other educational and political programs have also been held addressing a variety of issues.

- The 25th anniversary of the Building's purchase was celebrated in 2004 through a series of events, including an

evening program that featured a short documentary about The
Women's Building and the production of the play *She Rises
Like a Building to the Sky*.

- The Annual Celebration of Craftswomen fair continues to
  be held at Fort Mason over two weekends in November and
  December. The fair provides a forum for women artists and
  raises a significant part of the Building's annual operating
  budget.

- In 2009, the *Maestrapeace* mural was extended into the
  Building. It now covers the walls of the lobby and the stairwell
  up to the mezzanine level, with ribbons bearing the names
  of women associated with the Building, its staff, board, and
  volunteers.

The staff of the organization continues to be relatively small, as
does its annual budget. The Board of Directors, seven to ten women,
works to support the staff to make sure the assets of the Building remain secure. The economic recession that hit in 2008 affected The
Women's Building as it did other struggling nonprofit organizations;
donations dropped and grant opportunities declined. Though major construction is behind them, the women of the organization still
struggle to put aside reserves to pay for maintenance of the facility.
Even after thirty years, it is still a challenge to explain to major donors
and foundations why giving money to maintain a building is a political act. But the strong tradition of funding itself with small donations
from a large community is helping the Building to weather the tough
times.

2010 marked the 100th anniversary of the Building. In commem-
oration of this anniversary, Flyaway Production, a women's aerial
dance troupe, approached the Building about doing a performance
with the Building. In September 2010, the performers worked from
the fire escape, windows, and rooftop on the Lapidge Street side of the

Building to create an original dance piece. Spectators filled Lapidge Street, craning their necks to watch the performance. With the mural featuring Rigoberta Menchú as the backdrop, it was easy to see the Building thriving for another century.

APPENDIX

One of the important services the Women's Building offered the movement was providing fiscal sponsorship for emerging organizations. Though this program came to an end after 2002, during the previous forty years dozens of organizations were sponsored by the SFWC. Here is a partial list of those organizations:

Groups that went on to form their own non-profit organization:

San Francisco Women Against Rape
La Casa de las Madres Feminist Credit Union
Women's Alcoholism Coalition/Women's Alcoholism Center
The Women's Foundation
Lavender Youth Recreation and Information Center (LYRIC)
Lesbian Visual Artists
Options for Women over 40
The Women's Philharmonic
The Girls After School Academy
Women's Cancer Resource Center
Sisters & Allies Training Project
Maestrapeace Mural Project

Other former projects, with range in size from 2 people to large collectives and active for short periods to years.

Arts:

Fat Lip Readers Theater
Reel Women
Riot Act Theatre Company
Sistah Boom
Working Women Festival
WRY CRIPS Disabled Women's Theater Arts
Mothertongue Feminist Theatre Collective
Women's Arts Project

Health/Physical Welfare:

Center for Self Affirming Soul Healing Africans
Bay Area Coalition for our Reproductive Rights
Circle Counseling Center
Coalition on Prostitution
Berkeley Clearinghouse on FEMICIDE
Prison Integrated Health Project
S.F. Network for Battered Lesbian and Bisexual Women
Child Abuse Strategic Action Project
Date Marital Rape Education Project
Disable Women's Alliance
Prostitution Research & Education Project
Vaccine Advocate Committed to Universal Prevention
Noble Jones Internation Foundation
CFIDS Action Network
Women Organized to Respond to Life-threatening Diseases
    (WORLD)
Sacramento Coalition for our Reproductive Rights
Choosing Choice

Education:

Meadow Livingstone Education Center

Sisters and Allies
Promotoras Latinas Communitarias de Salud
A Miner Miracle
Creating Political Fire thru Cultural Diversity
Generation Five
Community Youth Troopers
Loveworks Scholarship Fund
Herstory for Futures Unlimited
Women's Voices of Old Wives Tales
Sportsbridge
Homosexuality in Ancient Greece Project

Publications:

ICON/Dykespeak
Lesbian Contradiction
RADIANCE Magazine

Organizing:

Beijing 95 and beyond: Women of Color Strategic Planning
    Project
Venceremos Brigade
Temporary Workers Union
Bay Area Teen Voices
Older Lesbian Organizing Committee (OLOC)
Epicenter Switchboard
HASHA – Iranian Lesbians
Radical Women
Women Refusing to Accept Tenant Harassment (WRATH)
Women's Action to Gain Economic Security
Lesbian Uprising
Exotic Dancers Alliance

REFERENCES

Interviews:

Roma Guy, interviewed March 1992 by Michelle Michaelson

Tiana Arruda, interviewed March 1997 by Lee Jenkins

Diane Jones, interviewed August 1992 by Michelle Michaelson

Graciela Perez Trevisan, interviewed May 1996 by Lee Jenkins

Carmen Vazquez, interviewed 1993 by Frances Doughty

Regina Gabrielle, interviewed January 1996 by Patricia Kess

Cynthia Gissler, interviewed January 2005 by Susan Ford and Sushawn Robb

Document Citations – all from the GLBT Historical Society, Women's Building Collections

Ch 1
 Footnote 3) List from July 1972 coordinating committee notes, Main Collection, Series 1, Subseries A, Box 1, file 8

Footnote 5) May 1975 meeting notes Main Collection, Series 1, Subseries A, Box 2, file 1

Footnote 6) The BAFFCU Bulletin, October 1979, final edition, Main Collection, Series 1, Subseries B, Box 7, file 4

Ch 2

Footnote 7) Violence Against Women Conference program, Main Collection, Series 1, Subseries A, Box 5, file 19

Ch 3

Footnote 9) SFWC Newsletter, Dec. 1977, Main Collection, Series 1, Subseries A, Box 4, file 3

Footnote 10) Women's Building of Bay Area Fact Sheet, Main Collection, Series 1, Subseries C, Box 7, file 7

Run in the Park poster, Main Collection, Box 66, file 1g

Table 1, Main Collection, Series 1, Subseries A, Box 2

Ch 4

Footnote 14) SFWC Newsletter, Feb. 1979, Main Collection, Series 1, Subseries A, Box 3, file 8

Footnote 15) Tiana's comments on transition, Main Collection, Series 1, Subseries C, Box 7, file 16

Ch 5

Vida Gallery poster, Main Collection, Box 65, file 9g

Ch 6

Footnote 20) Planning and Evaluation Committee, Memo Re: Proposal for the Women's Building, February 24, 1983. GLBTHS, WBA. Collection 3, Series 1, box 1

Footnote 21) Statement of Purpose, Main Collection, Series 2, Subseries A, Box 8, file 7

Craftsfair poster, Main Collection, Box 65, file 10c

Table 2, Main Collection, Series 2, Subseries A, Boxes 14-15

Ch 8

International Women's Day poster, Main Collection, Box 67, file 3a

Ch 9

Footnote 30) Regina's resignation letter – Collection 3, Series 1, Subseries 2, Box 2, file 19

Footnote 33) community letter – Collection 3, Series 1, Box 1, file 1

Ch 10

Maestrapiece Poster, Main Collection, Box 66, file 1g

We support the Women's Building poster, Box 66, file 1d

Table 3, Collection 3, Series 2, Box 4

ACKNOWLEDGEMENTS

Most projects associated with the San Francisco Women's Building take a village to bring them to fruition. This book was no exception. Special thanks to my editor, Patricia Heinicke, for pointing out the gaps and organizing the material so readers won't get lost. Thanks also to readers of early drafts for their input and kind words of encouragement: Max Elbaum, Diane Jones, Carmen Vazquez, Roma Guy, Marge Nelson, Susan Pedrick and Susan Ford. Karen Lenoir provided fast and superb proofreading skills. I have said it elsewhere, but the Gay, Lesbian, Bisexual and Transgender Historical Society deserve multiple acknowledgements. Without their work of preserving archival material from the movement and its leaders, this kind of history could not be written. The organization, and all of the volunteers who work with the various collections they hold, deserve the appreciation and support of everyone who values history. Thanks are also due to Teresa Mejia, the current Executive Director of the Women's Building, and to her staff and board, for the patience and support in seeing this project through. To my Tuesday night girls, Karen and Janette, thanks for the meals, cooking lessons and conversation that helped keep me healthy. Last, but far from least, I extend my gratitude to my girlfriend, Mercilee Jenkins. Her work in gathering the oral histories of founders was essential to the content of the book and the play brings the period to life in a way my narrative never could. Her moral support and encouragement got me through the periods when I was tempted to give up.

ABOUT THE AUTHORS

Sushawn Robb began her organizing career while still in junior high school, organizing fellow students to participate in the first Earth Day activities. In the years since, she has been involved in many campaigns and organizations, including Seattle Reproductive Rights Alliance, Committee for Justice for Gene Viernes and Silme Domingo, Alliance Against Women's Oppression, Line of March, Venceremos Brigade, Queer Nation (SF), *CrossRoads*, Committees of Correspondence and *War Times*. She has been a friend of the S.F. Women's Building since 1981, serving on the Board of Directors from 1994 to 2000, and working with the Women's Building History Project from 2002 to the present. She currently works as a Park Ranger for a regional park system in the S.F. Bay Area.

Mercilee Jenkins is a playwright, poet and performance artist. Her most recent play, *Oasis Detroit*, (previously entitled *The Fabulous Ruins of Detroit*) was selected for the 2008 Theatre Bay Area Playwrights Showcase and has been presented as work-in-progress in San Francisco, Phoenix, Chicago and Detroit. Her work encompasses scholarly articles, performance texts, poetry, and several produced plays including *A Credit to Her Country*, *The Two-Bit Tango*, *She Rises Like a Building to the Sky*, and *Menopause and Desire*. She co-edited an anthology of essays and performance pieces entitled *Sexualities and Communication in Everyday Life*, which was published in 2007. She received the Lesley Irene Coger Award for Distinguished Performance from the National Communication Association in 2004 and the Distinguished Performance Award from Western States Communication Association in 2009. She is a professor of Communication & Performance Studies at San Francisco State University.

CPSIA information can be obtained at www.ICGtesting.com
Printed in the USA
LVOW060300090312

272312LV00002B/9/P